# REGIONAL PATTERNS OF INDUSTRIAL GROWTH IN INDIA

# REGIONAL PATTERNS OF INDUSTRIAL GROWTH IN INDIA

DINESH N. AWASTHI

*Foreword by*
Y.K. ALAGH

CONCEPT PUBLISHING COMPANY, NEW DELHI 110059

The Indian Council of Social Science Research gave the financial support towards the publication of this work. However, the responsibility for the contents of the book — facts, opinions, conclusions, etc. — is entirely that of the author and not of the ICSSR.

ISBN 81-7022-327-X

*First Published 1991*



*Published and Printed by*
Ashok Kumar Mittal
Concept Publishing Company
A/15-16, Commercial Block, Mohan Garden
New Delhi 110059

*Lasertypeset by*
Microtech Advance Printing Systems (Pvt.) Ltd.
H-13, Bali Nagar
NEW DELHI 110015

# FOREWORD

DR. DINESH N. AWASTHI'S work on Regional Patterns of Industrial Growth in India is an important contribution to the much vexed question of optional policies for regional diversification. Dr. Awasthi's work was done at the Sardar Patel Institute of Economic and Social Research, which has a tradition of serious work on the subject. His contribution is analytical and goes a long way in exploring the structural determinants of the regional spread of industrialisation in India.

Dr. Awasthi finds that regional inequality in industrialization in India is decreasing. Subsequently, Prof. J.C. Sandersara has independently arrived at the same finding. However, the absolute distance between the industrial and other States is still large. Awasthi then goes on to debunk some earlier studies which had argued that linkage effects would lead to faster growth. He finds that the spread and growth of unorganised industry is independent of the organised sector, at least in the regional matrix. Again contrary to popular belief, as shown by earlier work by Isher Ahluwalia and Alagh, Kashyap, Shah and Awasthi, agricultural and industrial growth are not always interrelated at the State level.

The more interesting part of his work is the use of an analytical framework which uses demand and supply side factors to explain the regional spread of industrialisation. Demand side factors are important, he finds, and are getting to be more so as India's economy diversifies. He finds only agglomeration economies and power supply important on the supply side.

Dr. Awasthi's work argues very sensibly that competitive incentive policies do not necessarily help, and both direct and indirect government policies towards industrialisation must, to be effective, rely on an understanding of the basic structural factors at play.

This book will be read with interest by scholars and policy-makers.

Y.K. ALAGH

# ACKNOWLEDGMENTS

STUDY OF Economics attracted me to acquire further understanding in the domain of regional analysis. I chose it as a theme of my research work leading to the degree of Ph.D. I had rightly anticipated that this work will provide me an opportunity to peep into a variety of issues, interrelated with a variety of diverse patterns of socio-economic fabrics of the States of India. I was further encouraged to undertake this research work at Sardar Patel Institute of Economic and Social Research, Ahmedabad, as the Institute already had a very rich tradition of research in the area of Regional Analysis.

During the course of the research work, most of the time I found the task very interesting, challenging and sometimes frustrating! I am thankful to my supervisor and to the faculty members of the Institute. My deepest feelings of gratitude are for Prof. S.P. Kashyap who constantly inspired, fostered and channellised my efforts in the right direction. But for his analytical clarity and sober checks, the vast landscape of the present theme would not have taken its present shape.

I am grateful to Prof. Y.K. Alagh not only for taking keen interest in the progress of my work at each stage but also for very kindly writing foreword to the book. My grateful thanks are also due to Prof. K.K. Subrahmanian who provoked very thoughtful discussions which helped me substantially in deriving conceptual clarity. Prof. G.V.S.N. Murty and Prof. V.P. Bharadwaj extended crucial help in sorting out the econometric issues involved in the analysis. For this, I am grateful to them. I have also been benefited by the discussions with Prof. T.S. Papola, Prof. Amitabh Kundu, Prof. Ravi Dholakia and Prof. Atul Sarma at various stages of my work.

Indian Council of Social Science Research facilitated me to take up the research work on a full time basis, by awarding the Fellowship. I am thankful to the authorities of ICSSR for the Fellowship and also for the publication grant which facilitated me getting my thesis published. My grateful thanks are due to Sardar Patel Institute of Economic and Social Research for providing the facilities to carry out this work.

Co-operation extended by administrative staff of SPIESR in facilitating my task also deserves special thanks. The valuable help from my other colleagues and friends at SPIESR is also gratefully acknowledged. I specially thank Shri Y.V. Pantulu for his sustained help on Computer. Shri M.C. Madhavan did an excellent work by typing the draft of the thesis within a short time at his disposal. I am thankful to Shri Madhavan and Shri K.P. Sateesan and Mrs. Prema Madhavan for typing the thesis very neatly.

The pleasure of the friendly help which I received from my friends Jayshree, Rakesh, Tulsi, Jeemol, Rohitbhai, Dr. Devendra Kothari, Anil, Kiran, Surjeet and Kewal will remain as fresh as ever. Let me also confess that my wife Amita deserves at least half of the credit in this endeavour. I am also grateful to Shri Ashok Kumar Mittal, Concept Publishing Company for publishing of the work efficiently.

I am solely responsible for all the limitations this work carries.

DINESH N. AWASTHI

# CONTENTS

*Foreword* 5

*Acknowledgments* 7

*List of Tables* 10

1. Introduction 13

2. Some Issues 22

3. Performance of the Industrial Sector 42

4. Trends in Regional Industrial Inequalities 78

5. Industrial Structure and Regional Growth 102

6. Inter-Industry Linkages and Regional Industrial Growth 125

7. Inter-Regional Variations in India: Some Explanation 147

8. The Summing Up 184

*Appendices* 189

I. The Database 189

II. Aggregation of NIC Corresponding to ASI Classification Code 195

*Bibliography* 199

*Index* 218

# LIST OF TABLES


3.1 All India Growth Rates: Registered Manufacturing Sector (Use-based and Input-based Classification) During 1061-69, 1969-78 and 1961-78 **45**

3.2 Classification of Industries According to their Growth Performance between 1961-69, 1969-78 and 1961-78: Value Added **46**

3.3 Changes in Shares of Major Industry Groups in the Registered Manufacturing Sector: Use-Based and Input-Based Classification (1961, 1969, 1978) **50**

3.4 Classification of Industries According to their Shares in Value Added and Changes Therein **53**

3.5 Classification of Industries According to Growth Rates (1961-78) and Their Shares – (1961); Value Added **55**

3.6 Share of the States in All India: Value Added (Important Industries) – 1961 **57**

3.7 Share of the States in All India: Value Added (Important Industries) – 1969 **61**

3.8 Share of the States in All India: Value Added (Important Industries) – 1978 **64**

4.1 Percentage Share of Value Added generated in Manufacturing Sectors as a Proportion of State Domestic Product **81**

4.2 Rank Co-efficients of Correlation between the Various Segments of Manufacturing and Co-efficient of Variation of the Segments **84**

4.3 Per Capita Value Added Generated in the Manufacturing Sector by the States **86**

4.4 Annual Compound Rates of Growth by States **88**

4.5 Relative Shares of States in the Factory Sector **91**

4.6 Indices of Regional Industrial Inequality in India **95**

4.7 Trends in Regional Industrial Inequality Across States **97**

5.1 Industrial Base/Specialisations of Regions in India **107**

5.2 Industrial Specialisation Coefficient for the States – 1961, 1969, 1978 **117**

5.3 A Shift and Share Analysis of Value Added in the States of India Registered Manufacturing (Factory) Sector 1961-69 and 1969-78 **120**

6.1 Growth Rates, Hirschman Compliance Indices and Linkage Balance Indices of the Census Sector by State: Value Added **128**

6.2 Correlation Co-efficient (ρ) between the various Linkage Indices and Overall Rate of Growth ($G_i$) of the State (1969-70 to 1978-79) **129**

7.1 Estimated Regression Equations by Considering Demand Side Variables **162**

7.2 Estimated Regression Equations by Considering Supply Side Variables **165**

7.3 Estimated Regression Equations by Considering both Demand and Supply Side Variables together **167**

7.4 Estimated Regression Equations Considering the Components of the Agglomeration Economies and Infrastructure **172**

7.5 Estimated Regression Equations for Interregional Inequality Trends **175**

# 1

# INTRODUCTION

## PROLOGUE

THE PROBLEM of inter-regional economic disparities, though more acute in underdeveloped countries, is a widespread phenomenon. Irrespective of the level and state of economic development, the problem exists and persists (Robinson, 1969).[1] Heston (1967) has argued that, as economic development proceed, the major source of regional variations in income will be from industries rather than from agriculture. The regional dimension of the process of industrial development, therefore, has attracted attention of a large number of economists, the world over.

It is also widely observed that almost all countries are trying to industrialise as fast as possible. For, industrialisation is considered as *sine qua non* of the economic development and a panacea for the vicious problem of economic backwardness. It is considered not only a key to raising real per capita income (Moore, 1969) or reducing the real per unit cost of goods and services culminating into better standard of living for the people; but also a vital catalyst for a larger transformation of the economy through linkages (Hirschman, 1985) and creation of external economies (Rosenstein Rodan, 1961).

However, the indiscriminate struggle for industrialisation in many countries has resulted into a regionally unbalanced and lopsided economic growth, which manifests through a few islands of prosperity amidst the sea of pauperised regions. This unevenness raise several backwardness and poverty, why should it lead to such uncalled for consequences? Why all regions do not or may not industrialise enough to achieve a higher degree of economic prosperity? What are the bottlenecks, being faced by a depressed region, for economic growth? Though there are no unique answers to these questions, some tentative explanations have been put forward which are discussed below:

## PROCESS OF REGIONAL GROWTH

One of the arguments has been that regional growth is essentially an inequilibriating phenomenon due to the locational and structural variations between regions.[2] Historically, growth takes place only on some points in the space because "natural resources are not evenly distributed among regions of a nation. Access to major markets (including foreign) is essentially unequal. . . . Inherited 'know-how' and labour skills are also unequally distributed, though such inequality is subject to change (Isard and Reiner, 1961 : 23). Thus, as Myrdal (1958: 38) puts it, "naturally geography sets the stage".

Myrdal observes that there is an inherent tendency in the free play of market forces not only to create but increase the inequalities between regions through "backwash effects", emanating from the process of 'cumulative-causation'. For, once growth takes off in any region due to whatever social, political, economic or historical reasons, it gets accentuated there, via migration, interregional trade and transfer of capital, etc. due to the snowballing effect. This in turn leads to the deprivation and pauperisation of other regions of their locally generated capital, workers skilled and share of tertiary activity, and welfare services (Hirschman, 1958). And this unhampered operation of market forces tends of work against the development of poorer regions (Myrdal, 1958).[3] He further notices that this tendency is more pronounced in the poor countries compared to the rich ones.

But as growth proceeds, the regional inequalities tend to decline due to the existing complimentarities between regions (Hirschman, 1958). This hypothesis was vindicated by Williamson (1965) in a study of a large number of countries with marked difference in their level of economic development. He found that in the early stages of development the economic inequalities increased and in the later (higher) stages they tend to converge.[4] The regional income inequality curve is likely to be an inverted 'U' with respect to the level of economic development of the nation (Kuznets, 1958; Williamson, 1965).

The increasing inequalities in the early stages of economic development, are not likely to decline, so easily, on their own. For, the unabated concentration of industries at few points in space has its roots in the fact that the spread effects are usually too weak to make any serious dent in the problem of regional imbalances, compared to the backwash effects.[5] If the process of cumulative-causation is allowed to persist for a longer period, it is likely to result in social tension and political discontent. Therefore, arguments have been put forth in favour of government intervention for countermanding such equations.

Policy-makers also realise that not all regions share the fruits of economic growth equitably owing to the unequal access to the social, political and economic opportunities. The feeling is reinforced with the acceptance of 'growth with social justice' as a major goal by most of the countries following 'egalitarian policies'. As a result there is a new thrust on balanced regional development.

## RELEVANCE FOR INDIA

Researchers have emphasised the need for studies at the regional level to understand the process of uneven regional industrial growth (Chinitz, 1971; Alonso, 1968). This becomes all the more imperative in the case of a vast country such as India with its enormous socio-economic and cultural diversities. It is rightly argued that the

> . . . treatment of Indian development on a State level is an essential part of any detailed economic study of India. . . . India as a whole is merely the sum of its parts and it seems unrealistic, if not impossible, to treat India as a whole without accounting for the widely differing experience of the constituent States (Macrae, 1971 : 341).

Indian planning by and large has been limited to allocation of investment over sectors and sub-sectors. The spatial dimension has remained neglected for a long time. The glaring regional disparities in the level of economic development in general and industrial development in particular are the manifestations of such a process. This provides a compelling rationale for a regional approach to the planning process (Alagh, 1962 and 1969; Nath, 1967; Kashyap, 1979). Moreover its federal structure, with semi-autonomous States demanding equity in the process of the development of the national economy, has certain undeniable political compulsions for adopting a regional approach to the planning (Subrahmanian, 1971; Misra, 1972; Chakravarty, 1972).

## HISTORICAL BACKGROUND

India is among those countries which remained under the foreign yoke for a considerable period. Consequently, the development of the country was guided by the economic interests of its colonial masters. They paid attention to the development of only those regions of their colony which served their economic interests most. This is how historical forces guided the development of port towns such as Bombay, Calcutta and Madras, which in turn worked as a nucleus for the development of Maharashtra, West Bengal and Tamil Nadu respectively. On the other hand, resource rich regions such as Bihar, Orissa and Madhya Pradesh lagged behind.

The discriminatory development of some regions, by the British Raj, was made possible by linking the hinterland with the port towns by railways. These port towns worked merely as output of the metropolitan economy (Chattopadhyaya and Raza, 1975). It is argued that development of the Presidencies during the British period was realised at the cost of Bihar, Orissa, Assam and Maharashtra (excluding Bombay) (Thavaraj, 1972). This gave rise to the economic dualism. Digby observes:

> There are two Indias: the India of the Presidency and the Chief Provincial Cities, of the railway system, of the hill stations. . . . There are two countries: Anglostan, the land especially ruled by the English, in which English investments have been made; and Hindustan, practically all India, fifty miles from each side of the railway lines (Digby, 1901: 291-92).

This observation is vindicated if we look at the nature of the concentration of industries across space in the British India. Before World War I, industrial investment was confined to two nodes: Bombay and Calcutta. During the thirties, some more centres emerged on the industrial map of the country such as Ahmedabad, Delhi, Kanpur, Madras, Madurai and Coimbatore, which were engaged primarily in the cotton textile manufacturing. This spread was further aided by the creation of local markets through tariff protection for the whole of India (Bagchi, 1972).

However, the concentration and lopsided development continued unabated. The extent of regional imbalance in industrialisation is glaring if we look at the distribution of companies at work in 1913-14 and 1938-39, by States. During 1913-14, the total number of companies in the provinces of Bengal was 973 (35.46%), Bombay 613 (22.3%) and Madras 427 (15.6%). Taken together, these three States having three major port towns accounted for more than 73 per cent of the companies at work in 1913-14. During 1938-39 Bengal increased its share by six per cent at the expense of Bombay and Madras. These three Presidencies again maintained their dominance with approximately 68 per cent share of the total companies at work in 1938-39 (Sharma and Chauhan, 1969).[6] Even in 1946 this picture did not alter when the first Census of Manufacturing (CMI) was conducted:

> . . . the three major provinces West Bengal, Madras and Bombay accounted for 68 per cent of the total factory strength . . . (CMI, 1949 : 7).

Thus, it is clear that the regional pattern of industrialisation which emerged during the Imperial rule was highly uneven and of the enclave type across regions which gave birth to a severe rural-urban dichotomy.

## THE PROBLEM

Since Independence India has been trying to attain a rapid rate of growth through industrialisation within the framework of a highly uneven spatial structure with a centre-periphery syndrome.[7] This has further aggravated the problem of inter-regional inequality in the level of industrial development, where early starters continue to dominate the industrial scene of the country.

The government policies in the post-Independence period have been somewhat regressive as far as balanced regional industrial development is concerned. Almost all the policies have only marginally affected the location dynamics of industries even after more than 35 years of planning. The regional distribution of industries, by and large, represents the same picture of industrial concentration as under the British Rule (Pathak, 1980; Bhatt, 1981; Kundu and Raza, 1981). Some researchers, however, maintain that the inter-regional inequalities in the level of industrial development have declined over the past 30 years as a result of government intervention. They emphasise that industrial concentration would have been further aggravated in its absence (Pathak, 1971; Gupta, 1973).

Many attempts have been made in the literature to examine the nature of industrial dispersal across regions in India. However, most of the studies have been descriptive. Very few studies have attempted to offer some explanation for the location dynamics of industries across States/regions. Further, the treatment of the problem of inter-regional industrial inequalities has been inadequate. There is a dearth of information especially on the nature and the determining factors of the industrial spread across space in India. In fact we are not really sure as to what has been happening at the regional level in the industrial economy of India. Therefore, the need for such studies, which could fill this void, can hardly be exaggerated. In the present study our endeavour is to bridge this gap to some extent.

## OBJECTIVES

The present study makes an attempt to explore into the nature and causes of regional industrial disparities across States in India. In brief, the main aim of this exercise is to understand the 'what', 'where' and 'why' of the regional dispersal of industries in a general macro-economic framework. More specifically the objectives of the present study are:

(i) to examine the regional industrial structure of the various State economies with reference to the national economy;
(ii) to measure the extent and direction of inter-regional disparities in terms of some selected variables like fixed capital, employment and or/value added;
(iii) to ascertain the nature and pattern of the structural changes in the industrial base of the various States, and the growth profile thereof, during 1961 to 1978-79; and
(iv) to identify and isolate some of the factors determining the regional industrial growth and explaining inter-regional variations in the level of industrialisation.

## COVERAGE AND DATA BASE

For the purpose of our analysis we have covered 17 major States/regions.[8] (Andhra Pradesh, Assam, Bihar, Gujarat, Haryana, Himachal Pradesh, Jammu and Kashmir, Karnataka, Kerala, Maharashtra, Orissa, Punjab, Rajasthan, Tamil Nadu, Uttar Pradesh, West Bengal and one Union Territory, that is Delhi) which, taken together, account for approximately 99 per cent of the total fixed capital, employment, value-added or output of the nation as a whole, between 1961 and 1978-79. Each State is a unit of observation in the study. The analysis refers to the period 1961 to 1978-79. ASI data at the three-digit level have been used too specify 53 industrial sectors covered in the study. The database and its nature has been specified in the relevant chapters. Various statistical econometric techniques, e.g. growth rates inequality measures, shift and share analysis, input-output technique, regression analysis etc., have been employed to analyse various aspects of the problem.

Data for the analysis have been obtained mainly from the various issues of (i) *Annual Survey of Industries*, (ii) *Statistical Abstract of India*, (iii) *Operational Statistics of the Industrial Development Bank of India*, (iv) *Reserve Bank of India Bulletin*, (v) *National Accounts Statistics*, (vi) *Annual Reports* of the various Ministries of the Government of India, such as Railways, Company Affairs, Industrial Development, Finance etc., (vii) *The Technical Note* to the Sixth Plan (1978-83); and (viii) Reports of the various rounds of the National Sample Survey.

## PLAN OF THE STUDY

The present study is divided into seven chapters (excluding Ch. 1 i.e. Introduction).

Chapter 2 provides a brief review of the major studies relating to inter-regional industrial disparities, changes therein and explanations thereof; with reference to the regional economies of India. The dynamics of industrial structure of the national economy has been analysed in Chapter 3. An attempt has been made to identify the more important industries in the national economy which, in turn, have bearing on the regional growth profiles. The growth profile of various States has also been discussed in the backdrop of this analysis. In Chapter 4, an attempt has been made to gauge the extent of inter-regional inequalities in industrial development. The trend in these inequalities between 1961 and 1978-79 has also been analysed. A shift and share analysis has been carried out for the manufacturing (factory) sector of the various States in Chapter 5. The attempt is to ascertain the underlying sources responsible for the varied performance of the various State/regional economies a reflected by the change in their industrial structure. The impact of inter-industry linkages on the growth profiles of the State in an input-output (I-O) framework is examined in Chapter 6, using the 89 sector I-O table used for the Sixth Five Year Plan of the Government of India. In Chapter 7, the role of various factors in explaining inter-regional variations is examined with the help of multiple regression models. In the last chapter (Chapter 8), we have discussed the major findings of the study and their implications.

## NOTES

1. For example in Pakistan, value added generated in industries in Karachi exceeded the figure for whole of the erstwhile East Pakistan (UNIDO, 1971 : 454); in Greece, Metropolitan Athens accounted for 45 per cent of the nations industrial employment (Michalopoulous, 1971 : 145); most of the industry in Kenya is located around Nairobi; similarly in Zambia, Ivory Coast, Ethiopia and Uganda, industry is concentrated in one of two centres of districts (Jack, 1971 : 117). Similarly Sao Paulo in Brazil accounted for half of the industrial production and employment in 1959; Metropoli Manila with 4.2 per cent of the country's total population shared half of the industrial employment as well as value added in 1959. In Argentina, Buenos Aires accounted for 52.5 per cent of the industrial establishment and 63.4 per cent of workers in 1963 (UNIDO, 1971 : 454); and 3 out of 32 federal States in Mexico accounted for 58.9 per cent of the total value of manufacturing output (Lamadrid; 1971 : 558). In the case of developed countries also, the position is not very different. For example, in United States, the north-eastern part of the country accounts for 7 per cent of the area and 70 per cent of the industrial employment of the country (Ulliman, 1964 : 153). In France, 49 per cent of the total turnover in industrial enterprises is accounted for by the Parisian region (Penoril, 1969 : 80), Budapest, with 3 per cent of the total area, accounts for about 45 per cent of the industrial employment and even greater percentage of industrial production (Koszegi, 1969 : 296); Similarly heavy concentration of industries in the South-East region of U.K. and in the Northern part of the Italy are well known.
2. An exhaustive survey of the literature is not aimed at here. For details, see Isard (1956); Alonso (1964); Meyers (1968); Lefeber (1968); Brown (1969) and Richardson (1973), among others.
3. However, Myrdal's proposition was challenged by Salvatore who argued that the free play of market forces may not necessarily be the direct cause for widened regional inequalities. This phenomenon might also be a result of factors, purely internal to the region. Citing the case of Italy, he argued that operation of the market mechanism was rather helpful to the development of the Italian South. (Salvatore, 1972 : 518-538).
4. Some of the other studies vindicating 'the convergence hypothesis' are: Perloff *et al.* (1960); Chenery (1962); Alonso (1968); Chaudhary (1971); Koropeckyj (1972) and Richardson (1973).

5. While Myrdal defines forces of divergence as 'backwash effects' and convergence as 'spread effects' Hirschman (1958) refers to them as 'polarisation and trickling down' effects respectively.
6. Percentages are worked out from the table "State-wise distribution of the companies in a certain year", page 49 of the book.
7. These issues are discussed in greater detail in the next chapter.
8. For arguments in favour of taking States, as regions for such analysis, see (Singh, 1972 Bhattacharya, 1973).

# 2

# SOME ISSUES

IN MANY countries, industrial/economic activity gets started at some point in space owing to some natural, historical or political reasons, and tends to get concentrated in and around that point. Though natural resources do play a crucial role in determining the location of economic activity, the historical forces often assume a more strategic role in the pattern of economic development of the country/region. The problem of inter-regional disparities in the level of industrial development has aroused lot of interest among researchers in India, which has resulted into several studies in the recent past. Despite the data constraints, some studies in the recent past. Despite the data constraints, some studies have made useful contribution in the area. There are three main strands of analysis in which these studies could conveniently be classified:

(a) Studies which compare the industrial growth performance of the regions and analyse the trend in regional industrial inequalities;
(b) Studies which focus on the regional industrial structures and the emerging patterns of industrial base of various region/States; and
(c) Studies which offer some explanations for the behaviour of regional variations in the level of industrial development in India.

We propose to bring out the major contributions of various researchers and trace some missing links in what follows:

## TRENDS IN REGIONAL INDUSTRIAL INEQUALITIES

Scholars have taken keen interest in understanding the nature of regional inequalities in industrialisation despite the limitations of data and the problems emerging due to the changes in the State boundaries and the coverage of industries. Most of the studies have analysed the available data for the factory (manufacturing) sector for the post-Independence period. Though some paltry spatial dispersal of the industries was noticed in the thirties when some other industrial centres emerged on the industrial map of India (e.g. Ahmedabad, Delhi, Kanpur, Madras, Madura, Coimbatore) due to the advent of the sugar and cotton textile industries (Bagchi, 1959), the Bombay, Calcutta and Madras presidencies dominated the industrial scene of the country.[1] The extent of regional industrial disparities was quite glaring at the time of independence. Even as late as 1961, the Census of India noted with concern the unabated tendency of industrial concentration in a few metropolitan centres.

Some of the early attempts to measure the extent of inter-regional industrial inequalities were made by Dhar and Sastry (1967), Lahiri (1969), and Saradamoni (1969). These studies observed that the inequalities have declined over time. For example Dhar and Sastry, using power consumption as a proxy for manufacturing output across States, observed that the inter-regional inequalities have reduced between 1951 and 1961 on the basis of the decline observed in the value of the coefficient of variation over time. However, the conclusions reached by these studies are subject to limitations at least on two counts: (i) the conclusions drawn are based only on two points in time; and (ii) the measurement is based on some proxies and inadequate database.

In the recent past, some attempts were made to overcome these limitations by Gupta (1973) Seth and Gulati (1974), Seth (1974), Dholakia (1979), Nair (1982) and Udai Sekhar (1985). The studies, by the large, vindicate Sandesara's observation that organised industry has contributed towards narrowing the inter-State imbalances. It seems fairly clear that, but for the counterweight of industry, the imbalances would have probably widened (Sandesara, 1974 : 558).[2]

Contrary to these findings, Nadkarni (1969) found that the regional disparities in manufacturing have increased between 1960-65, using the coefficient of variation in per capita value added. Similarly Jhuraney (1976) found that the inequalities in the regional distribution of employment in the manufacturing sector has further aggravated between 1961 and 1974. Examining the dispersion of the companies at work and their paid-up capital during 1975-76 and 1978-79, Barathawal (1980) observed that the private sector is almost linearly related with the level of regional industrialisation and the new firms are attracted in proportion to the already existing firms in a particular city or region as well as in a particular industry group. Thus one can plausibly infer that regional disparities must have increased over time owing to the cumulative-causation process. However, these studies too suffer from the limitations posed by inadequate and partial coverage of time and the database.[3] Absolute dependence of the coefficient of variation as a measure of inequality further limits the reliability of the conclusion.

Therefore, the debate whether the regional disparities have converged or not remains somewhat inconclusive. We do not yet have standard estimates of growth rates and index of the levels of industrial development for alternative indicators such as output, employment, capital stock etc., for each of the major States for a sufficiently long period, which may enable use to reach to a more concrete conclusion. Thus, the need of an indepth analysis to ascertain the regional inequalities is obvious.

## REGIONAL INDUSTRIAL STRUCTURE

Another stream of research efforts has gone into analysing the industrial structure of various regional economies at inter-State as well as intra-State levels. Alagh *et al.* (1971a) portrayed the industrial base of 16 major States of India, using employment data. The study observed that the industrial scene of most of the States is still dominated by resource based industries. They also noticed a remarkable stability in the level of regional industrial specialisation between 1956 and 1965, implying that hardly any structural shift took place across States during this period.

In another study, using the input-output technique, Lakdawala *et al.* (1974) attempted to identify 'technological clusters' and 'empirical spatial clusters' of industries to examine the degree of technological interdependence of industries with each another across space.[4] While comparing these two clusters, the study observed that, in general, 'empirical clusters' were smaller than the 'technological clusters'. It implies that in the regional context of India, full-scale development of technologically interrelated industries has yet not taken place, apart from a few highly developed regions. This is perhaps to be expected in the initial phase of industrialisation. This finding further corroborates earlier findings of Alagh *et al.* (1971b) and Alagh (1972) at the inter-State level. The finding, that the developed regions by and large have more diversified industrial structure compared to the less developed ones was vindicated even at the intra-State level.[5]

Though these studies provide a valuable insight into the nature of spatial distribution of industries across States in India, they do not offer any explanation for the emerging patterns and their dynamics over time. They also do not throw any light on the role industrial composition plays in the growth performance of a region.

## DETERMINANTS OF THE REGIONAL INDUSTRIAL VARIATION IN INDIA

Three broad research groups could be noticed while looking into the causes of industrial variations across regions in India.[6] Researchers explaining the variations in terms of historical forces belong to the first group. The second group of researchers has tried to analyse role of public policies in achieving balanced regional development of the industrial economy of India. The third group explains the variations in the level of industrial development in terms of some market forces, indirectly affecting factor prices and cost of production.

### Historical Forces and Regional Industrial Variations

Studies belonging to this group contend that the answers to the existing regional industrial inequalities ought to be sought in the process of the economic history of the regions.[7] India remained under British rule for a considerable period. And the interest of the rulers was to use the 'dependent colony' as a supplier of the raw material for the British industries. Incidentally, the vast population of India also ensured a captive market for British manufacturers. Attempts of the British to keep India as a captive market for their manufacturers are described elsewhere (Dutta, 1902; Hurd, 1973). While the industrial revolution was sweeping throughout England, India was undergoing a systematic process of de-industrialisation (Bagchi, 1975). In the process, only those regions of the colony could develop which served the economic interest of the colonial masters most. The development of port towns such as Bombay, Calcutta and Madras was incidental to these historical and political forces. This in turn had wider ramifications on the regional development in India for a long time. After Independence these port towns became the hub of industrial activities, though initially these urban centres acted merely as outposts of the metropolitan economy in the colony (Chattopadhyaya and Raza, 1975).

The development of the three Presidencies, viz. Calcutta, Bombay and Madras, having three major port towns with the same name, gave birth to a severe rural-urban dichotomy. It is also argued that the development of the Presidencies took place at the cost of hinterlands (Thavaraj, 1972), consisting of Assam (Misra, 1980), Bihar and Orissa (Bagchi, 1974; Gupta, 1981), and Maharashtra (excluding Bombay) (Savur, 1980). Thus, the metropolitan satellite relationship changed from an inter-national to international scale, culminating in a centre-periphery syndrome.

A question emerges as to what was the process due to which industrial concentration took place in a few port towns. It is often argued that the regional distribution of industries was rather a consequence of the railway freight policy (Hashim, 1969), and the uneven public sector investment in basic overheads made by the government keeping their own economic interest and strategic needs (Thavaraj, 1972).[8] Researchers feel that the regional spread of industries during pre-independence days did not always reflect the locational advantage or disadvantage (Savur, 1980). Not only this, the dominant emergence of port towns might have been different if based on locational logic.

> . . . the choice of Calcutta was largely fortuitious, likewise Madras, and had there been planning in existence two or three hundred years ago, the main ports of the east-coast might easily have been elsewhere. . . . It is from the accident of first 'contacts' that we have it where we have it (Census of India, 1941 : 27).

Some of the region specific institutional factors also had played an important role. For example, in the case of Punjab and Haryana, Pandit (1978) observed that factors like historically available local skills owing to agricultural prosperity (probably an outcome of the heavy public investment made in Punjab in irrigation by the British) and induced early development of agricultural implements, machines and certain other tools manufacturing were instrumental in the industrial development of these regions. On the other hand Gupta (1981) found in the case of Bihar that lack of 'sub-nationalism' had acted as a stumbling block in the industrial development of the region.[9] He observes

> . . . the Indian sub-continental syndrome is testimony for the fact that the States have progressed had sufficiently sub-national consciousness; (and) by keeping sub-nationalism at a low key, the capitalists of Western India (Marwari's ai d Gujaratis) spread to the eastern region under the banner of nationalism. . . . Close liaison between the Western Indian capitalists and Bihar political leaders came in way of development of an indigenous industrial class. The situation has not substantially changed even after ndependence (Gupta, 1982 : 1500).

These studies offer some explanations for the industrial development and underdevelopment of the various regions in India. A more important question which, by and large, remains unanswered is: whether such mechanism still operates in the country, despite government efforts? Some of the researchers have tried to answer this question while analysing the impact and efficacy of the public policies towards balanced regional industrial development. We review this stream in the subsequent section.

**Public Policy and Balanced Regional Development**

It is often argued that government's policies, in the post-Independence period, have resulted in greater regional imbalances (Pathak, 1980). Most of the large industrial units have taken advantage of the colonial setting in which the axis of the development converged on metropolitan cities, oriented to the ports (Kundu and Raza, 1981). This calls for a closer scrutiny of the planning process in the post-Independence period.[10]

It is alleged that Indian planning, by and large, has been limited to allocation of investment over time, sectors and sub-sectors, whereas there is no explicit spatial dimension in the formal planning models (Chakravarty, 1977; Alagh, 1962; Kashyap, 1979). The government, however, was well aware of the regional disparities and its consequences right from the inception of the planning era in 1951. For example, the First Five Year Plan (1951-56) noted with concern that

> . . . greater attention will have to be paid to the development of the States and regions which have remained backward. Since, industrial development in India has so far been on an unbalanced basis and it has been concentrated in a few selected areas (First

Five Year Plan, 1951 : 442).

The emphasis was more sharp in the Industrial Policy Resolution of 1956 which observed

> In order that industrialisation may benefit the economy of the country as a whole, it is important that disparities in the levels of development between different regions should be progressively reduced. . . . Only by securing a balanced and co-ordinated development of the industrial agricultural economy *in each region*, can the entire economy attain higher standards of living (emphasis ours).

The Third Five Year Plan document, which contained one full chapter on Balanced Regional Development, noted that : "A balanced development of different parts of the country, the extension of benefits of economic progress to less developed regions and widespread diffusion of industry are among the major aims of planned development" (Third Five Year Plan, 1961 : 44). This spirit was carried forward in all the subsequent plans and policy documents with increasing stress. The government used following policy instruments in order to achieve balanced regional industrial development.

(i) Industrial licensing;
(ii) Location of public sector undertakings;
(iii) Extension of infrastructural facilities through industrial estates;
(iv) Distribution and pricing policy; and
(v) Incentives to industrially backward areas.

*Industrial Licensing:* As noted earlier, the balanced regional development was an implicit aim of the various plans. The government envisaged licensing as an instrument to achieve the objective; through the Industries (Development and Regulation) Act, 1951. In other words, the underlying message was to grant more licences for big industrial units in the backward regions, and at the same time control the industrial expansion of already highly developed areas/towns (Krishnaiah, 1976).

However, contrary to the expectations, Mitra (1965) found that between 1953 and 1961, 35.77 per cent out of the total 1978 licences issued, went to the three top industrial centres, viz. Bombay, Calcutta and Madras. A more recent study also shows that though there is a slight shift in licences, the 'top' still remains the 'top'. For, out of 750 licences issued in 1982, 102 were cornered by Maharashtra, followed by Gujarat getting 93 licences (Aguiar and Ravindranath, 1983).[11]

Therefore, one can broadly infer that the regional pattern of industrial licensing continues to be weighted in favour of the high and middle income States (Kolanjiyil, 1978). Licensing as a policy instrument for reducing regional disparities has not been successful.

*Location of Public Sector Projects:* It was postulated that the location on public sector undertaking in backward areas will benefit the regions in a variety of ways.[12] Consequently most of the public sector projects were initially located in backward States such as Bihar, Orissa and Madhya Pradesh. However, most of these location decisions were an outcome of economic compulsions like resource endowment of the regions.

Some researchers argue that investment in public sector undertakings in backward areas has reduced regional disparities (Pathak, 1971; Gupta, 1973). On the other hand some other researchers feel that this policy has not been an unqualified success. For, the projects which have come up in backward States are not necessarily integrated with the local economy and instead have linkages outside the regions (Patnaik, 1973; Prasad, 1976; Goel, 1975; Nair, 1980; Sarma, 1982; Ramadhyani, 1984).[13] It is also argued that the public sector investment has been regionally regressive, particularly after the sixties, due to the changes in the sectoral priorities (Alagh *et al.*, 1982; Udai Sekhar, 1983).

Thus, it appears that location of some public sector undertakings in the backward regions has had only a marginal impact. It is doubtful if investment of this nature will have any serious impact on the backward regional economies unless priority is given to those industries which have high regional rather than sectoral linkages.

*Industrial Estates:* The crucial role of infrastructure in the economic development was recognised by the government and it was accepted that "Growth and diversity of economic activity can take place only if infrastructure required for this is provided in an adequate manner" (Third Five Year Plan, 1961 : 149). The Government of India launched an industrial estates programme in 1955 to spread infrastructure more widely (Bredo, 1960) creating, thereby, more external economies for the entrepreneurs willing to locate their units in a relatively backward area (Alexander, 1963). One of the objectives of the scheme was to disperse industries away from the metropolitan regions (Mathur, 1971; Bharati, 1978).

Studies conducted during the mid-sixties and early seventies to assess the effectiveness of the programme have raised serious doubts about the success of the programme (Alexander, 1963; Nagia, 1971; Bandopadhyaya, 1969; Udaisekhar 1983). It is alleged that wrong locational choice and inadequate infrastructural facilities have further aggravated the problem (Sanghvi, 1976). Moreover, instead of integrating with local regional economies, most of the relatively successful industrial estates have links with the national economy (Kashyap *et al.*, 1975). Even these so-called successful estates are, by and large, concentrated in and around the urban industrial areas, thereby mocking at the goal of regional decentralisation of industries. Therefore, it is often argued that the policy of induced industrialisation through industrial estates has proved to failure (Adhvaryu, 1983).

*Distribution and Pricing Policy:* Certain inputs such as cement, coal and steel are crucial for the operation of industrial units. Therefore, with an eye on the objective of regional equality in India, the government has pursued a policy of equalising the price and controlling the distribution of these inputs throughout the country through railway freight charges and retention prices.

It is often argued that this type of control results into various kinds of market distoration and leads to certain irrationalities in industrial locations. For example, 'postage stamp rates' for certain critical industrial raw materials such as cement, steel and coal, have tended to negate the location advantages of any particular place (Rao and Sundaram, 1973). Since regional production of these inputs is determined by the locational advantage in terms of raw material and transport cost, the policy of freight equalisation acts as a subsidy to the 'non-producing' (of key inputs) regions. It is observed that had the Indian Railways charged market rates for coal transportation, there would have been greater motivation for industrialists to locate their units near the coal-fields (Lefeber and Chauduri, 1964); the existing rate structure of the railways induced producers to seek location near market centres rather than near the source of raw material (Raina, 1969; Singh, 1983).[14] Therefore, by and large, this policy of freight equalisation has not only helped developed States to develop faster, leading to further imbalances in the regional development; where the interest of the backward but resource rich regions such as Bihar, Orissa or Madhya Pradesh are neglected. Thus the freight policy of the government has been counterproductive as far as balanced regional industrial development is concerned.

*Financial Incentives:* The failure of the policies of industrial dispersal led the government to appointing two committees in 1968. The first (the Pande Committee) was to recommend objective criterion for identifying industrially backward regions. The other (the Wanchoo Committee) was to recommend fiscal and financial incentives for setting up industries in backward regions.

Based on the reports of these two committees, the government declared 296 (about 60%) districts as industrially backward, and introduced a Central Capital Investment Subsidy Scheme in 101 of the totally backward districts. These backward areas were given further incentives in terms of income-tax concession, sales tax subsidy, special facilities to import raw materials and hire-purchase of machinery for small scale units.

The distribution of this subsidy till 1978-79 among the various regions shows that more than 55 per cent of the capital subsidy went to only 25 eligible districts of *industrially advanced States* (Dua, 1980). It is also argued that even if subsidy can be successfully utilised for achieving balanced regional industrial development, its ability to generate employment is suspected on *a priori* grounds.[15] Therefore, researchers have strongly advocated labour or infrastructure subsidy instead of capital subsidy (Alagh and Pathak, 1973; Nagia, 1980; Asthana, 1980).

*Commercial Banks:* Before their nationalisation, commercial banks had no role to play in the direction of balanced regional development. After the nationalisation they also came into the ambit of the government directions. Earlier, a commercial bank always waited for a region to develop to a certain level before it started business there. After nationalisation, the government expected that finances will start flowing to the backward regions. However, evidence shows that funds have tended to flow from backward regions to the developed ones. Thus, the former have continued to contribute to the growth of the latter and banking operations, on the whole, seem to have been regressive in this respect.[16]

*Non-Banking Financial Institutions:* The Government of India, through development banks, has evolved many incentive schemes to attract industries to backward districts. The industrial Development Bank of India (IDBI) acts as an apex industrial financial institution co-ordinating the operation of other institutions such as industrial

Finance Corporation of India (IFCI), industrial Rehabilitation Bank of India, Unit Trust of India, Life Insurance Corporation of India and State Financial Corporations. The operational statistics of the IDBI shows that, between 1964 and 1984, the backward areas of four developed States (Maharashtra, Gujarat, Karnataka and Tamil Nadu) together received 42.6 per cent of total backward area finance. If we include Andhra Pradesh and West Bengal, the percentage increases to 56 per cent; whereas the total share of backward States (Assam, Bihar, Himachal Pradesh, Jammu and Kashmir, Kerala, Madhya Pradesh and Orissa) taken together was barely 15.9 per cent, marginally above (15.2%) that of Gujarat alone. Similarly, net financial assistance sanctioned by the IFCI, between 1948 and 1984, to these backward States totalled only 14.7 per cent against 58.6 per cent for the six developed States. The picture does not change in the case of the operations of other non-banking financial institutions. Therefore, it appears that though the net share of backward regions is increasing in the degree of assistance provided by these institutions, the beneficiaries are the backward areas of the developed States only. Plausibly it might have helped in reducing intra-state industrial regional inequalities, but their role in the context of inter-state industrial imbalances is at best suspect.

The State governments also play a crucial role in shaping regional industrialisation. Most of the governments have established some or the other agency to promote industrial development such as Industrial Development Corporations, industrial Investment Corporations, Small Industries Development Corporations, etc. apart from financial corporations at States' level.

However, there seems to be a cut-throat competition among the States in attracting enterprises. Any new incentive declared by any on State government is usually instantly initiated by other States.[17] Consequently promotional measures and concessions available to the entrepreneur, across States, are not very dissimilar (Godbole, 1978 : 79 : 86).[18] However, States do differ in the degree of success which possibly could be attributed to the efficiency of the implementing machinery and the outlook of the State government. Developed States such as Gujarat, Maharashtra, Tamil Nadu, Karnataka and Andhra Pradesh are able to attract more entrepreneurs than States such as Assam, Bihar, Orissa and Kerala.[19]

From the above discussion it clearly emerges that the planning policies adopted by the government has, by and large, failed to deliver goods. And market forces are strong enough to hold the industrial concentration in a few developed regions despite government will. What, then, are those uncontrolled market forces?

**Determinants of Inter-regional Industrial Variation**

Apart from the colonial legacy or historical and political process as an explanation for the inter-regional industrial imbalances in India, it is argued that factors like availability of infrastructure in terms of transport, power and means of communications, agglomeration economies, size of the market, linkages – inter-industry (technological) and marketing, availability of cheap and submissive labour, urbanisation, entrepreneurship, level of agricultural development, and the like ones strongly affect the industrial development of any region. Thus it can be postulated that the regional variations in the level of industrial development will prevail to the extent the aforesaid factors vary across States. We try to assess the impact of one or a group of these above factors.

*Level of Agricultural Development:* Interdependence between agriculture and industry is too well known (Rudra, 1964; Hayami, 1969; Raj, 1984). It is a widely accepted proposition that as per capita income increases there will be a distinct shift, in the sectoral allocation, towards industries (Kuznets, 1957; Hoffman, 1958; Clark, 1960). Initially an increase in per capita income can be realised only from agriculture. This increase in income is likely to lead to (i) higher demand for manufactured goods (initially consumer goods) owing to higher income elasticity; and (ii) investible surplus for investment in industries, because of the increasing rate of savings. Of course, in later stages even industries are found to provide a push to the agricultural growth (Hayami, 1969).

It is argued that regional variations in the level of industrial development are some sort of reflection of the regional variations in the level of agricultural development. This proposition was empirically vindicated by Papola (1979), Pandit (1978), Singh (1981) and Kaur (1983) at intra-State level. In the inter-State context Alagh *et al.* (1982) also observed a positive association between the two. However, Raj (1976) believes that development of small scale industries depends on agriculture to a large extent, but it may not hold good in the case of large scale industries. Nair (1982) also found, it to be true more in the case of small scale than large scale industries. However, this type of proposition treats agriculture as only a supply side variable.

As a matter of fact, agricultural development assumes greater importance when treated as a demand side variable. For, it is likely to encourage industrialisation in the region via demand for agricultural inputs like fertilizer, tools and implements, etc. At the same time, enhanced incomes of the farmers also result in a higher demand for consumer goods. Moreover, it is also noticed that there is a tendency for economic activities to concentrate in areas of greatest population density and that the most densely populated agricultural areas in the pre-industrial age often turned out to be areas of greater industrial growth (Clark, 1967). This leads to another factor, viz. market, which probably could explain the regional variations.

*Market Size:* Agricultural development may give an initial boost, but the level and scale of operation of industries is likely to be limited by market size. This is normally determined by the size of population and the purchasing power of the buyer, apart from inter-industry demand. Purchasing power, again, depends on the per capita income as well as income distribution. The bigger size of the market also may give rise to economies of scale.

Chenery (1960), using international cross-section data for the 1950s, observed that size of the country (i.e. market) in terms of population was of crucial importance in the intercountry variation in the level of industrial development. Using a somewhat similar methodology, Gupta (1971) observed that larger States (in terms of population) had better growth performance compared to the smaller ones between 1951 and 1961. Similarly, Sastry (1970) observed that per capita income, population and urbanisation explained inter-regional variations in the net industrial output in India during the same period.

It can also be argued that the federal structure of Indian polity, with almost unrestricted inter-regional trade, is likely to limit the effectiveness of the size of the market. After all, unlike national economies, regional economies within a country are open economies. Therefore, local demand can be met through imports.[20]

However, the market in India is highly segmented and regional in character, owing to the relative immobility of factors (Gandhi, 1979; Sridharan and Chakraborty, 1979), and small magnitude of inter-regional trade (Mehta, 1955; Manne, 1967). In fact, the emergence of trade-blocks, each consisting of a group of States, was observed empirically by Hashim (1970), who noted very high concentration of inter-regional trade of each region with a very few other regions.[21] This further hints possibility of concentration of industries in a few regions within each trade block and in a few urban metropolitan centres within these regions, leading to regional variations.

*Urbanisation and Agglomeration Economies:* Co-existence of industrialisation and urbanisation in the process of economic growth is a widely observed phenomenon (Lampard, 1955; Richardson, 1973). The relationship between urbanisation and industrialisation is indirect and circuitous (Breese, 1969). Though it is argued that urbanisation is a by product of industrial development in India (Acharya, 1956; Suri, 1968), it is also argued that the latter is not a precondition for the former (Banerjee, 1969). For example, a slower tempo of urbanisation was observed in a decade of rapid industrialisation between 1951 and 1961 (Bose, 1961: 1970). However, today industry goes to the urban centres rather than urbanisation growing in and around new industrial locations (Bose, 1969; Pathak, 1975; Rakesh Mohan, 1983).

Whatever be the circuit or direction of causation the case for a strong relationship between urbanisation and industrialisation does exist. It can be argued that variations in the level of industrial development are related to variations in the level of urbanisation across States in India.[22] It has been further corroborated in a recent empirical study by Udai Sekhar (1983) that employment in household industry tends to concentrate more in smaller size towns, which primarily caters to the local demand; whereas location of the non-household industry in larger towns and cities is dictated by factors like economies of scale, technology and availability of infrastructural facilities.

The most significant feature of urbanisation is the concentration of population which in turn exercises a localised effect on several new Commercial and trade units. Moreover, an increase in city-size leads to an increase in industrial activity (Rao, 1975; Kashyap *et al.*, 1980). For, an increase in city size generally leads to improved capital as well as labour productivity due to the agglomeration economies like scale economies, access to larger pool of skilled labour, availability of specialized auxilliary industrial and repair facilities (Mera, 1973; Segal, 1975; Richardson, 1977). Improvement in transport and communication further facilitates the growth in these centres. These focal points attract skilled and unskilled workers and encourage entrepreneurship, leading to further industrial growth (Lampard, 1955; Richardson, 1973).

Lakdawala *et al.*, (1974), for the first time, attempted to isolate the effect of agglomeration economies and concluded that the clustering of industrial activities across various regions confer productivity advantages.[23] On the basis of a field survey of 130 units in Maharashtra, Godbole (1978) also found that agglomeration economies are crucial for increasing the attractiveness of an area. However, these studies are not only partial in regional coverages but measure the agglomeration economies only in an indirect and somewhat crude manner. It might, therefore, be rewarding to assess the potential of urbanisation and agglomeration economies more comprehensively.

*Technological/Scaler Linkages and Regional Imbalances:* Once industry starts at some place, it generates external/agglomeration economies through technological as well as scalar linkages. Alagh *et al.* (1971a), Nair (1982), Papola (1979), Hashim (1978 & 1979) and Thomas (1979), among others, noticed that medium and small size enterprises, left to themselves are attracted towards those regions which are also already industrially developed. Some other studies, using an input-output framework, observe that inter-industry linkages *per se* have very little bearing on the growth performance of regional industrial economies in India. However, it is difficult to accept this proposition because the input-output tables used for the analysis by Kashyap and Desai (1974) and Venkataramaiah (1983) pertain to the technology existing in 1965, which is likely to have become obsolete. Moreover, these studies ignore the demand side altogether. Awasthi (1983) tried to incorporate the demand side in terms of the sectoral income elasticities; but reached a similar conclusion. But in this case also, the sectoral income elasticities were that of the nation and do not reflect the region specific demand. Therefore, a fresh testing of the hypothesis is likely to shed more light on the impact of linkages in regional industrial growth performance.

*Availability of Infrastructure:* Infrastructure has been found to be a very important factor in explaining the regional variations at inter- as well as intra-State level.[24] Hashim (1978/79) observed that infrastructure significantly explained the regional variations in addition to per capita fixed capital, and workers per thousand population, in the large scale manufacturing sector between 1961 and 1965. These findings were further confirmed by Papola (1979); Singh (1981); Kaur (1983) and Sarma (1982) who found that availability of transport, power and institutional finance in easy terms play a very crucial role.

However, Papola (1981) argued that any of the factors do not work successfully in isolation; and are able to attract new industrial activity, only when supported by government efforts. Therefore, any effort to assess contribution of infrastructural facilities has to be made in totality and not in isolation as has usually been done so far.

*Human Capital:* It is argued in the literature that owing to the relative unavailability of human factors, industries are adapting themselves to the market (Seth, 1975). Following Schumpeter, it was also suggested that shortage of entrepreneurs with a capacity to recognise and exploit opportunities and introduce innovations, may also lead to stagnation and backwardness of the regions (Myrdal, 1958; Hirschman, 1958; Pathak, 1973).

Pandit (1978), in his study of 'footloose industries' in Punjab and Haryana, found that the displaced population, which came to Punjab (after the partition in 1947) was well endowed with entrepreneurial qualities, which transformed the industrial map of Punjab and Haryana.[25] The study also revealed how a regular supply of submissive and cheap labour force can be favourable for the emergence of the industrial sector in a region; and concluded that this "provides some of the major cause of the location of footloose industries in this region" (Pandit, 1978 : 262).[26]

However, these observations are based on the case studies of small-scale units in different regions and reflect only entrepreneurs' views. It appears from the studies as if organised labour force is detrimental to the growth of industries; and strong trade union movement necessarily leads to conflict.[27] It is also often argued that strong trade unions and their activities play a positive role in the process of industrialisation (Ross and Hartman, 1960; Kannappan, 1970; Brown and Medoff, 1978; Clark, 1980). Our only argument is that this proposition needs a more careful observation, before generalising in inter-regional context.

## CONCLUDING OBSERVATIONS

While reviewing the literature, we noticed that most of the aspects of interregional industrial variations in India have been treated inadequately. Analysis of the role and relation of the factors like urbanisation/agglomeration, entrepreneurship and labour problems, government policies and the like in the process of industrialisation, by and large, remains inconclusive. However, the factors chosen randomly and treated in isolation hardly throw any light on the process of regional industrial growth. Moreover, quantification of the relationships has been mostly carried out in the framework of descriptive statistics like correlations or standard deviations.

It is of course not our purpose to undermine the importance of such studies. They do provide a framework and direction for further expeditions. The findings also provide some important directions for policy and planning. However, the need for a study which attempts at the problem more comprehensively, can hardly be denied. This study, therefore, is an effort in investigating the pattern, nature and causes of regional disparities in industrial development of India between 1961 and 1978 in a more comprehensive manner.

## NOTES

1. For, even on the eve of Independence in 1948, Bombay State accounted for 34.7 per cent of the total workers engaged in manufacturing and 44.8 per cent of the total value of net industrial output, followed by West Bengal with 31.7 per cent and 23.7 per cent of employment and value of net industrial production respectively. If we include Madras, the three presidencies together accounted for approximately 76.7 per cent of the total industrial workers and 77.0 per cent of the total output. (Chandra, 1963).
   If we look at the sectoral concentration of industries in various States in 1948, approximately 81.9 per cent output of textiles was contributed by Bombay and Madras States. Similarly West Bengal and Bombay States accounted for 76.1 per cent of engineering and electric goods and 80.6 per cent of the chemical industry. The sugar industry was mostly confined to Uttar Pradesh (55.6%), Bombay (28.6%) and Bihar (14.3%). These four States taken together accounted for as much as 84.5 per cent of total sugar production. (Chandra, 1963).
2. Udai Sekhar (1963) found that the inter-regional inequalities have converged continuously. With the help of Thiel's Inequality Index and the Hirschman-Herfindahl Index, constructed for all the years between 1960 and 1975 using value added and employment data (for the organised sector), he observed that the former index exhibits a decline of 40 per cent in terms of value added and 30 per cent in employment. The decline observed in the case of the latter index was to the extent of 18 and 15 per cent respectively between 1960 and 1975.
3. Barathawal's total dependence on the total pertaining only to the corporate sector or employment only in the large scale public and private sector tends to limit the general applicability of his conclusions.
4. Technological clusters indicate the technological inter-dependence between industries/industry groups; whereas the Empirical Spatial clusters of industries are those clusters of group of industries which tend to grow together in different regions (Lakdawala, *et al.*, 1974 : 9).
5. For example, see Godbole (1978), Papola (1979), Awasthi and Shah (1981); Ramakrishna Sarma (1982); Kaur (1983), among others, who studied inter district variations with reference to Maharashtra, Uttar Pradesh, Gujarat, Andhra Pradesh and Haryana respectively.

6. However, at the outset is may be noted that it is not possible to clarify these studies into the watertight compartments. For, they overlap in context in most of the cases. We have adop'ed this three-fold classification purely for the sake of convenience.
7. The theoretical base of such studies can be traced back into a mix of the propositions better known as 'Cumulative-Causation Theory" *a la* Myrdal (1958), Hirschman (1958) and Rosenstein Rodan (1963); 'Growth Role Theory' of Perroux (1971); Boudeville (1966), Friedmann (1966); and 'Centre-Periphery' concept of Prebisch (1962); later developed as 'Dependency Theory' having base in Marxism, by Griffin (1966); Frank (969); Luxemburg (1951); Baron (1957); Amin (1976), Furtado (1976), Sunkel (1969) and Casanova (1969), among others. Main stress of these scholars has been that the underdevelopment of the underdeveloped regions has its roots in the development process of the developed regions; where the later developed at the cost of the former regions.
8. For example the British industrialists found that the export of raw cotton to Britain fell steeply due to the lack of good internal transport. Hence, to ensure regular supply of raw cotton, they thought of covering at least the strategic cotton growing areas with railways. It was also expected that, in addition, it would further their interest of selling the finished products in the hinterland. That is why the first section of the Bombay-Baroda and Central India's Railways (BBCIR) was laid by 1860 and the Ahmedabad section by 1863 (Edward, 1941), Importance of Bombay was further enhanced with opening the the Suez Canal in 1869, which instantly brought Bombay a thousand miles closer to England, compared to Calcutta or Madras (Thorner). Thus industrial development was rather incidental to the development of railways (Hashim, 1969) which helped Britain to retain India more securely as one of her principal markets (Ramadhan, 1946; Habib, 1975).

   Similarly the regional pattern of British public investment in railway, power, irrigation and roads adversely affected the future of balanced regional development. Between 1860 and 1947, Punjab received the largest share in public expenditure accounting for 22 per cent of the total share. Madras State was static, whereas the share of Bombay and Sind put together claimed progressively increasing share of investment. The share of United Province was quite impressive looking at its size. The share of all other regions taken together was surprisingly less than even the total public investment in Punjab alone (Thavaraj, 1972). Thus balanced or judicious regional development became the first casualty.
9. In a somewhat similar fashion Bagchi trying to explain the industrial development of Western India and backwardness of the Eastern Indian States observed "that some, at least of the difference between the burdens of exploitation as between Eastern and Western India can be attributed to the fact that dominant capitalist class in Western India had a very large Indian component, whereas the capitalist strata dominating manufacturing, plantation and the mining and large scale banking and external trade in Eastern India was almost entirely European, particularly before World War I" (As quoted by Shaibal Gupta, 1981 : 150). The study holds good even in the case of Assam (Misra, 1980; Goswami, 1981).
10. As noted earlier, government intervention was seen as crucial in thwarting the free interaction of market forces. Left to the free play of market forces, economic activities show a tendency to concentrate at a few geographically advantageous

points, and only strong political will and government intervention can curb this tendency. Plausibly that is why Government of India has been serious about the lopsided regional development, and has been promulgating various policies, from time to time, directed towards achieving a more balanced regional development.

11. Even within the States the picture is not very different; for example, 54.29 per cent of the licences issued to Maharashtra between 1952 and 1975 went to Greater Bombay alone. If we include Thane (20.19%) and Pune, (10.0%); 3661 of the total 4332 licences went only to these three districts in Maharashtra (Godbole, 1978:15:16).
12. For example, it was envisaged that such locations will create much needed infrastructure, enhance trade and commerce activities and in turn will create employment opportunities for the local population. It was also envisaged that due to the initial impact of public sector undertakings, the dorment entrepreneurial potential will find a meaningful outlet for its development and growth through the prospective ancillary industries. See Nath (1971); Ghosh and Ghosh (1980); Sarma (1982); Dhingra and Jhurany (1974-75), among others.
13. For example, the lead industry in Bhilai was closely linked with the distant economy of Bombay; small scale and ancillary industries based on the lead industry developed in far off regions completely by-passing the next village economy (Goel, 1975).
14. For example, Mitra (1983) contends that the pricing and transport subsidy has adversely affected the industrial development of West Bengal, Bihar and Orissa. Similarly, in case of cement, southern and western India, with concentration of the cement industry has lost its locational advantage *vis-a-vis* northern and eastern regions (NCAER, 1979).
15. Capital subsidy, by its very nature, will lead to high capital as well as technological intensity leading to low employment generation. Low income generation for the masses is the logical outcome, which has serious repercussions on income distribution.
16. For example in 1956 the share of four industrially developed States, viz. Gujarat, Maharashtra, Tamil Nadu and West Bengal, in credit was 72 per cent against the deposit of 61 per cent (Lal, 1974). Even in 1980, this picture did not alter much. For, these very States accounted for 48.78 per cent of the credit against 46.04 per cent share of the deposits during 1980-81 (*Economic Survey*, 1980-81 : 106).
17. I am grateful to Prof. Ashok Mitra, ex-Finance Minister of West Bengal, for drawing my attention to this point.
18. For a comparison of incentives offered by various State governments, see *Scope for Industries in Different States — Incentives and Facilities for industrial Location*, India Investment Centre, 1976, New Delhi.
19. "Gujarat and Maharashtra are much more dynamic in selling themselves to firms and much faster at processing applications and sanctions than any other States in India. Tamil Nadu comes third. From what I have heard, Kerala is not particularly good in this respect, which may have to do why firms are not moving to the State" (Mackie, quoted in Oomen, 1981 : 86).
20. For example Pandit (1975) observes that local market has not been of much consequence in the industrial development of Punjab and Haryana; since these States sold most of their industrial products in markets outside the regions and purchased inputs form as distant places as Bihar.

21. For example, Hashim (1970) noticed that about five developed regions accounted for 60 to 99 per cent of the trade in any region. If trade balance constraints are imposed, the regional pattern of the industrial-mix is significantly altered, except in the case resource base industries (Mathur and Hashim, 1972 : 969). Similarly Thakkar (1971) found that about half of the Gujarat's trade was with the adjoining regions of Rajasthan, Madhya Pradesh and Maharashtra.
22. Urbanisation has been found as an important determinant of the regional variations in the level of industrial development in India. See Dhar and Sastry (1969), Wadhva and Kashyap (1983).
23. Desai (1974) empirically evaluated the advantages of clustered industrial activities in case of the cotton textile industry in Gujarat, Maharashtra, Rajasthan and Delhi, and concluded that owing to the emergence of the cotton textile complex Gujarat has an edge over other regions in productivity and has a comparative advantage in the industry.
24. For, infrastructure provides industry with basic services necessary for productive process. It includes transportation, power, water supply and communication. These facilities are expected to give rise to external economies. Perhaps that is why investment in transport and power facilities is the heart of the 'big push' argument. See for details, Rosenstein Rodan (1961) alongwith the comments of Furtado (1961) and Nurkse (1961); Singer, (1960); among others. For Indian context, see Sinha (1968); Antia (1973); Aiyar (1973).
25. Similarly it is also said that Gujarat's industrial development owes much to its historical tradition of entrepreneurship. So are Marwaris, but Rajasthan still remains an industrially backward region. Similarly in Maharashtra, most of the industrial activity is controlled by Gujarat is and Parsies. Probably, entrepreneurs move to the opportunities. However, local availability of entrepreneurs may be of some consequence as far as small-scale industries are concerned. But growth of large scale industries is a function of the economically attractive location rather than local availability of entrepreneurs.
26. In a study of the mobility of small scale entrepreneurs out of Kerala, based on the field investigation of 124 entrepreneurs of Kerala origin and having their units in Tamil Nadu or Karnataka, Oomen noticed that "the most important single reason reported about the choice of location was the availability of cheap labour" (1981 : 78). He further observed that "Workers of Kerala are much more conscious of their rights; the social and political atmosphere of Kerala also is more conducive to asserting them. This is why small scale entrepreneurs are not able to reconcile with" (p.82). Studies by Papola (1979), Kaur (1983) and Godbole (1978) also have reached somewhat similar conclusions.
27. Circumvention of labour laws and regulations by industrialists in general and the exploitative nature of small scale units are too well known.

# 3

# PERFORMANCE OF THE INDUSTRIAL SECTOR

IN THE preceding chapter we observed that the distribution of industries was highly uneven across States on the eve of Independence. Hardly any noticeable change was observed in the location dynamics of industries, even after the first decade of planned development. Despite the fact that States are parts of the same economy, they differ widely in terms of their growth experience. Before we examine the emerging industrial patterns at the regional level, it will be rewarding to analyse the industrial performance at the national level. For, the regional planning process reflects the national planning, accompanied by somewhat similar efforts at the State level. Moreover in a federal set-up like that of India, any discussion on regional development, we believe, must be carried out in the backdrop of the national scenario. This chapter attempts a brief sketch of the growth of the manufacturing sector at the all India level.

## DATABASE

The mjor source of data for this and the three subsequent chapters is the *Annual Survey of Industries (ASI)*, published by the Central Statistical Organisation (CSO). We have used information for the registered factory sector, i.e. census and sample sectors, as published by CSO. The analysis, spatial as well as temporal, has been made in terms of variables like fixed capital, employment and value added. We have also used some information provided by the National Accounts Statistics, with reference to the unorganised segment of the manufacturing sector, wherever necessary.[1] In all the 53 industrial groups, roughly corresponding to the sample sector's level of disaggregation, have been used for the purpose of analysis.[2]

## THE METHODOLOGY

Growth performance of the industrial sector in an economy can be measured in terms of various economic variables such as fixed-capital, employment, output or value added etc. One or a combination of different variables is generally employed for the purpose. We have taken three variables for our analysis viz., fixed capital, employment and value added.[3] By and large they represent investment, employment, and income aspects of the manufacturing sector respectively.[4]

For the purpose of temporal assessment of the performance of the manufacturing sector we have used simple statistical measures like percentage shares and changes, compound growth rates[5] and trend rated of growth,[6] etc.

## PERFORMANCE OF THE REGISTERED MANUFACTURING (FACTORY) SECTOR IN INDIA: 1961-1978

India started with a small and narrow industrial base, confined mainly to the consumer goods sector, in 1951. During the subsequent years of planning, performance of the industrial sector has been quite impressive in terms of quantity as well as quality. As envisaged in the Mahalanobis model, India has broadened and diversified its industrial base to capital and intermediate goods sectors during the Second and Third Plan periods (Medhora, 1968; Shirokov, 1973).

The initial spurt in the growth rates till the mid-sixties, however, could not be sustained in the years that followed. A plethora of literature has emerged during the mid-seventies, indicating stagnation after 1965-66.[7] There is evidence to suggest that the growth of industrial production suffered a set-back during 1965-67 recession, from which it is yet to recover.[8] However, all the sectors did not suffer alike during the recession. For example, the decline in the growth of capital goods sector was more pronounced than any of the other sectors (Shetty, 1978; Ahluwalia, 1985). Therefore, the growth performance of the various industry groups at all India level is being analysed in order to capture the broad trends over a period of 18 years, i.e., between 1961 and 1978 and its sub-periods.[9]

### The Growth Trends

The growth performance of the registered manufacturing (factory) sector in India has been quite satisfactory during the past two decades. In terms of value-added it grew at an average compound growth rate of 5.89 per cent per annum between 1961 and 1978. The same period experienced 3.97 per cent per annum rate of growth in employment and an impressive 8.91 per cent in terms of fixed capital. The highest growth rate attained by fixed capital is indicative of a capital deepening process in the registered manufacturing sector in India. However, it was the first sub-period (1961-69), when fixed capital grew at a substantially higher rate (14.13%), compared to value-added and employment which registered 5.70 and 3.86 per cent growth per annum respectively. During the second sub-period (1969-78), fixed capital grew at the low pace (3.86%) per annum (see Table 3.1). This probably reflects the government policy of giving big push to the heavy and capital intensive 'investment goods sector' during the Second and the Third Five Year Plans, following the Mahalanobis Model. It was possibly the long gestation period involved in the process due to which fixed capital grew at a relatively higher rate than employment or value added in the first sub-period.

*The Growth Trends: Broad Industrial Classification*

The capital goods sector registered highest rate of growth (7.53% per annum), followed by basic goods (7.03% per annum), intermediate goods (4.77%) and consumer goods sector, which remained at the bottom, with 3.76 per cent rate of growth per annum between 1961 and 1978 in terms of value added (see Table 3.1). Except the consumer goods sector which grew by only 6.62 per cent per annum, all the other sectors experienced a marked spurt (more than 13 per cent per annum) in terms of fixed capital in the first sub-period. Incidentally, the latter groups comprise mostly non-traditional and relatively new industries with high capital intensity. During the second sub-period, not only the tempo of growth of these sectors got subdued, but even became negative, at least in the case of the capital goods sector (–0.009% per annum). On the contrary, the relative rates of growth in all the sectors, including consumer goods, were higher in terms of value added as well as employment.[10] It is interesting to note that it is the non-durable consumer goods sector where employment grew at the fastest rate (4.59%) during the second sub-period while it had experienced the lowest growth (0.68% per annum) during the first sub-period. The durable consumer goods segment, which is relatively

TABLE 3.1: All India Growth Rates: Registered Manufacturing Sector (Use-based and Input-based classification): 1961-1969, 1969-1978 and 1961-1978

*(per cent per annum)*

| Industry Groups | Value-added[1] | | | Trend[2] | Employment[1] | | | Tend[2] | Fixed capital | | | Tend[2] |
|---|---|---|---|---|---|---|---|---|---|---|---|---|
| | 1961-69 | 1969-78 | 1961-78 | 1961-78 | 1961-69 | 1961-78 | 1961-78 | 1961-78 | 1961-69 | 1969-78 | 1961-78 | 1961-78 |
| A *Use-based Classification* | | | | | | | | | | | | |
| Aggregate for all industries | 5.70 | 6.07 | 5.89 | 5.56 | 3.86 | 4.08 | 3.97 | 3.94 | 14.13 | 3.86 | 8.91 | 6.22 |
| 1. Basic goods | 6.35 | 7.63 | 7.03 | 5.87 | 7.23 | 4.54 | 5.80 | 5.73 | 15.90 | 3.08 | 3.93 | 6.41 |
| 2. Intermediate goods | 4.67 | 4.87 | 4.77 | 6.53 | 4.38 | 4.32 | 4.35 | 3.91 | 13.14 | 4.21 | 8.32 | 6.35 |
| 3. Capital goods | 9.65 | 5.68 | 7.53 | 7.55 | 6.55 | 1.71 | 3.96 | 3.47 | 13.69 | -0.009 | 6.22 | 5.31 |
| 4. Consumer goods | 3.42 | 4.07 | 3.76 | 3.55 | 1.11 | 4.37 | 2.82 | 3.12 | 6.62 | 2.10 | 4.20 | 3.45 |
| (a) Durables | 9.31 | 5.54 | 7.30 | 7.97 | 6.97 | 1.72 | 4.16 | 4.04 | 10.24 | 1.35 | 5.44 | 4.65 |
| (b) Non-durables | 3.09 | 3.96 | 3.55 | 3.25 | 0.68 | 4.59 | 2.73 | 3.05 | 6.34 | 2.17 | 4.11 | 3.35 |
| B *Input-based Classification* | | | | | | | | | | | | |
| 1. Agro-based | 2.88 | 3.55 | 3.23 | 3.08 | 0.74 | 4.36 | 2.64 | 2.93 | 5.92 | 2.17 | 3.92 | 3.05 |
| 2. Metal-based | 8.37 | 5.98 | 7.10 | 6.77 | 6.89 | 2.62 | 4.61 | 4.06 | 15.31 | 1.53 | 7.80 | 4.83 |
| 3. Chemical-based | 6.77 | 8.21 | 7.53 | 8.05 | 6.84 | 5.83 | 6.30 | 7.01 | 16.07 | 4.31 | 9.68 | 10.20 |
| 4. Non-metallic mineral-based | 5.76 | 3.80 | 4.72 | 4.34 | 3.47 | 3.50 | 3.49 | 3.04 | 6.99 | 0.83 | 3.68 | 3.23 |

1. Values are compound rates of growth between respective two points of time.
2. Values depict trend rates of growth, estimated as $\log y = a+bt$; where $y$ is value of the variable and $t$ stands for time. All the values are significant at one per cent level of significance.

*Notes:* (a) Data are at 1970-71 prices
(b) Excludes sectors like electricity, gas and water supply; except at aggregate.
(c) For aggregation scheme of various classification, see Appendix 1.

*Source:* Annual Survey of Industries.

TABLE 3.2: Classification of Industries According to their Growth Performance[1] between 1961-69, 1969-78 and 1961-78 : Value Added

*(Compound per annum)*

| | Favourable[2] Growth in 1969-78/1961-69 *n* = 24 | Unfavourable[2] Growth in 1969-78/1961-69 *n* = 29 |
|---|---|---|
| High Growth Industries (n=26) | 329(20.08,20.02:22.13); 243(12.30,2.81:19.80); 370(11.44,11.09:12.19); 385(10.85,8.97:9.14); 381(10.65,5.38:13.92); 312(10.32,3.81:14.89); 233(9.71,4.41:13.70); 311(9.23,8.08:10.69); 339(6.32,4.99:8.03); 341(5.92,5.69:8.30); 319(5.75,5.21:6.16). *n* = 11 | 393(19.29,37.17:8.75); 241(14.12,12.69); 213(13.43,18.27:18.21); 202(13.21,19.42:9.95); 204(11.59,15.62:9.15); 321(10.49,9.01:1.43); 360(9.65,12.42:6.43); 271(9.35,11.36:4.61); 383(7.82,10.95:7.68); 389(7.54,12.40:0.50); 392(7.50,14.19:4.25); 384(7.35,9.13:6.54); 391(7.03,13.39:5.32); 399(7.02,7.12:2.00); 206(6.50,10.57:2.34). *n* = 15 |
| Low Growth Industries (n=27) | 260(5.07,4.33:6.37); 211(4.70,3.43:8.22); 331(4.27,1.36:6.68); 251(4.00,-3.12:5.37); 291(3.89,1.78:5.56); 231(3.09,2.20:5.26); 220(2.65,3.07:3.71); 207(2.13,0.65:2.22); 239(1.30,1.24:1.71); 208(0.35,-7.48:13.52); 203(-0.25,1.51:6.60); 209(-0.35,-0.51:0.92); 205(-0.57,-3.38:5.40) *n* = 13 | 232(5.38,9.48:1.34); 332(5.09,6.43:5.08); 394(4.85,7.01:—0.18); 212(4.25,26.38:-10.10); 293(3.83,16.36:-1.48); 334(3.74,6.05:1.99); 300(3.70,4.99:0.90); 386(3.36,10.54:-0.33); 333(2.17,11.78:1.28); 350(2.01,6.50:-0.25); 280(1.77,7.42:-3.14); 214(1.75,13.79:-7.17); 382(1.34,5.72:-1.57); 342(-1.67,4.55:-1.51). *n* = 14 |

1. High and Low Growth Industries are marked on the basis of aggregate trend growth rate of all the industries at all India level (5.56) being used as a cut off point. All the industries with trend growth rate, more than 5.56 per annum are defined as 'High Growth Industries', all the remaining industries are 'Low Growth Industries'.
2. Within the parentheses, the first value is trend rate of growth between 1961-78; the second value is annual compound rate of growth between 1961-69 (I sub-period) and the second between 1969-78 (II sub-period).

*Notes:* (a) Favourable/unfavourable growth industries are defined in terms of their growth performance in the second sub-period (1969-78) compared to the I sub-period (1961-69). If performance was better in the II sub-period, it implied that the growth is favourable and vice versa.

(b) *n* stands for the number of industry groups in a particular sub-set.

modern, by and large, confirmed to the growth pattern of the non-traditional sectors like intermediate or basic goods industries (see Table 3.1).

*A Further Disaggregation*

We analysed overall growth performance of the factory sector according to broad industrial classifications, viz. use-based and input-based groups. It is quite likely that all the industries pertaining to respective sectors and sub-sectors did not behave alike during the period of analysis. Therefore, we carried out analysis of 53 major industry groups (at 3 digit level of industrial classification). Taking overall compound growth rate of the registered manufacturing sector between 1961 and 1978 as cut-off point we can divide all the 53 major industry groups into two sub-groups viz. (i) industries growing above the national rate of growth, defined as high growth industries, and (ii) industries growing below the national average as low growth industries (which will include even absolutely declining industries, registering negative rate of growth) (Table 3.2). These two groups can further be subdivided according to the performance of industries during the two sub-periods, i.e. 1961-69 and 1969-78. Accordingly we can define (i) industries growing at an increasing rate, where they perform better in the second sub-period (1969-78), and (ii) industries growing at a decreasing rate where the growth rate in an industry in the second sub-period is less than that of the first sub-period.

As noted earlier, the registered factory segment in India grew at approximately 5.56 per cent per annum in terms of value-added. Taking this value (5.56) as a cut-off point, we observe that the industry groups are divided into almost two equal parts, where first 26 industries having registered the growth above the bench mark (5.56) and the rest 27 industries falling below the national rate of industrial growth during 1961-78 (see Annexure 3.1 to the chapter).

*High Growth Industries* : If we incorporate the periodisation scheme, in all 11 industry groups were observed to have growth above the national growth rate and at an increasing rate. In this group petroleum and coal products (329) registered the highest rate of growth (20.02 per cent per annum) in terms of value added, followed by tailoring umbrella and textile garments (243), manufacturing of electric machinery and apparatus (370), motorcycles and bicycles (385), boat and ship building (381), including oils (312), manufacturing of thread, cordage and ropes of all types (233), industrial heavy organic and inorganic chemicals, fertilizers and pesticides (311), non-metallic mineral products, n.e.c. (339), iron, steel and ferro-alloys (341), and paints, drugs and medicines, varnish, cosmetics, perfumes and other chemical products n.e.c. (319).

The other sub-group of fast growing industries belongs to these 15 industries which have experienced a higher overall rate of growth, i.e. above the national level growth rate, but are growing at a declining rate over time. It is reflected by their low growth profile in the second sub-period compared to the first period (1961-69). In this sub-group watches and clocks (393) experienced the highest rate of growth of 19.29 per cent per annum, second only to the petroleum and petroleum products (329) among all the industries performing above the national average. The other groups following watches and clocks are, manufacturing of foot-wear except rubber and plastic (241), malt liquor, malt, country liquor and toddy (213); manufacturing of dairy products (202); canning and preservation of fish and sea foods (204); petroleum refineries (321); manufacturing of machinery and machine tools, except electrical machinery (360); paper and paper products (271); manufacturing of motor vehicles and parts (383); manufacturing of transport equipments n.e.c. (389); photographic materials (392); repair of motor vehicles n.e.c. (384); medical, surgical and scientific equipment (391); miscellaneous industries, n.e.c. (399); and backery products (206).

*Low Growth Industries:* The 27 industries which have performed below the national industrial rate of growth, in terms of value-added, constitute the group of low growth industries. However, in this group also, there are as many as 13 industry groups which have registered increasing trend over time (see Table 3.3). The industries which improved their performance in the second sub-period (1969-78) compared to the first sub-period (1961-69) are: furniture and fixtures (260); distilling and rectifying of spirit (211); structural clay products (331); wood and wood products (251); tanning and curing of leather (291); manufacturing of textiles (231); tobacco and tobacco products (220); sugar, *gur* and *khandsari* (207); other textiles n.e.c. (239); cocoa, chocolate and sugar, candy (208); canning and preservation of food products (203); food products n.e.c. (209); and grain mill products (205). Though the overall performance of these industries has been far from satisfactory, they have shown a revival over time. Another interesting feature of this group is that most of these industry groups belong to the consumer goods sector (especially non-durable segment) which experienced a very low growth during the first sub-period, showed revival in the second sub-period (see Table 3.3).

The other sub-group of this segment of industries which not only performed below the national mark in terms of value-added but also faced a declining trend over time constitutes 14 industry groups viz. knitting mills (232); glass and glass products (332); jewellery and mint (394); wine industries (212); leather products (300); air-craft (386); earthenware and chinaware (333); metal products and parts except machinery and transport (350); printing and publishing (280); soft drinks and carbonated water (214); railway locomotive (382); and non-ferrous basic industries (342) (see Table 3.3).[11] It is disheartening to note that this group constitutes some of the important industry groups belonging to the capital goods and basic goods sectors, so crucial for the rapid pace of industrialisation. If the trend in sectors such as iron and steel, cement, metal products and parts, all railway locomotives is not revived, the future of industrial development of the country is likely to be in jeopardy. It calls for a rethinking on the industrial policies being pursued by the Government of India.

The picture of industrial growth by and large remains unchanged even if we take the other two variables, viz. employment and fixed capital, into consideration.[12] For example in the case of 11 industries, viz., 243, 385, 321, 312, 211, 331, 291, 207, 229, 209 and 205, the growth trend in employment and fixed capital is increasing one in conformity to the value added. Similarly 16 industries, viz., 393, 202, 204, 321, 271, 383, 392, 384, 232, 212, 334, 300, 350, 280, 214, 382, which are increasing at a decreasing rate in terms of employment and fixed capital, again confirm to the decreasing trend observed in the case of value added.

In the remaining 26 industry groups it is difficult to discern any trend when all the three variables are considered together. However, industries where value added shows an increasing trend, accompanied by declining trend in employment and fixed capital, indicate more efficient use of the factors of production. In all seven industry groups viz., 370, 311, 389, 399, 341, 319 and 260 represent the trend. Opposite trend is reflected by two industry groups, viz., 293 and 342 hinting thereby an inefficient use of the factors of production (see Annexure 3.1 to the chapter).[13]

TABLE 3.3: Changes in the Shares of Major Industry Groups in the Registered Manufacturing Sector: Use-based and Input-based classification (Years: 1961, 1969, 1978)

(per cent)

| Industry Groups | Value-added | | | Employment | | | Fixed capital | | |
|---|---|---|---|---|---|---|---|---|---|
| | 1961 | 1969 | 1978 | 1961 | 1969 | 1978 | 1961 | 1969 | 1978 |
| A *Use-based Classification* | | | | | | | | | |
| Total | 100.00 | 100.00 | 100.00 | 100.00 | 100.00 | 100.00 | 100.00 | 100.00 | 100.00 |
| 1. Basic goods | 15.26 | 16.66 | 20.26 | 9.04 | 11.64 | 12.63 | 30.39 | 40.51 | 43.96 |
| 2. Intermediate goods | 10.34 | 10.51 | 9.08 | 7.94 | 9.02 | 8.38 | 9.57 | 9.84 | 10.42 |
| 3. Capital goods | 13.47 | 19.70 | 22.00 | 13.75 | 18.40 | 15.84 | 13.73 | 16.92 | 14.16 |
| 4. Consumer goods | 60.93 | 53.13 | 48.66 | 69.27 | 60.94 | 63.15 | 46.31 | 32.73 | 31.46 |
| (a) Durables | 2.05 | 2.79 | 3.19 | 3.17 | 4.13 | 3.80 | 2.32 | 1.79 | 1.89 |
| (b) Non-durables | 58.88 | 50.34 | 45.47 | 66.10 | 56.81 | 59.35 | 43.95 | 30.94 | 29.57 |
| B *Input-based Classification* | | | | | | | | | |
| 1. Agro-based | 55.63 | 46.36 | 40.65 | 63.52 | 53.49 | 56.46 | 41.90 | 28.26 | 27.82 |
| 2. Metal-based | 28.39 | 36.04 | 38.35 | 26.37 | 35.27 | 31.15 | 36.18 | 45.36 | 42.96 |
| 3. Chemical-based | 12.09 | 13.65 | 17.37 | 4.94 | 5.89 | 7.17 | 15.75 | 22.01 | 24.84 |
| 4. Non-metallic mineral-based | 3.89 | 3.95 | 3.63 | 5.17 | 5.35 | 5.22 | 6.17 | 4.37 | 4.38 |

*Notes:* (a) Shares in the value-added and fixed capital are at 1970-71 prices.
(b) Details of individual category are provided in Appendix II.
(c) Excluding Electricity, gas and Water Supply.

*Source:* Based on Annexure 3.2.

In another case, fixed capital showed a sharp decline compared to employment or value added. It indicates increase in value added owing to more intensive use of labour. In all 10 industries viz., 329, 233, 360, 391, 206, 339, 231, 220, 333, 203 constitute this group. Contrary to this, the industry group 394 grew at a relatively higher rate in terms of fixed capital compared to the other two variables which indicates somewhat growing inefficient use of capital.

In the third group, comprising five industries, we observe that employment is growing at a relatively much faster rate compared to the value added and fixed capital in four industry groups viz., 241, 213, 332 and 208. It is difficult to explain the reason for this and perhaps it is a case of inefficient use of labour.[14] However, in industry group 251, growth of employment declined, accompanied by higher growth in fixed capital followed by highest rate of growth attained by value-added. It indicates that the industry group is becoming more capital intensive, and that the increase in capital is being accompanied by higher productivity.

It may not be appropriate to explain the behaviour of various industries only in terms of growth rates. It is quite possible that an industry group, despite its high rate of growth, may not be able to affect the overall pattern of industrial structure, especially if the industry group in question has a very meagre weight in total manufacturing. Moreover, sometimes these growth rates appear to be abnormally high owing to their rudimentary base in the initial period. Hence it is difficult to rely on the growth profile of various industry groups exclusively on the basis of growth rates.[15] Therefore, it might be more useful to take the stock of weights (shares) of these industries before arriving at any conclusion.

## Shares of Industry Groups

The industrial structure changes with the level of economic development (Kuznets, 1969; Clark, 1971); and a uniform pattern of sectoral change is observed by researchers in the process of industrialisation (Hoffman, 1958; Chenery, 1960). It is argued that in the early stages of industries development, traditional (most of the consumer goods) industries claim a relatively higher share of employment, output or capital. Later, these traditional industries tend to give way to the non-traditional sectors such as capital goods and intermediate goods in the process of industrial development (Hoffman, 1958 : 11).

*The Share: Broad Industry Groups*

As mentioned earlier, India diversified its industrial structure substantially during the sixties. It is evident from Table 3.3 that the traditional sectors comprising mostly non-durable consumer goods lost their share heavily in favour of capital and basic goods sectors, particularly in terms of value added, between 1961 and 1978. Despite its unchanged rank in value added and employment, the consumer goods sector accounted for only 48.66 per cent share in value-added, 63.15 per cent in employment and barely 31.46 per cent in fixed capital in 1978. Thus, it virtually has interchanged its position with basic industries which increased its share to 43.96 per cent in fixed capital by 1978. Out of the remaining two, the capital goods sector enhanced its share from 13.47 per cent in 1961 to 22 per cent in 1978 in terms of value added, whereas intermediate goods lost around 1.26 per cent of their share of value-added between 1961-1978.

A somewhat similar picture emerges if industries are classified according to their inputs. The agro-based industry group, which incidentally is constituted by most of the traditional industries, lost it share heavily in favour of relatively modern industries like chemical-based and to an extent metal based industries between 1961 and 1978, at least in terms of value-added and fixed capital. However, non-metallic mineral products do not show much changes over time.

*The Shares: Disaggregated Analysis*

We attempt to capture the nature and pattern of shift in the shares of major industry groups in total value-added between 1961 and 1978 at a more disaggregated (3 digit level of ASI) level. It is observed that textile manufacturing (231), with 25.99 per cent share in value added in 1961, emerges prominent, though it declines into approximately 20.28 per cent by the terminal year. Some of the other important groups in 1961 are 209 (9.26%); 341 (6.96%); 311(6.19%); and 319 (4.5%) (see Table 3.4). It is also clear from the table that in due course some of the important consumer goods industries like 205, 207, 209, 220, 231 and 280 lost their shares in favour of relatively modern industries such as 311, 319 and 370.

TABLE 3.4: Classification on Industries According to their Shares[1] in Value added and Changes Therein[2]

*(per cent)*

| | Favourable Shift 1978/1961 (*n* = 25) | Unfavourable Shift 1978/1967 (*n* = 28) |
|---|---|---|
| High Share Industries (*n*=16) | 341(6.96, 9.47); 319(6.19, 6.78); 311(4.57, 8.47); 360(4.34, 8.24); 370(3.34, 6.94); 383(2.12, 3.92). *n* = 6 | 231(25.99, 20.28); 209(9.26, 4.79); 207(4.47, 2.44); 220 (3.26, 2.45); 350(2.98, 2.05); 383(2.96, 1.76); 300(2.47, 1.68); 342(2.46, 1.29); 280(2.33, 1.32); 205(2.01, 1.01). *n* = 10 |
| Low Share Industries (*n*=37) | 27(1.34, 2.05); 339(0.97, 1.20); 384(0.92, 1.38); 381(0.45, 0.95); 385(0.39, 0.73); 206(0.32, 0.37); 391(0.18, 0.35); 211(0.17, 0.19) 243(0.16, 0.43); 202(0.15, 0.61); 213(0.15, 0.22); 312(0.13, 0.26); 233(0.09, 0.16); 329(0.07, 0.88); 389(0.05, 0.06); 241(0.03, 0.18); 204(0.02, 0.08); 392(0.02, 0.05); 393(0.01, 0.22). *n* = 19 | 334(1.27, 10.3); 321(1.24, 1.19); 251(1.13, 0.58); 239(0.93, 0.50); 399(0.86, 0.76); 331(0.74, 0.62); 332(0.50, 0.49); 333(0.41, 0.23); 260(0.39, 0.38); 291(0.35, 0.29); 386(0.21, 0.19); 232(0.17, 0.16); 394(0.16, 0.11); 214(0.14, 0.08); 203(0.07, 0.06); 208(0.05, 0.04); 212(0.04, 0.02); 293(0.01, 0.01). *n* = 18 |

*Notes:* (1) Classification of the high and low shares is based on the percentages in the year 1961. An industry is a high share industry if its share was found to be equal to or more than 2, otherwise is a low share industry.

(2) Favourable shift is defined when share of a particular industry increased in the year 1978 compared to 1961; otherwise the shift was defined unfavourable.

(a) Within parentheses, first value pertains to the year 1961 and second to 1978. The percentage is that of the aggregate value-added in a particular year.

*Source:* Based on Annexure 3.2 to the chapter.

Classified according to their importance or weight in the industrial structure of the country along with trends in their share over time, all the industries could broadly be grouped into four sets: high share with favourable shift; high share with unfavourable shift; low share with favourable shift; and low share with unfavourable shift.[16] According to this classification we find that six industries belonging to the first group : those with high share and favourable shift are 341, 319, 311, 360, 370 and 383, while 10 industries having high share but experiencing unfavourable shift between 1961 and 1978 are 231, 209, 207, 220, 350, 382, 300, 342, 280 and 205. It is interesting to note again that most of the traditional industries which accounted high share in 1961 lost in favour of some of the relatively non-traditional or modern industries. An almost similar trend emerges in the case of low share industries. The picture is not much different even if we consider employment or fixed capital in lieu of value added (see Annexure 3.2 to the chapter).

## Identifying Important Industry Groups

No clear trend is discernible if we compare growth profile of industries with their share in the base year. Most of the high share industries experienced low growth in value-added, while the majority of the industries having relatively low share registered a high rate of growth between 1961 and 1978. Most of the industries (approximately 57%) reveal negative association between growth and the share (see Table 3.5).

Therefore, as noted earlier, simply high growth of an industry does not signify its importance in the industrial structure and *vice-versa*. It mainly depends on the weight, in terms of its share an industry carriers in the industrial structure. It is plausibly high-share industries which play a crucial role in the overall growth. However, taking two per cent share as a cut-off-point for isolating more important industries eliminates the possibility of considering those industries which have a high potential for growth. Even one per cent share appears to be restrictive. Therefore, in order to have better combination of growth and share of industries, it will be reasonable to include all those industries which contribute at least 0.5 per cent share in any of the variables.

TABLE 3.5: Classification of Industries According to Growth Rates (1961-78) and Their Shares (1961) : Value added.[1]

(per cent)

| Total = 53 | High Growth Industries $n = 26$ | Low Growth Industries $n = 27$ |
|---|---|---|
| High Share Industries $n$=16 | 341(6.96, 5.92); 319(6.19, 5.75); 311(4.57, 9.23); 360 (4.34, 9.65); 370(3.34, 11.44); 383(2.12, 7.82). $n = 16$ | 231(25.99, 3.09); 209(9.26, -0.35); 207(4.47, 2.13); 220(3.26, 2.65); 350(2.98, 2.01); 382(2.96, 1.34); 300(2.47, 3.70); 342(2.46, -1.67); 280(2.33, 1.77); 205(2.01, -0.57) $n = 10$ |
| Low Share Industries $n$=37 | 271(1.34, 9.35); 321(1.24, 10.49); 339(0.97, 6.32); 384(0.92, 7.35) 399(0.84, 7.02); 381(0.45, 10.65); 385 332(0.50, 5.09); 333(0.41, 2.17); 260(0.39, 5.07); 291(0.35, 3.89); (0.39, 10.85); 206(0.32, 6.50); 391(0.18, 7.03); 243(0.16, 12.30); 213(0.15, 13.43); 202(0.15, 13.12); 312(0.13, 10.32); 233(0.09, 9.71); 329(0.07, 20.08); 389(0.05, 7.54); 241(0.03, 14.12); 204(0.02, 11.59); 392(0.02, 7.50); 393(0.01, 19.29). $n = 20$ | 334(1.27, 3.74); 251(1.13, 4.00); 239(0.93, 1.30); 331(0.74, 4.27); 386(0.21, 3.36); 232(0.17, 5.38); 211(0.17, 4.70); 3.90(0.16, 4.85); 214(0.14, 1.75); 203(0.07, -0.25); 208(0.05, 0.35); 212(0.04, 4.25); 293(0.01, 3.83). $n = 17$ |

*Notes:* Within parenthesis the first value represents share of the industry group in aggregate value added in 1961 and the second value is the trend rate of growth of that industry group between 1961 and 1978. Cut off point for high growth industries is 5.56 per cent per annum and high share industry is an industry having ≥ 2 per cent share in the value added.

*Source:* Tables 3.2 and 3.4.

Accordingly we identify 35 industry groups for the purpose of further analysis, especially at the regional level.[17] These 35 industries together account for approximately 97.22 per cent of value-added, 98.23 per cent of employment and 98.25 per cent of fixed capital in 1961. These proportions were 97.15, 96.63 and 97.80 respectively in 1978.[18] On the basis of this identification we attempt to portray the distribution of these 'important industry groups' in the various States in the next section.

## DOMINANCE OF THE REGIONS IN THE 'IMPORTANT' INDUSTRY GROUPS

The purpose of this exercise is to trace dominance of the States in various industries. For, it can be postulated that the high industry States (in terms of their shares in the total value-added generated in the organised manufacturing sector at the national level) will also have significant share of important industries and *vice-versa.*

Tables 3.6 to 3.8 display shares of various States in the selected 35 industry groups.[19] In 1961, Maharashtra and West Bengal dominated in almost all the major industry groups. Out of the 35 industry groups Maharashtra claimed more than 10 per cent of the shares in as much as 32 industry groups and West Bengal in 30 industry groups. States such as Gujarat and Tamil Nadu, though did not dominate to that extent in any specific industry group, had significant share of quite a few industries. For example Gujarat's share in some of the predominant industries 231, 209, 319, 360, 311 and 21.34, 9.76, 9.53, 7.10 and 18.02 per cent respectively in 1961. Tamil Nadu had 12.22, 10.93, 5.75, 7.68, 9.20 and 8.95 per cent share in the industry groups 231, 209, 319, 207, 360 and 311 respectively, of course, along with other industry groups (see Table 3.6). Two other States, Bihar and Uttar Pradesh, had significant share, though only in a few, but very important industries at the national level. For example, Uttar Pradesh claimed 39.07 per cent share of the nation's sugar, gur and khandsari industry (207). Similarly, Bihar claimed 30.31 per cent share of the iron and steel industry group (341) in 1961, along with other industries, which is evident from the table.

On the other hand States such as Karnataka, Madhya Pradesh, Kerala, Andhra Pradesh and Assam hardly any significant concentration of 'important' industries. For example, Karnataka hardly crosses 3 percent share in the top ten industry groups except in 207, 220 and 360.

TABLE 3.6: Share of the States in All-India: Value Added (Important Industries) — 1961

*(per cent)*

| Name of the States | Industry Code | | | | | | | | | | |
|---|---|---|---|---|---|---|---|---|---|---|---|
| | 231 (1) | 209 (2) | 341 (3) | 319 (4) | 207 (5) | 360 (6) | 311 (7) | 370 (8) | 220 (9) | 350 (10) | 382 (11) |
| 1. Andhra Pradesh | 1.39 | 2.34 | 1.20 | 1.46 | 8.51 | 1.02 | 1.81 | 1.83 | 26.99 | 1.00 | — |
| 2. Assam | 0.05 | 29.13 | 0.02 | 0.27 | 0.10 | 0.08 | — | — | — | 0.27 | 1.44 |
| 3. Bihar | 0.31 | 1.02 | 30.31 | 0.98 | 10.87 | 2.02 | 5.36 | 4.60 | 7.29 | 1.36 | 2.30 |
| 4. Gujarat | 21.34 | 9.76 | 3.21 | 9.53 | 0.75 | 10.03 | 18.32 | 3.09 | 5.93 | 4.69 | 3.84 |
| 5. Haryana | — | — | — | — | — | — | — | — | — | — | — |
| 6. Himachal Pradesh | — | — | — | — | — | 0.05 | — | — | — | — | — |
| 7. Jammu & Kashmir | 0.22 | 0.08 | — | 0.02 | — | — | 0.05 | — | — | 0.04 | — |
| 8. Karnataka | 2.72 | 2.50 | 2.03 | 2.61 | 6.33 | 6.36 | 1.01 | 3.00 | 6.74 | 1.55 | 0.51 |
| 9. Kerala | 0.89 | 11.26 | 0.66 | 2.47 | — | 0.80 | 3.01 | 2.43 | 2.40 | 0.71 | — |
| 10. Madhya Pradesh | 4.40 | 0.95 | 5.17 | 0.93 | 1.96 | 1.06 | 1.10 | 0.10 | 6.39 | 1.15 | — |
| 11. Maharashtra | 30.83 | 11.45 | 14.58 | 56.60 | 18.98 | 29.27 | 44.59 | 30.37 | 19.74 | 32.02 | 14.92 |
| 12. Orissa | 0.09 | 0.02 | 10.23 | 0.16 | 0.05 | 0.35 | — | — | 0.44 | 1.02 | 0.09 |
| 13. Punjab[1] | 2.81 | 1.29 | 3.80 | 0.14 | 4.10 | 7.82 | 0.92 | 2.24 | — | 5.61 | 2.10 |
| 14. Rajasthan | 0.72 | 0.06 | 0.62 | 0.04 | 0.07 | 0.23 | — | 0.66 | 0.21 | 0.28 | 7.72 |
| 15. Tamil Nadu | 12.22 | 10.93 | 2.15 | 5.75 | 7.68 | 9.20 | 8.95 | 4.14 | 8.36 | 7.81 | 1.16 |
| 16. Uttar Pradesh | 5.32 | 4.79 | 2.13 | 2.55 | 39.07 | 5.17 | 3.11 | 7.10 | 2.87 | 5.73 | 12.26 |
| 17. West Bengal | 14.18 | 13.90 | 22.96 | 17.32 | 1.50 | 23.45 | 11.73 | 37.15 | 2.36 | 34.01 | 53.51 |
| 18. Delhi | 2.40 | 0.30 | 0.81 | 0.80 | — | 2.30 | 0.22 | 2.89 | 0.26 | 2.90 | — |

*(Contd.)*

TABLE 3.6 *(Contd.)*

| Name of the States | | Industry Code | | | | | | | | | | |
|---|---|---|---|---|---|---|---|---|---|---|---|---|
| | | 231 (1) | 209 (2) | 341 (3) | 319 (4) | 207 (5) | 360 (6) | 311 (7) | 370 (8) | 220 (9) | 350 (10) | 382 (11) |
| 1. Andhra Pradesh | — | — | 2.81 | 3.74 | 17.11 | 3.42 | 6.69 | 14.21 | 2.88 | 4.39 | 5.11 | 4.61 |
| 2. Assam | — | — | 0.95 | — | 3.35 | — | — | 27.39 | 13.20 | — | 0.82 | 2.26 |
| 3. Bihar | — | 15.00 | 2.38 | 5.54 | 10.50 | 10.50 | 10.86 | — | 1.24 | 13.71 | 1.29 | 1.99 |
| 4. Gujarat | 1.00 | 7.33 | 5.76 | 6.73 | 3.10 | 7.54 | 10.75 | — | 2.96 | 9.71 | 9.87 | 8.14 |
| 5. Haryana | — | — | — | — | — | — | — | — | — | — | — | — |
| 6. Himachal Pradesh | — | — | — | — | — | — | — | | — | — | — | 0.44 |
| 7. Jammu & Kashmir | — | — | 0.12 | — | — | — | — | — | 0.19 | — | — | 0.24 |
| 8. Karnataka | 1.25 | — | 1.31 | 9.22 | 2.70 | 4.43 | 6.30 | — | 24.79 | 3.15 | 6.64 | 4.39 |
| 9. Kerala | 4.38 | 0.86 | 2.33 | — | 1.53 | 1.48 | 4.45 | — | 20.83 | 0.17 | 9.45 | 3.63 |
| 10. Madhya Pradesh | — | 2.21 | 1.22 | — | 9.25 | 2.58 | 12.66 | — | 1.26 | 4.83 | 5.67 | 1.17 |
| 11. Maharashtra | 47.88 | 26.62 | 32.64 | 31.65 | 15.70 | 17.24 | 8.21 | 58.40 | 16.12 | 27.62 | 26.86 | 22.98 |
| 12. Orissa | — | 0.49 | 0.95 | — | 3.16 | 1.36 | 2.22 | — | 1.20 | 0.19 | — | 0.90 |
| 13. Punjab | 1.82 | 3.26 | 2.98 | 1.78 | 4.02 | 5.86 | — | — | 1.49 | 1.33 | 6.79 | 1.75 |
| 14. Rajasthan | — | 1.05 | 0.77 | — | 1.13 | — | 4.08 | — | 0.25 | 3.12 | 3.59 | 0.36 |
| 15. Tamil Nadu | 5.11 | 2.39 | 16.99 | 16.25 | 13.67 | 6.82 | 14.73 | — | 1.59 | 9.43 | 13.02 | 18.39 |
| 16. Uttar Pradesh | 0.07 | 5.52 | 6.72 | 8.35 | 6.08 | 9.11 | 6.11 | — | 1.16 | 1.61 | 2.99 | 9.40 |
| 17. West Bengal | 46 | 35.09 | 13.96 | 16.39 | 14.64 | 29.56 | 12.93 | — | 12.91 | 17.42 | 5.75 | 11.60 |
| 18. Delhi | 0.93 | — | 8.09 | 0.31 | 1.85 | 0.07 | — | — | 0.22 | 3.30 | 2.10 | 7.19 |

*(Contd.)*

TABLE 3.6 *(Contd.)*

| Name of the States | | Industry Code | | | | | | | | | | |
|---|---|---|---|---|---|---|---|---|---|---|---|---|
| | | 231 (1) | 209 (2) | 341 (3) | 319 (4) | 207 (5) | 360 (6) | 311 (7) | 370 (8) | 220 (9) | 350 (10) | 382 (11) |
| 1. Andhra Pradesh | 2.42 | 0.65 | 0.10 | 15.82 | 3.55 | 0.29 | 0.87 | 3.31 | 1.71 | 2.41 | — | 1.13 |
| 2. Assam | 1.21 | 0.11 | — | 0.30 | — | — | — | — | — | — | — | — |
| 3. Bihar | 1.68 | 21.60 | 3.68 | 1.39 | 4.65 | 0.70 | 1.12 | 0.46 | 1.48 | 3.98 | 47.14 | — |
| 4. Gujarat | 12.19 | 10.71 | 13.24 | 2.41 | 19.66 | 2.27 | 0.98 | 0.58 | 2.17 | 18.70 | — | 3.26 |
| 5. Haryana | — | — | — | — | — | — | — | — | — | — | — | — |
| 6. Himachal Pradesh | — | — | — | — | — | — | — | — | — | — | — | — |
| 7. Jammu & Kashmir | 0.44 | — | — | — | — | — | 0.31 | 0.11 | — | — | — | 0.16 |
| 8. Karnataka | 2.42 | 11.52 | 0.70 | 1.51 | 2.88 | — | 1.46 | 2.31 | 4.76 | — | — | 1.35 |
| 9. Kerala | 1.40 | 15.84 | 1.44 | 6.44 | 2.93 | 0.44 | 1.52 | — | 4.86 | — | — | 13.63 |
| 10. Madhya Pradesh | 0.27 | 2.49 | — | — | 11.32 | 0.82 | 1.87 | 0.20 | 5.63 | 2.54 | — | 3.21 |
| 11. Maharashtra | 37.93 | 15.67 | 23.28 | 24.20 | 3.39 | 16.80 | 65.01 | 4.52 | 47.05 | 28.00 | 4.65 | 18.95 |
| 12. Orissa | 0.20 | 0.61 | 0.82 | — | 0.43 | — | 0.12 | 1.12 | — | — | — | |
| 13. Punjab | 3.04 | 1.58 | 2.35 | — | 2.49 | 13.83 | 2.36 | 2.71 | 1.38 | 1.33 | — | 15.31 |
| 14. Rajasthan | 1.55 | — | 0.06 | — | — | 0.20 | — | — | 0.50 | — | — | — |
| 15. Tamil Nadu | 14.17 | 5.30 | 5.62 | 3.71 | 14.07 | 33.05 | 6.77 | 46.69 | 8.43 | 4.65 | — | — |
| 16. Uttar Pradesh | 4.78 | 0.11 | 23.83 | — | 0.25 | 5.02 | 1.99 | 23.36 | 1.36 | 20.82 | — | 18.49 |
| 17. West Bengal | 11.84 | 13.07 | 24.35 | 44.17 | 32.92 | 24.45 | 12.26 | 12.76 | 17.07 | 15.80 | 49.16 | 20.40 |
| 18. Delhi | 4.43 | 0.49 | 0.52 | — | 2.42 | 2.30 | 2.56 | 2.56 | 2.84 | 1.99 | — | 1.50 |

*Notes:* 1. Includes Haryana.
*Source:* Annual Survey of Industries, Factory, (Census + Sample Sector), Central Statistical Organisation, Govt. of India, New Delhi.

Similarly Madhya Pradesh accounts for 6.39 per cent in tobacco and tobacco products (220), 5.17 in iron, steel and ferro alloys (341) and 4.40 per cent share in textile group (231); Andhra Pradesh accounts for 26.99 per cent in 220 and 8.51 per cent in sugar, *gur* and *khandsari* (207); Assam, 29.13 per cent in industry group miscellaneous food products (n.e.c.) (209) and Kerala accounts for 11.26 per cent share of industry group 209 and 3.01 per cent of the industry group 311 (see Table 3.6).

It is apparent from the table that other States such as Orissa, Rajasthan, Himachal Pradesh and Jammu and Kashmir had very small shares in most of the industry groups. And if we find high proportion of some important industry groups in these States, the industry in general will be very low ranking in terms of its proportion in the total value-added of the country; exceptions like the industry group 341 in Orissa (10.23%) and the group 382 in Rajasthan (7.73%) hardly change the general case.

The situation has remained more or less unchanged in the later years also. For example, Maharashtra continues to dominate the industrial scene though without improving its share (in fact it lost some of its share to other States). But West Bengal seems to emerge as a net loser in quite a few significant industries. The gainers have been States such as Gujarat, Tamil Nadu, Uttar Pradesh, Andhra Pradesh, Madhya Pradesh and Rajasthan which over time gained significant share of some of the important industries.

Tables 3.7 and 3.8 reveal that though six States viz. Maharashtra, West Bengal, Gujarat, Tamil Nadu, Bihar and Uttar Pradesh continue to dominate the first ten industry group, the degree of dominance has tended to decline substantially. Consequently a tendency of greater spatial spread is evident among the various industry groups. States such as Andhra Pradesh, Karnataka and Madhya Pradesh have shown greater vitality whereas Assam has lost its initial advantage in some of the important industry groups. Kerala has remained almost static, with a somewhat unusual upward swing in 1969. Among the remaining States, while Rajasthan, Orissa, Punjab and Haryana seem to have broaden their base, the performance of Jammu and Kashmir has been anything but impressive.

Thus, it is clear that the industrial structure of the country has been heavily concentrated in a few industries (the ten industry groups account for almost 72 per cent share in the total value added generated in 1978). These industries in turn, are concentrated in a few States.

TABLE 3.7: Share of the States in All-India: Value Added (Important Industries) — 1969

*(per cent)*

| Name of the States | Industry Code | | | | | | | | | | |
|---|---|---|---|---|---|---|---|---|---|---|---|
| | 231 (1) | 209 (2) | 341 (3) | 319 (4) | 207 (5) | 360 (6) | 311 (7) | 370 (8) | 220 (9) | 350 (10) | 382 (11) |
| 1. Andhra Pradesh | 1.39 | 3.36 | 1.37 | 1.42 | 12.15 | 3.38 | 6.42 | 4.45 | 28.12 | 0.86 | 0.61 |
| 2. Assam | 0.19 | 24.72 | 0.11 | 0.10 | 0.10 | 0.33 | 0.26 | 0.06 | — | 0.45 | 1.52 |
| 3. Bihar | 0.59 | 1.00 | 21.68 | 0.42 | 5.53 | 4.62 | 7.34 | 1.30 | 12.13 | 3.70 | 1.77 |
| 4. Gujarat | 20.30 | 8.32 | 3.67 | 10.69 | 0.83 | 10.19 | 20.60 | 2.85 | 6.10 | 4.87 | 2.26 |
| 5. Haryana | 0.96 | 0.32 | 1.69 | 0.89 | 0.83 | 5.63 | 0.35 | 1.02 | — | 4.40 | 1.79 |
| 6. Himachal Pradesh | 0.01 | 0.01 | 0.07 | 0.02 | — | 0.23 | 0.04 | 0.13 | — | 0.14 | — |
| 7. Jammu & Kashmir | 0.03 | 0.10 | 0.02 | 0.08 | — | — | 4.08 | 0.01 | — | 0.05 | — |
| 8. Karnataka | 3.18 | 5.22 | 0.53 | 1.36 | 6.12 | 5.20 | 2.77 | 9.36 | 10.31 | 3.59 | 2.98 |
| 9. Kerala | 1.07 | 17.87 | 0.36 | 2.21 | 0.15 | 0.49 | 6.55 | 0.97 | 3.15 | 1.15 | — |
| 10. Madhya Pradesh | 4.17 | 1.55 | 7.80 | 0.49 | 0.30 | 1.19 | 2.94 | 7.37 | 4.42 | 0.91 | 1.08 |
| 11. Maharashtra | 32.13 | 11.03 | 14.89 | 60.19 | 23.27 | 29.46 | 32.00 | 34.42 | 12.96 | 40.81 | 11.99 |
| 12. Orissa | 0.38 | 0.08 | 13.77 | 0.09 | 0.46 | 0.21 | 0.41 | 0.46 | 0.15 | 0.29 | 0.61 |
| 13. Punjab | 2.27 | 1.44 | 2.50 | 0.25 | 0.36 | 4.48 | 0.51 | 0.84 | 0.05 | 3.94 | 0.29 |
| 14. Rajasthan | 1.40 | 0.35 | 0.44 | 0.16 | 0.41 | 0.45 | 0.80 | 0.27 | 0.10 | 0.30 | 6.12 |
| 15. Tamil Nadu | 9.87 | 8.46 | 6.06 | 4.50 | 11.80 | 16.99 | 6.03 | 9.17 | 2.67 | 7.30 | 12.94 |
| 16. Uttar Pradesh | 5.02 | 5.73 | 2.87 | 0.99 | 36.68 | 4.71 | 6.03 | 4.72 | 15.99 | 6.82 | 21.65 |
| 17. West Bengal | 15.27 | 9.81 | 21.85 | 13.26 | 1.15 | 10.53 | 6.39 | 20.84 | 3.00 | 21.42 | 33.99 |
| 18. Delhi | 1.72 | 0.61 | 0.82 | 1.50 | — | 1.34 | 0.36 | 1.43 | 0.53 | 2.17 | 0.35 |

*(Contd.)*

TABLE 3.7 *(Contd.)*

| Name of the States | Industry Code | | | | | | | | | | | |
|---|---|---|---|---|---|---|---|---|---|---|---|---|
| | 300 (1) | 342 (2) | 280 (3) | 383 (4) | 205 (5) | 271 (6) | 334 (7) | 321 (8) | 251 (9) | 339 (10) | 239 (11) | 384 |
| 1. Andhra Pradesh | 2.10 | 0.90 | 3.43 | 0.37 | 8.98 | 2.89 | 10.23 | 6.99 | 2.69 | 4.88 | 2.42 | 7.93 |
| 2. Assam | — | 0.02 | 0.73 | — | 4.56 | 0.03 | 0.56 | 26.49 | 16.53 | — | 0.20 | 1.24 |
| 3. Bihar | 1.66 | 14.30 | 2.52 | 33.87 | 4.91 | 3.76 | 9.20 | 11.73 | 4.41 | 11.25 | 0.16 | 2.13 |
| 4. Gujarat | 0.93 | 3.20 | 3.35 | 0.78 | 3.14 | 9.23 | 10.21 | 8.04 | 4.70 | 9.64 | 15.52 | 10.38 |
| 5. Haryana | 2.84 | 1.19 | 1.80 | 1.75 | 1.31 | 4.53 | — | — | 1.83 | 0.89 | 3.50 | 1.40 |
| 6. Himachal Pradesh | — | — | 0.38 | — | — | — | 0.18 | — | 0.06 | 0.97 | — | 1.37 |
| 7. Jammu & Kashmir | — | — | 0.30 | 0.03 | 0.19 | — | 0.19 | — | 0.18 | 0.46 | — | 0.31 |
| 8. Karnataka | 3.12 | 2.60 | 3.13 | 6.92 | 4.20 | 7.43 | 9.74 | — | 13.01 | 3.17 | 3.91 | 8.03 |
| 9. Kerala | 5.15 | 0.71 | 2.78 | — | 1.26 | 3.60 | 1.31 | 7.99 | 16.88 | 0.66 | 6.91 | 4.18 |
| 10. Madhya Pradesh | 0.87 | 0.77 | 1.00 | 0.20 | 7.28 | 11.88 | 11.24 | — | 4.91 | 3.91 | 5.58 | 2.23 |
| 11. Maharashtra | 24.87 | 17.25 | 41.15 | 25.53 | 22.92 | 19.09 | 10.40 | 38.00 | 12.61 | 35.46 | 26.47 | 21.43 |
| 12. Orissa | — | 0.44 | 1.15 | — | 3.49 | 11.43 | 1.50 | — | 3.44 | 0.22 | 0.01 | 1.36 |
| 13. Punjab | 1.81 | 0.08 | 0.60 | 2.71 | 3.33 | 0.05 | — | — | 1.07 | 0.34 | 6.86 | 1.37 |
| 14. Rajasthan | — | 1.12 | 0.97 | 0.02 | 1.18 | 0.03 | 10.20 | — | 0.34 | 4.04 | 5.81 | 1.45 |
| 15. Tamil Nadu | 12.51 | 5.02 | 11.53 | 19.36 | 8.37 | 4.06 | 14.37 | — | 3.20 | 10.65 | 12.19 | 14.66 |
| 16. Uttar Pradesh | 4.33 | 20.89 | 5.70 | 0.90 | 7.67 | 3.22 | 2.82 | — | 1.29 | 1.66 | 3.25 | 7.08 |
| 17. West Bengal | 37.48 | 31.02 | 12.33 | 7.08 | 13.64 | 18.61 | 8.97 | — | 11.84 | 8.21 | 6.22 | 8.06 |
| 18. Delhi | 2.24 | 0.43 | 6.42 | 0.36 | 3.03 | 0.06 | — | 0.68 | 0.43 | 3.00 | 0.98 | 5.01 |

*(Contd.)*

TABLE 3.7 *(Contd.)*

| Name of the States | Industry Code | | | | | | | | | | | |
|---|---|---|---|---|---|---|---|---|---|---|---|---|
| | 399 (24) | 331 (25) | 332 (26) | 381 (27) | 333 (28) | 385 (29) | 260 (30) | 291 (31) | 243 (32) | 202 (33) | 329 (34) | 203 (35) |
| 1. Andhra Pradesh | 1.54 | 1.21 | 1.10 | 23.21 | 4.25 | 0.95 | 1.18 | 2.85 | 1.25 | 5.33 | — | 1.35 |
| 2. Assam | 0.54 | 0.56 | — | 0.33 | — | 0.28 | 0.21 | — | — | — | 6.48 | 1.32 |
| 3. Bihar | 2.51 | 10.02 | 3.79 | 1.82 | 7.08 | 0.11 | 0.70 | — | 1.09 | 7.62 | 68.32 | 1.38 |
| 4. Gujarat | 8.76 | 15.40 | 14.44 | 1.11 | 18.51 | 2.22 | 4.88 | 0.36 | 3.18 | 21.48 | — | 2.30 |
| 5. Haryana | 0.82 | 0.77 | 6.64 | — | 4.42 | 18.97 | — | — | — | — | — | — |
| 6. Himachal Pradesh | 0.22 | — | — | — | — | — | — | — | — | — | — | 0.67 |
| 7. Jammu & Kashmir | 3.74 | 0.02 | — | — | — | — | — | 0.06 | — | — | — | 0.24 |
| 8. Karnataka | 3.11 | 14.12 | 1.13 | 2.15 | 3.30 | 0.95 | 2.20 | 1.13 | 6.45 | 14.31 | — | 17.20 |
| 9. Kerala | 0.68 | 18.04 | 0.68 | 6.19 | 4.27 | 1.20 | 3.00 | — | 2.87 | 4.00 | — | 11.16 |
| 10. Madhya Pradesh | 0.09 | 5.12 | 0.15 | — | 3.11 | 1.28 | 0.86 | — | 2.58 | 0.14 | — | 5.63 |
| 11. Maharashtra | 26.90 | 20.56 | 24.52 | 27.55 | 6.91 | 36.11 | 58.24 | 5.46 | 53.90 | 17.10 | 20.24 | 23.25 |
| 12. Orissa | 1.21 | 0.82 | 0.10 | — | 0.31 | — | 1.25 | 0.38 | — | 2.67 | — | — |
| 13. Punjab | 1.94 | 0.42 | — | — | 0.49 | 10.89 | 0.94 | 0.35 | 1.23 | 4.89 | — | 1.55 |
| 14. Rajasthan | 0.74 | 0.37 | 0.80 | — | 2.35 | 0.17 | 0.73 | — | 2.22 | 2.22 | — | — |
| 15. Tamil Nadu | 17.78 | 5.74 | 5.08 | 3.87 | 13.72 | 14.82 | 6.47 | 69.06 | 7.55 | 2.51 | -27.70 | — |
| 16. Uttar Pradesh | 6.62 | 1.05 | 21.77 | — | 0.81 | 1.67 | 1.21 | 13.32 | 1.68 | 11.96 | — | 15.86 |
| 17. West Bengal | 17.73 | 4.80 | 19.32 | 33.71 | 27.54 | 7.67 | 14.04 | 6.16 | 7.51 | 1.64 | 32.62 | 15.93 |
| 18. Delhi | 3.93 | 0.94 | 0.44 | — | 2.68 | 2.04 | 3.55 | 0.30 | 8.11 | 4.00 | — | 1.54 |

*Source*: As in Table 3.6.

TABLE 3.8: Share of the States in All-India: Value Added (Important Industries) — 1978

*(per cent)*

| Name of the States | Industry Code | | | | | | | | | | |
|---|---|---|---|---|---|---|---|---|---|---|---|
| | 231 (1) | 209 (2) | 341 (3) | 319 (4) | 207 (5) | 360 (6) | 311 (7) | 370 (8) | 220 (9) | 350 (10) | 382 (11) |
| 1. Andhra Pradesh | 2.09 | 3.47 | 1.92 | 1.49 | 4.76 | 3.70 | 1.27 | 10.21 | 30.65 | 1.59 | 2.92 |
| 2. Assam | 0.32 | 23.90 | 1.49 | 0.88 | 0.38 | 0.28 | 0.12 | 0.20 | 0.09 | 0.38 | 2.42 |
| 3. Bihar | 0.33 | 0.53 | 0.16 | 2.80 | 7.48 | 5.24 | 8.00 | 1.67 | 16.59 | 0.65 | 0.89 |
| 4. Gujarat | 20.35 | 8.15 | 20.23 | 11.40 | 3.86 | 8.39 | 17.71 | 3.08 | 4.62 | 7.15 | 1.12 |
| 5. Haryana | 1.99 | 0.33 | 3.21 | 0.44 | 1.07 | 6.94 | 0.62 | 2.32 | — | 6.29 | 2.93 |
| 6. Himachal Pradesh | 0.01 | 0.01 | 12.61 | 0.06 | — | 0.78 | 0.24 | 0.06 | — | 0.09 | — |
| 7. Jammu & Kashmir | 0.32 | 0.14 | 0.05 | 0.26 | — | 0.05 | 0.09 | 0.05 | 0.11 | 0.09 | — |
| 8. Karnataka | 3.06 | 2.95 | 2.91 | 2.88 | 9.09 | 4.70 | 3.04 | 12.80 | 9.35 | 5.65 | 4.20 |
| 9. Kerala | 1.46 | 7.89 | 0.32 | 2.27 | 0.43 | 0.82 | 0.71 | 2.46 | 4.10 | 1.97 | — |
| 10. Madhya Pradesh | 4.35 | 0.81 | 8.63 | 1.86 | 1.51 | 0.81 | 2.61 | 8.72 | 4.97 | 1.19 | 0.89 |
| 11. Maharashtra | 27.92 | 13.08 | 12.21 | 57.09 | 33.55 | 30.51 | 29.17 | 24.68 | 11.58 | 38.09 | 9.40 |
| 12. Orissa | 0.45 | 0.47 | 9.48 | 0.22 | 0.06 | 0.77 | 11.81 | 0.32 | 0.83 | 0.17 | 0.78 |
| 13. Punjab | 2.47 | 7.03 | 2.90 | 0.29 | 2.85 | 1.98 | 1.18 | 1.32 | 0.28 | 5.21 | — |
| 14. Rajasthan | 2.21 | 1.35 | 0.60 | 0.22 | 0.49 | 1.84 | 2.91 | 2.06 | 0.20 | 0.71 | 3.57 |
| 15. Tamil Nadu | 11.86 | 12.05 | 6.78 | 5.46 | 8.94 | 15.71 | 10.55 | 6.08 | 3.02 | 6.86 | 15.10 |
| 16. Uttar Pradesh | 5.84 | 8.15 | 4.00 | 2.73 | 25..62 | 5.70 | 6.98 | 9.17 | 9.80 | 7.17 | 15.63 |
| 17. West Bengal | 13.81 | 9.08 | 22.98 | 8.30 | 0.64 | 10.09 | 2.28 | 11.61 | 3.01 | 13.46 | 39.21 |
| 18. Delhi | 0.91 | 0.41 | 0.71 | 1.00 | — | 1.00 | 0.68 | 2.35 | 0.64 | 2.95 | 0.50 |

*(Contd.)*

TABLE 3.8 *(Contd.)*

| Name of the States | Industry Code | | | | | | | | | | | |
|---|---|---|---|---|---|---|---|---|---|---|---|---|
| | 300 (12) | 342 (13) | 280 (14) | 383 (15) | 205 (16) | 271 (17) | 334 (18) | 321 (19) | 251 (20) | 339 (21) | 239 (22) | 384 (23) |
| 1. Andhra Pradesh | 3.13 | 0.19 | 3.81 | 0.58 | 16.82 | 9.34 | 12.82 | 3.03 | 1.92 | 8.78 | 6.21 | 8.92 |
| 2. Assam | — | — | 0.69 | 0.03 | 2.58 | 1.30 | — | 25.33 | 24.18 | 3.79 | 0.14 | 1.76 |
| 3. Bihar | 1.20 | 9.59 | 3.63 | 25.60 | 2.50 | 4.54 | 11.98 | 8.42 | 0.56 | 6.25 | 0.29 | 1.93 |
| 4. Gujarat | 1.08 | 1.63 | 5.47 | 1.37 | 3.19 | 5.05 | 8.98 | 5.17 | 5.12 | 9.71 | 17.55 | 8.53 |
| 5. Haryana | 11.51 | 2.19 | 2.39 | 2.61 | 4.07 | 6.74 | 2.10 | — | 1.16 | 6.66 | 0.39 | 2.16 |
| 6. Himachal Pradesh | — | — | 0.33 | — | 0.16 | — | 0.17 | — | 0.18 | 0.64 | — | 0.99 |
| 7. Jammu & Kashmir | — | — | 0.26 | 0.02 | 0.48 | — | — | — | 1.31 | 0.41 | — | 0.60 |
| 8. Karnataka | 3.42 | 8.07 | 4.73 | 8.15 | 3.95 | 7.58 | 7.77 | — | 12.07 | 10.82 | 9.28 | 9.24 |
| 9. Kerala | 7.73 | 4.91 | 2.10 | — | 0.46 | 3.98 | 0.93 | 8.12 | 16.07 | 0.66 | 5.23 | 3.40 |
| 10. Madhya Pradesh | 0.28 | 8.06 | 3.65 | 1.07 | 6.53 | 5.72 | 15.37 | — | 5.71 | 3.29 | 3.48 | 2.13 |
| 11. Maharashtra | 18.53 | 21.30 | 20.77 | 24.13 | 7.32 | 19.03 | 2.35 | 34.55 | 11.29 | 22.74 | 28.47 | 19.54 |
| 12. Orissa | — | 3.30 | 10.82 | 0.03 | 2.54 | 10.58 | 3.50 | — | 3.02 | 0.70 | 0.04 | 1.08 |
| 13. Punjab | 1.64 | 1.01 | 0.17 | 4.46 | 11.96 | 0.30 | — | 0.01 | 0.83 | 0.17 | 7.23 | 2.53 |
| 14. Rajasthan | 4.76 | 8.79 | 0.55 | 0.31 | 1.78 | 0.03 | 11.05 | — | 0.07 | 3.71 | 2.76 | 1.90 |
| 15. Tamil Nadu | 13.62 | 4.30 | 14.20 | 20.32 | 13.80 | 8.89 | 13.44 | 3.05 | 2.94 | 10.49 | 9.60 | 14.81 |
| 16. Uttar Pradesh | 12.36 | 14.42 | 4.97 | 1.27 | 9.52 | 4.97 | 1.85 | — | 2.00 | 2.61 | 0.51 | 7.90 |
| 17. West Bengal | 18.90 | 11.24 | 11.90 | 8.49 | 10.02 | 11.66 | 6.84 | 11.56 | 3.43 | 6.72 | 7.82 | 8.06 |
| 18. Delhi | 1.51 | 0.33 | 9.50 | 1.41 | 2.01 | 0.25 | 0.10 | 0.18 | 0.39 | 1.75 | 0.28 | 4.30 |

*(Contd.)*

TABLE 3.8 (*Contd.*)

| Name of the States | Industry Code | | | | | | | | | | | |
|---|---|---|---|---|---|---|---|---|---|---|---|---|
| | 399 (24) | 331 (25) | 332 (26) | 381 (27) | 333 (28) | 385 (29) | 260 (30) | 291 (31) | 243 (32) | 202 (33) | 329 (34) | 203 (35) |
| 1. Andhra Pradesh | 2.15 | 1.69 | 1.99 | 18.97 | 2.24 | 2.77 | 1.06 | 2.28 | 1.14 | 6.68 | — | 2.98 |
| 2. Assam | 1.15 | 0.05 | — | 0.50 | — | — | 0.21 | — | — | — | 3.21 | 1.97 |
| 3. Bihar | 1.52 | 14.60 | 5.82 | 1.02 | 7.71 | 0.01 | 0.31 | — | 1.11 | 6.00 | 45.94 | 0.03 |
| 4. Gujarat | 7.28 | 10.90 | 16.69 | 1.11 | 16.04 | 1.30 | 3.19 | 0.72 | 3.07 | 16.52 | 19.13 | 9.16 |
| 5. Haryana | 0.82 | 3.16 | 4.65 | — | 12.79 | 17.83 | — | — | 1.99 | 2.04 | — | 0.42 |
| 6. Himachal Pradesh | 0.14 | — | — | — | — | — | 0.10 | — | — | — | — | — |
| 7. Jammu & Kashmir | 2.40 | — | — | — | — | — | 0.21 | — | — | — | — | — |
| 8. Karnataka | 2.11 | 6.56 | 2.88 | 3.05 | 12.81 | 4.21 | 3.19 | 1.33 | 7.11 | 12.38 | 0.27 | 3.92 |
| 9. Kerala | 0.63 | 12.03 | 0.36 | 10.84 | 2.36 | 0.32 | 1.74 | — | 2.11 | 2.70 | — | 21.33 |
| 10. Madhya Pradesh | 0.90 | 3.05 | — | — | 1.90 | 0.22 | 0.63 | — | 2.09 | 0.10 | 0.28 | 7.15 |
| 11. Maharashtra | 29.05 | 7.42 | 29.93 | 37.02 | 4.77 | 40.05 | 77.50 | 4.43 | 40.52 | 14.09 | 11.20 | — |
| 12. Orissa | 1.37 | 25.66 | 0.62 | — | 0.51 | — | 0.42 | 0.40 | — | 2.41 | 0.03 | 22.94 |
| 13. Punjab | 3.68 | 0.08 | — | — | 0.10 | 15.57 | 0.39 | 2.76 | 1.26 | 10.16 | — | — |
| 14. Rajasthan | 1.29 | 1.15 | 0.26 | — | 1.78 | — | 0.30 | — | 6.08 | 1.73 | — | 2.21 |
| 15. Tamil Nadu | 14.30 | 9.71 | 1.41 | 1.21 | 24.57 | 8.74 | 2.16 | 74.97 | 8.71 | 18.05 | 11.03 | — |
| 16. Uttar Pradesh | 8.90 | 1.88 | 17.62 | — | 3.86 | 4.97 | 0.42 | 6.27 | 1.39 | 6.30 | 0.09 | 1.30 |
| 17. West Bengal | 17.70 | 1.29 | 17.44 | 26.17 | 6.83 | 1.33 | 5.29 | 5.86 | 2.12 | 1.28 | 8.81 | 9.70 |
| 18. Delhi | 3.62 | 0.30 | 0.15 | — | 1.49 | 2.53 | 2.25 | 0.65 | 21.95 | 6.26 | — | 14.32 |

*Source:* As per Table 3.6.

More striking is the dominance of a few States not only in the important industry groups but also in most of the industries which are not so important even in 1978 (see Table 3.8).

## CONCLUDING OBSERVATIONS

An attempt was made to analyse the performance of the registered manufacturing sector at all India and regional levels between 1961 and 1978. We observed that:

(1) though the overall growth of the manufacturing sector has been quite impressive at all India level, all the industry groups did not behave uniformally between 1961 and 1978. More so, if the entire period is divided into somewhat two equal sub-periods. However, we observed a clear trend of traditional industries being replaced by modern industries. For example, agro-based industries or consumer industries (especially non-durable) have lost their share heavily in favour of chemical based industries, metal based industries or basic and capital goods sectors between 1961 and 1978. Another interesting observation is that though the consumer goods sector grew at a relatively slow rate, its sub-sector viz., consumer durables, grew at a relatively higher rate than the manufacturing sector as a whole. It indicates that even within the sector, there is a shift in favour of modern industries;

(2) industry groups with a very high rate of growth are not necessarily very important in terms of their potential to effect overall growth of the industrial sector *per se*. Some times these exceptionally high rates of growth are more a statistical illusion, because they derive high values of growth rates because of their very low base in the initial year. Consequently, even a small absolute increase result in a very high rate of growth;

(3) in all, 35 industry groups emerge as important industry groups, based on minimum 0.5 per cent share of individual industry in either of the national value added, employment or fixed capital in any of the years 1961, 1969 and 1978; and

(4) while analysing the distribution of important industries across States, it is observed that the industrial structure of the country in the first instance is heavily concentrated in a few industries; and these industries in turn are concentrated in few regions. The

regions with high concentration of industries not only have a dominant share of important industries but also of those industries which are not so important at the national level. Therefore, the growth and decline of various regional industrial economies can plausibly be explained in terms of their industrial structure and shifts therein. Put in other words, the industrial structure of the various regions provides a major clue for explaining regional industrial disparities over time in India. However, before pondering over the causes of the inter-regional industrial variations, it will be interesting to know the trend and extent of regional disparities existing across the regions/States in India.

## NOTES

1. For a detailed discussion on the data base, its limitations and adjustments made, see Appendix I.
2. A detailed aggregation scheme is presented in Appendix II.
3. Fixed Capital and value added are in constant terms at 1970-71 prices.
4. The reason for taking value added in lieu of output is that value-added is considered a more comprehensive indicator of industrial growth. For, it represents net cost of the output and is relatively free from the input biases across industries. For further arguments see, Rosen (1959).
5. For computing compound growth rates we used the following method
   $P_t = P_o (1 + r)^t$
   Where
   $P_o$ = value if the base year,
   $P_t$ = value in the terminal year,
   $r$ = growth rate;
   $t$ = time variable, i.e., number of years.
6. For calculating trend rate of growth we used a sem-log linear regression model as follows
   $log\ Y = \alpha + \beta_t$
   Where $Y$ = value of any variable over time;
   $t$ = time and $\beta$ is the trend co-efficient.
7. Our purpose here is not to probe into the various aspects of the industrial stagnation during the post mid-sixties. However, for a lively debate on the subject, see : Rudra (1967); Bagchi (1970); Raj (1976 and 1984); Srinivasan (1977); Srinivasan and Narayana (1977); Vaidyanathan (1977); Patnaik and Rao (1977); Mitra (1977); Nayyar (1978); Shetty (1978); Chakravarty (1979); Desai (1981); Rangarajan (1982); Varshney (1983) and, more recently, a detailed study by Ahluwalia (1985).
8. However, Raj (1984) contends that the phenomenon of industrial stagnation is illusory to an extent and there is a clear trend of reversal. It is more a sort of cyclical phenomenon than a State of stagnation. Also see Bardhan (1984) for a

critique on Raj.

9. We divide the series 1961-78 into two, more or less, equal sub-periods, i.e., 1961-1969 and 1969-1978, for the purpose of analysis. Year 1969 is taken as cut off point. For it is believed that the recession touched the rock bottom in 1967-68, and started recovering thereafter. Therefore, the choice of 1969 as cut-off point is quite logical for observing the trend in a periodisation scheme.
10. This is further confirmed, if we look at the growth profile of the industry groups, based on input base classification. For, the metal based industry group (by and large covering investment goods industries, i.e. basic goods and capital goods sector), recorded higher rate of growth of fixed capital during the first sub-period. So is the case of chemical based industries, known for their high capital intensive nature, whereas in the second sub-period, value-added as well as employment overtook the growth rate in fixed capital, observed during the earlier period.
11. Henceforth only the industry code will be mentioned for indicating any specific industry group.
12. However, the rank order of employment or fixed capital growth by-industry does not always match with the value added performance. They differ depending upon the capital or labour intensive nature of the industry.
13. It is also plausible that the industries in this group being relatively new, involved a long gestation period, where some workers were engaged in commissioning and maintenance of the plants. Later they achieved better capacity utilisation resulting in faster growth of value added compared to the fixed capital and employment.
14. It is also possible that industry composition might have changed towards greater labour intensity which is not being captured even at three digit level of disaggregation.
15. For example industry group like watches and clocks (393) with a meager weight (0.01 per cent in 1961 and 0.22 in 1978), in the aggregate value added might hardly have affected overall growth of the manufacturing sector despite its very impressive growth performance, e.g., 19.29 per cent per annum compound in terms of value-added, 12.34 per cent in terms of employment and 13.67 per cent in terms of fixed capital during 1961-78. Whereas the cotton textile industry (231), with its dominant share in the manufacturing sector grew barely at a rate of 3.0 per cent per annum, in terms of value added a rate much below the national rate of growth (5.56%) between 1961-78. This low growth rate will obviously have much a serious bearing on the growth of the industrial sector as a whole than the high rate of growth in the industries like watches and clocks (393).
16. Since the total number of industries under consideration is 53, average naturally approximates to 2 per cent. Therefore, an industry with more than or equal to 2 per cent share in the value added in 1961 is defined as high share industry or more important industry; otherwise it is low share or less important industry. Similarly if an industry has gained in terms of its share in value added between 1961 and 1978, it is defined having a favourable shift, otherwise the shift is unfavourable.
17. Thus, taking 0.5 per cent as cut-off point, in all 35 out of the 53 industry groups emerge as important for the purpose of further analysing the industrial structure in a more fruitful manner. It is plausible that these very industries will play a major role in determining the growth profile of the States or regions. Other remaining industries, unless concentrated in one or a few regions, will hardly have any crucial impact on the regional growth mechanism. Moreover, it is quite unlikely that these remaining industries will get concentrated within a very few regions,

given their 'foot loose' character. Identified 35 important industry groups are : 202, 203, 205, 207, 209, 220, 231, 239, 243, 251, 260, 271, 280, 291, 300, 311, 319, 321, 329, 331, 332, 333, 334, 339, 341, 342, 350, 360, 370, 381, 382, 383, 384, 385, 399.

18. However, under this scheme also some of extremely fast growing industries like 393, 241, 213, 312, 271, 391 and 206 with 19.29, 14.12, 13.43, 10.32, 9.71, 7.50, 7.03, 6.50, per cent compound rate of growth per annum, in terms of value-added, between 1961 and 1978, are left out. The first three industries are the second third and fourth fastest growing industries in the country. However, their share even in 1978 was merely 0.22, 0.18, 0.22, 0.26, 0.16, 0.05, 0.34, 0.37 per cent of the total value-added respectively a share quite insignificant for making any impact on the overall growth of a region.
19. Though the performance of the various regions will vary according to the variable considered; we consider value added (in real terms) as the best indicator. Other variables, like employment or fixed-capital, are likely to give a biased picture depending upon the factor proportions in specific industry groups. Moreover, value-added is a net outcome of the contribution of all the factors of production, it is expected to yield more reliable results for our kind of analysis.

*ANNEXURE 3.1*

**All India Compound Growth Rates: Major Industry Groups in Registered Manufacturing (Factory) Sector[1] Three Digit Classification[2] (Years 1961-1969, 1969-1978, 1961-1978)**

*(per cent per annum)*

| Sl.[3] No. | Indu-[3] stry Code | Industry group[3] | Value added[4] | | | Trend[5] Rate of growth 1961-1978 | Employment | | | Trend[5] Rate of growth 1961-1978 | Fixed capital | | | Trend[5] Rate of growth 1961-1978 |
|---|---|---|---|---|---|---|---|---|---|---|---|---|---|---|
| | | | 1961-1969 | 1969-1978 | 1961-1978 | | 1961-1969 | 1969-1978 | 1961-1978 | | 1961-1969 | 1969-1978 | 1961-1978 | |
| (1) | (2) | (3) | (4) | (5) | (6) | (7) | (8) | (9) | (10) | (11) | (12) | (13) | (14) | (15) |
| 1. | 329 | Petroleum and coal products | 20.02 | 22.13 | 21.13 | 20.08* | 19.97 | 13.32 | 13.16 | 12.16* | 48.45 | 10.84 | 27.18 | 14.53* |
| 2. | 393 | Watches and clocks | 37.17 | 8.75 | 21.31 | 19.29* | 22.94 | 7.37 | 14.44 | 12.34* | 22.93 | 11.63 | 16.81 | 13.67* |
| 3. | 241 | Foot-wear (except rubber and plastics) | 17.66 | 12.69 | 15.01 | 14.12* | 7.28 | 20.99 | 14.33 | 19.45* | 24.76 | 17.94 | 21.10 | 16.76* |
| 4. | 213 | Malt liquor, country liquor and toddy | 18.27 | 11.21 | 7.17 | 13.43* | 6.24 | 17.55 | 12.09 | 17.06* | 21.93 | 12.35 | 16.76 | 21.92* |
| 5. | 202 | Dairy products | 19.42 | 9.95 | 14.31 | 13.12* | 16.26 | 11.03 | 13.47 | 14.76* | 16.84 | 5.72 | 10.81 | 9.55* |
| 6. | 243 | Tailoring, Umbrella and textile garments | 2.81 | 19.80 | 11.48 | 12.30* | 3.64 | 15.37 | 9.70 | 10.36* | 9.98 | 16.24 | 13.25 | 14.02* |
| 7. | 204 | Canning and preservation of fish and sea food | 15.62 | 9.15 | 12.14 | 11.59* | 19.35 | 14.26 | 16.62 | 17.07* | 24.99 | 11.47 | 17.64 | 17.54* |
| 8. | 370 | Electric machinery and appliances | 11.09 | 12.19 | 11.67 | 11.44* | 9.33 | 4.74 | 9.33 | 6.78* | 18.43 | 3.17 | 10.09 | 8.79* |

*(Contd.)*

ANNEXURE 3.1 *(Contd.)*

| (1) | (2) | (3) | (4) | (5) | (6) | (7) | (8) | (9) | (10) | (11) | (12) | (13) | (14) | (15) |
|---|---|---|---|---|---|---|---|---|---|---|---|---|---|---|
| 9. | 385 | Motor cycles and bicycles | 8.97 | 9.14 | 9.06 | 10.85* | 5.47 | 7.31 | 6.44 | 6.92* | 3.96 | 6.81 | 5.45 | 4.56* |
| 10. | 381 | Ship and boat building | 5.38 | 13.92 | 9.82 | 10.65* | 1.16 | 6.47 | 3.94 | 3.45* | 6.04 | 19.47 | 12.95 | 11.78* |
| 11. | 321 | Petroleum refineries | 9.01 | 1.43 | 4.93 | 10.49* | 10.11 | -0.11 | 4.58 | 4.32* | 13.94 | -3.23 | 4.50 | 3.54*** |
| 12. | 312 | Inedible oil | 3.81 | 14.89 | 9.53 | 10.32* | 2.32 | 15.44 | 9.07 | 12.32* | 11.94 | 14.31 | 13.19 | 11.31* |
| 13. | 233 | Thread, rope and cordiges of all types | 4.41 | 13.70 | 9.23 | 9.71* | -0.11 | 7.65 | 3.93 | 5.44* | 13.81 | 1.73 | 7.24 | 7.61* |
| 14. | 360 | Machine and machine tools (except electric) | 12.42 | 6.43 | 9.21 | 9.65* | 7.98 | 2.50 | 5.04 | 4.66* | 19.94 | -1.59 | 8.01 | 6.39* |
| 15. | 271 | Paper and paper products | 11.36 | 4.61 | 7.73 | 9.35* | 6.31 | 3.12 | 4.61 | 4.75* | 10.35 | 1.98 | 5.84 | 4.65* |
| 16. | 311 | Industrial heavy chemicals | 8.08 | 10.69 | 9.45 | 9.23* | 8.15 | 5.44 | 6.71 | 7.95* | 16.25 | 4.52 | 9.89 | 11.79* |
| 17. | 383 | Motor vehicles and parts | 10.95 | 7.68 | 9.04 | 7.82* | 7.34 | 4.68 | 5.93 | 5.95* | 14.03 | 0.64 | 6.74 | 5.83* |
| 18. | 389 | Transport equipments, not elsewhere classified (n.e.c.) | 12.40 | 0.50 | 5.94 | 7.54* | 12.16 | -2.79 | 3.97 | 3.95* | 19.44 | -1.56 | 7.81 | 11.47* |
| 19. | 392 | Photographic material | 14.19 | 4.85 | 9.15 | 7.50* | 10.09 | 7.99 | 8.97 | 7.11* | 55.52 | 7.22 | 18.30 | 14.39* |
| 20. | 384 | Repair of motor vehicles | 9.13 | 6.54 | 7.76 | 7.35* | 7.24 | 2.11 | 4.50 | 4.22* | 8.93 | 0.91 | 4.61 | 3.20* |
| 21. | 391 | Medical, surgical and scientific industries | 13.39 | 5.32 | 9.05 | 7.01* | 12.98 | 3.38 | 7.80 | 7.10* | 25.41 | -0.74 | 10.80 | 6.80* |
| 22. | 399 | Miscellaneous industries (n.e.c.) | 7.12 | 2.00 | 4.38 | 7.02* | 5.20 | -4.11 | 0.16 | 0.93 | 9.03 | -1.68 | 3.21 | 4.65* |
| 23. | 206 | Bakery products | 10.57 | 2.34 | 6.13 | 6.50* | 9.74 | 4.13 | 6.74 | 6.36* | 14.25 | -0.71 | 6.07 | 7.18* |
| 24. | 339 | Non-metallic mineral products (n.e.c.) | 4.99 | 8.03 | 6.59 | 6.32* | 5.77 | 6.01 | 5.90 | 4.66* | 13.03 | 4.82 | 8.60 | 7.61* |
| 25. | 341 | Iron-steel and ferrous alloys | 5.69 | 8.30 | 7.06 | 5.92* | 7.44 | 4.64 | 5.95 | 5.20* | 17.59 | 1.73 | 8.91 | 3.89** |

*(Contd.)*

ANNEXURE 3.1 *(Contd.)*

| (1) | (2) | (3) | (4) | (5) | (6) | (7) | (8) | (9) | (10) | (11) | (12) | (13) | (14) | (15) |
|---|---|---|---|---|---|---|---|---|---|---|---|---|---|---|
| 26. | 319 | Other chemical (n.e.c) | 5.21 | 6.16 | 5.71 | 5.75* | 7.15 | 4.03 | 5.48 | 5.04* | 12.45 | 4.50 | 8.17 | 8.92* |
| 27. | 232 | Knitting mills | 9.48 | 1.34 | 5.09 | 5.38* | 4.92 | 1.47 | 3.08 | 3.45* | 10.49 | 5.10 | 7.61 | 7.12* |
| 28. | 332 | Glass and glass products | 6.43 | 5.08 | 5.72 | 5.09* | 2.14 | 2.17 | 2.16 | 2.02* | 8.97 | 1.39 | 4.57 | 4.57* |
| 29. | 260 | Furniture and fixtures | 4.33 | 6.37 | 5.41 | 5.07* | 0.66 | -0.80 | -0.11 | -0.43 | 3.61 | -0.69 | 1.31 | 0.94*** |
| 30. | 394 | Jewellery and mint | 7.01 | -0.18 | 3.13 | 4.85* | 5.91 | -1.82 | 1.74 | 3.79* | 1.44 | 3.92 | 2.78 | 3.10* |
| 31. | 211 | Distilling and rectifying spirit | 3.43 | 8.22 | 5.94 | 4.70** | 3.87 | 11.85 | 8.02 | 8.01* | 3.87 | 9.35 | 6.74 | 6.35* |
| 32. | 331 | Structural clay products | 1.36 | 6.68 | 4.15 | 4.27* | 2.57 | 3.31 | 2.96 | 2.60* | 1.76 | 3.32 | 2.59 | 1.49* |
| 33. | 212 | Wine industries | 26.38 | -10.10 | 5.53 | 4.25* | 11.33 | -4.89 | 2.42 | 1.85 | 27.85 | -1.29 | 11.49 | 7.43*** |
| 34. | 251 | Wood and wood products | -3.12 | 5.37 | 1.28 | 4.00* | 4.91 | 2.56 | 3.66 | 2.95* | 0.37 | 2.05 | 1.26 | 1.97* |
| 35. | 291 | Tanning and curing of leather | 1.78 | 5.56 | 3.76 | 3.89* | 0.37 | 6.21 | 3.42 | 3.21* | 9.24 | 15.05 | 12.28 | 12.95* |
| 36. | 293 | Leather products (n.e.c.) | 16.36 | -1.48 | 6.54 | 3.83** | 7.29 | 2.74 | 4.86 | 4.27* | 10.44 | 3.53 | 6.72 | 3.81* |
| 37. | 334 | Cement, lime plaster | 6.05 | 1.99 | 3.89 | 3.74* | 3.06 | 2.93 | 2.99 | 3.44* | 5.91 | -0.24 | 2.61 | 3.10* |
| 38. | 300 | Rubber and rubber products | 4.90 | 0.90 | 2.80 | 3.70* | 6.89 | 2.14 | 4.35 | 3.96* | 12.70 | 4.81 | 8.46 | 7.53* |
| 39. | 386 | Air craft | 10.54 | -0.33 | 4.64 | 3.36* | 11.25 | 3.64 | 7.16 | 4.44* | -3.32 | 3.30 | 0.13 | -0.54 |
| 40. | 231 | Manufacturing of textiles | 2.20 | 5.26 | 3.81 | 3.09* | -0.20 | 2.08 | 0.99 | 0.90* | 5.78 | 0.26 | 2.82 | 1.37** |
| 41. | 220 | Tobacco and tobacco products | 3.07 | 3.71 | 3.41 | 2.65** | -3.08 | 11.83 | 4.54 | 5.29* | 5.98 | 1.55 | 3.61 | 4.44* |
| 42. | 333 | Earthernware and chinaware | 11.78 | 1.28 | 6.09 | 2.17 | 3.61 | 0.33 | 1.86 | 1.34** | 10.00 | -3.18 | 2.81 | 2.33*** |
| 43. | 207 | Sugar, *gur* and *khandsari* | 0.65 | 2.22 | 1.48 | 2.13 | 2.21 | 12.67 | 7.62 | 9.96* | 5.06 | 5.91 | 5.51 | 4.92* |
| 44. | 350 | Metal products and parts (except machine & trans.) | 6.50 | -0.25 | 2.87 | 2.01* | 5.38 | -0.81 | 2.06 | 1.30* | 7.13 | -3.43 | 1.41 | 4.37 |
| 45. | 280 | Printing and publishing | 7.42 | -3.14 | 1.69 | 1.77** | 2.82 | -0.09 | 1.27 | 0.84** | 6.01 | -0.92 | 2.28 | 2.20* |
| 46. | 214 | Soft drinks and carbonated water | 13.79 | -7.17 | 2.16 | 1.75 | 18.42 | -2.75 | 6.69 | 8.51* | 12.49 | -0.35 | 5.50 | 8.42* |

*(Contd.)*

ANNEXURE 3.1 *(Contd.)*

| (1) | (2) | (3) | (4) | (5) | (6) | (7) | (8) | (9) | (10) | (11) | (12) | (13) | (14) | (15) |
|---|---|---|---|---|---|---|---|---|---|---|---|---|---|---|
| 47. | 382 | Railway locomotives | 5.72 | -1.57 | 1.80 | 1.34** | 3.91 | -4.08 | -0.39 | -1.73*** | 3.95 | -8.99 | -3.11 | -4.73* |
| 48. | 239 | Other textiles (n.e.c.) | 1.24 | 1.21 | 1.49 | 1.30 | -2.41 | 5.67 | 1.78 | 3.31* | -1.39 | 3.06 | 0.94 | 0.86 |
| 49. | 208 | Cocoa, chocolate and sugar candy | -7.48 | 13.52 | 3.10 | 0.35 | 3.02 | 0.97 | 1.94 | 1.61*** | 2.05 | -0.65 | 40.61 | 1.37 |
| 50. | 203 | Canning and food preservation | 1.51 | 6.60 | 4.17 | -0.25 | 5.67 | 6.63 | 6.17 | 5.81* | 7.23 | 5.04 | 6.07 | 6.84* |
| 51. | 209 | Food products (n.e.c.) | -0.51 | 0.92 | 0.24 | -0.35 | 0.90 | 4.39 | 2.73 | 3.17* | 1.04 | 1.17 | 1.11 | 0.21 |
| 52. | 205 | Grain mill products | -3.38 | 5.40 | 1.17 | -0.57 | 0.46 | 2.81 | 1.70 | 1.05*** | 3.22 | 3.92 | 3.59 | 2.49* |
| 53. | 342 | Non-ferrous basic industries | 4.55 | -1.51 | 1.29 | -1.67*** | 7.22 | 2.48 | 4.69 | 4.06* | 12.95 | 9.85 | 11.29 | 11.13* |
| All Industries | | | 5.70 | 6.07 | 5.89 | 5.56* | 3.86 | 4.08 | 3.97 | 3.94* | 14.13 | 3.86 | 8.91 | 6.26* |

*Notes:* (1) Excludes Electricity, Gas and water supply, except at aggregate (all India) level which includes total registered manufacturing (factory sector).

(2) Corresponds to 3 digit level of industrial classification of ASI (see Appendix II).

(3) Industry groups are given in descending order according to their trend rate of growth in value added.

(4) Data are at 1970-71 prices.

Trend rates of growth have been estimated as

Log $y = a + b^t$

otherwise all other compound growth rates are based on respective two points of time information. Level of significance of the trend values, based on $R^2$ value is:

* Significant at 1 per cent level of significance.

** Significant at 5 per cent level of significance.

*** Significant at 10 per cent level of significance.

*Source:* Annual Survey of Industries (ASI).

ANNEXURE 3.2

## Changes in the Shares[1] of Major Industry Groups in Manufacturing (Registered) Sector at all India level: Three Digit Classification – Years: 1961, 1969, 1978

(per cent)

| Sl.[2] No. | Industry[3] Code | Value added[4] | | | Employment | | | Fixed capital[4] | | |
|---|---|---|---|---|---|---|---|---|---|---|
| | | 1961 | 1969 | 1978 | 1961 | 1969 | 1978 | 1961 | 1969 | 1978 |
| (1) | (2) | (3) | (4) | (5) | (6) | (7) | (8) | (9) | (10) | (11) |
| 1. | 231 | 25.99 | 20.69 | 20.28 | 32.79 | 25.55 | 21.92 | 17.79 | 11.70 | 9.68 |
| 2. | 209 | 9.26 | 6.06 | 4.79 | 7.72 | 6.54 | 6.90 | 6.39 | 2.45 | 2.20 |
| 3. | 341 | 6.96 | 7.26 | 9.47 | 5.47 | 7.57 | 8.15 | 15.21 | 22.31 | 21.89 |
| 4. | 319 | 6.19 | 6.15 | 6.78 | 2.45 | 2.97 | 3.44 | 2.87 | 3.03 | 3.70 |
| 5. | 311 | 4.57 | 5.58 | 8.47 | 2.23 | 2.43 | 3.00 | 9.92 | 13.92 | 16.70 |
| 6. | 207 | 4.47 | 4.25 | 2.44 | 3.84 | 3.63 | 7.56 | 5.28 | 3.20 | 4.35 |
| 7. | 360 | 4.34 | 7.40 | 8.24 | 4.58 | 6.73 | 5.97 | 4.36 | 7.57 | 5.28 |
| 8. | 370 | 3.34 | 5.18 | 6.94 | 2.54 | 4.06 | 4.42 | 2.94 | 4.02 | 4.40 |
| 9. | 220 | 3.26 | 2.78 | 2.45 | 4.66 | 3.66 | 5.61 | 0.53 | 0.34 | 0.32 |
| 10. | 350 | 2.98 | 3.31 | 2.05 | 2.85 | 3.42 | 2.28 | 2.82 | 2.05 | 1.20 |
| 11. | 382 | 2.96 | 3.09 | 1.76 | 4.34 | 4.68 | 2.28 | 3.57 | 2.03 | 0.07 |
| 12. | 300 | 2.47 | 2.44 | 1.68 | 0.10 | 0.14 | 0.12 | 1.00 | 1.07 | 1.35 |
| 13. | 342 | 2.46 | 2.35 | 1.29 | 0.63 | 0.84 | 0.76 | 1.67 | 1.83 | 3.49 |

(Contd.)

ANNEXURE 3.2 (*Contd.*)

| (1) | (2) | (3) | (4) | (5) | (6) | (7) | (8) | (9) | (10) | (11) |
|---|---|---|---|---|---|---|---|---|---|---|
| 14. | 280 | 2.33 | 2.76 | 1.32 | 3.37 | 3.31 | 2.35 | 2.09 | 1.39 | 1.04 |
| 15. | 383 | 2.12 | 5.17 | 3.92 | 1.45 | 2.02 | 2.18 | 2.48 | 2.85 | 2.45 |
| 16. | 205 | 2.01 | 1.02 | 1.01 | 2.75 | 2.25 | 2.06 | 1.26 | 0.75 | 0.85 |
| 17. | 271 | 1.34 | 2.13 | 2.05 | 1.37 | 1.77 | 1.67 | 3.48 | 3.22 | 3.10 |
| 18. | 334 | 1.27 | 1.47 | 1.03 | 0.78 | 0.80 | 0.72 | 3.59 | 2.45 | 1.88 |
| 19. | 321 | 1.24 | 1.64 | 1.19 | 0.12 | 0.22 | 0.15 | 2.80 | 3.27 | 1.96 |
| 20. | 251 | 1.13 | 0.58 | 0.58 | 1.03 | 1.19 | 1.07 | 0.81 | 0.33 | 0.32 |
| 21. | 339 | 0.97 | 0.95n | 1.20 | 1.13 | 1.40 | 1.69 | 0.56 | 0.63 | 0.78 |
| 22. | 239 | 0.93 | 0.69 | 0.50 | 3.70 | 2.39 | 2.83 | 1.27 | 0.47 | 0.51 |
| 23. | 384 | 0.92 | 1.23 | 1.38 | 1.68 | 2.32 | 2.00 | 0.96 | 0.79 | 0.70 |
| 24. | 399 | 0.86 | 1.00 | 0.76 | 1.19 | 1.42 | 0.68 | 0.78 | 0.64 | 0.46 |
| 25. | 331 | 0.74 | 0.65 | 0.62 | 1.62 | 1.56 | 1.50 | 1.01 | 0.47 | 0.53 |
| 26. | 332 | 0.50 | 0.56 | 0.49 | 1.08 | 1.01 | 0.88 | 0.57 | 0.46 | 0.44 |
| 27. | 381 | 0.45 | 0.46 | 0.95 | 0.68 | 0.58 | 0.74 | 0.45 | 0.29 | 1.20 |
| 28. | 333 | 0.41 | 0.32 | 0.23 | 0.56 | 0.58 | 0.43 | 0.44 | 0.36 | 0.23 |
| 29. | 385 | 0.39 | 0.52 | 0.73 | 0.47 | 0.57 | 0.78 | 0.68 | 0.37 | 0.57 |
| 30. | 260 | 0.39 | 0.37 | 0.38 | 0.62 | 0.51 | 0.34 | 0.35 | 0.18 | 0.13 |
| 31. | 291 | 0.35 | 0.28 | 0.29 | 0.52 | 0.41 | 0.51 | 0.13 | 0.11 | 0.32 |
| 32. | 206 | 0.32 | 0.48 | 0.37 | 0.22 | 0.36 | 0.38 | 0.17 | 0.20 | 0.15 |
| 33. | 386 | 0.21 | 0.31 | 0.19 | 0.09 | 0.17 | 0.17 | 0.30 | 0.10 | 0.09 |
| 34. | 391 | 0.18 | 0.33 | 0.35 | 0.20 | 0.40 | 0.39 | 0.13 | 0.33 | 0.25 |
| 35. | 211 | 0.17 | 0.14 | 0.19 | 0.11 | 0.13 | 0.23 | 0.25 | 0.13 | 0.25 |

(*Contd.*)

ANNEXURE 3.2 *(Contd.)*

| (1) | (2) | (3) | (4) | (5) | (6) | (7) | (8) | (9) | (10) | (11) |
|---|---|---|---|---|---|---|---|---|---|---|
| 36. | 232 | 0.17 | 0.24 | 0.16 | 0.24 | 0.27 | 0.22 | 0.10 | 0.06 | 0.12 |
| 37. | 394 | 0.16 | 0.18 | 0.11 | 0.18 | 0.22 | 0.13 | 0.17 | 0.06 | 0.09 |
| 38. | 243 | 0.16 | 0.13 | 0.43 | 0.28 | 0.28 | 0.76 | 0.06 | 0.05 | 0.17 |
| 39. | 202 | 0.15 | 0.41 | 0.61 | 0.10 | 0.27 | 0.51 | 0.38 | 0.56 | 0.76 |
| 40. | 213 | 0.15 | 0.19 | 0.22 | 0.02 | 0.03 | 0.10 | 0.03 | 0.08 | 0.19 |
| 41. | 214 | 0.14 | 0.26 | 0.08 | 0.06 | 0.20 | 0.11 | 0.10 | 0.10 | 0.08 |
| 42. | 312 | 0.13 | 0.12 | 0.26 | 0.14 | 0.14 | 0.27 | 0.13 | 0.13 | 0.38 |
| 43. | 233 | 0.09 | 0.08 | 0.16 | 0.10 | 0.08 | 0.12 | 0.04 | 0.05 | 0.04 |
| 44. | 329 | 0.07 | 0.22 | 0.88 | 0.09 | 0.19 | 0.45 | 0.17 | 1.65 | 3.42 |
| 45. | 203 | 0.07 | 0.06 | 0.06 | 0.09 | 0.11 | 0.15 | 0.08 | 0.59 | 0.74 |
| 46. | 389 | 0.05 | 0.09 | 0.06 | 0.07 | 0.14 | 0.08 | 0.03 | 0.06 | 0.04 |
| 47. | 208 | 0.05 | 0.02 | 0.04 | 0.06 | 0.05 | 0.04 | 0.04 | 0.01 | 0.02 |
| 48. | 212 | 0.04 | 0.01 | 0.02 | 0.03 | 0.05 | 0.01 | 0.02 | 0.05 | 0.04 |
| 49. | 241 | 0.03 | 0.09 | 0.18 | 0.07 | 0.09 | 0.43 | 0.01 | 0.01 | 0.09 |
| 50. | 204 | 0.02 | 0.06 | 0.08 | 0.01 | 0.05 | 0.14 | 0.02 | 0.05 | 0.11 |
| 51. | 392 | 0.02 | 0.06 | 0.05 | 0.05 | 0.08 | 0.13 | 0.02 | 0.19 | 0.08 |
| 52. | 393 | 0.01 | 0.16 | 0.22 | 0.02 | 0.11 | 0.16 | 0.03 | 0.06 | 0.15 |
| 53. | 393 | 0.01 | 0.02 | 0.01 | 0.02 | 0.03 | 0.03 | 0.02 | 0.01 | 0.01 |
| | All industries[5] | 100.00 | 100.00 | 100.00 | 100.00 | 100.00 | 100.00 | 100.00 | 100.00 | 100.00 |

*Notes:* (1) Shares are proportions of the total values of all the industries taken together, except Electricity, Gas and Steam and water works.
(2) Industries are given in descending order according to their share in the value added in the year 1961.
(3) For settled classification and the names of various industry groups, see Annexure 3.1.
(4) Data used are at 1970-71 prices.
(5) Totals may not add up to 100 due to rounding off/to the second decimal point.

*Source: Annual Survey of Industries (Factory Sector).*

# 4

# TRENDS IN REGIONAL INDUSTRIAL INEQUALITIES

IN THE preceding chapter we analysed broad trends in the performance of the manufacturing sector in India and its regional industrial economies over a period of almost two decades, i.e. from 1961 to 1978. We observed that the performance has been very divergent across different sectors and over time. In the light of the above exercise, it is plausible that the experience at the national level may not have been shared uniformally by different regions/States in the country, depending on various factors such as government policies and market forces. Therefore, an evaluation of such issues obviously will involve an analysis of the actual trends in the location of industries across States.

In this chapter we have attempted to trace the trends in the inter-State distribution of industry, and the extent of inter-regional inequalities during the past 18 years.

## METHODOLOGY

The analysis of the trend in the distribution of industries (as reflected by value added, employment or fixed-capital) across States and over time was carried out with the help of percentages and growth rates.

While reviewing the studies on the trends in regional inequalities, we observed that the conclusion varied depending upon the measure of inequality used and the years (base and terminal) considered for the purpose of comparison.[1] It is often argued that none of the measures of inequality can be treated as precise of flawless. A plethora of literature is available, widely discussing the weaknesses and strengths of the inequality measures. Therefore, to arrive at a fairly reliable conclusion, various measures of inequalities such as co-efficient of variation (weighted and unweighted), variance, Gini coefficients, Thiel's inequality index and Hirschman-Herfindahl index have been worked out for all the years between 1961 and 1978 (except 1972 for which data are not available).[2] It is hoped that such an exercise would help in overcoming the limitations arising out of the selection of the technique or the point of time.

To further examine the trend over time and the extent of decline/increase in the level of inequalities, we fitted regression equations with time '*t*' and its square as the dependent variable and various indices (each of them individually) as dependent variables using the model

$$I_x = \alpha + \beta_1 t_1 + \beta_2 t_2$$

where, $I_x$ = inequality index, $t_1$ and $t_2$ stand for the time and square of time respectively. $\alpha$ and $\beta$ are parameters.

## DATABASE

The same database as used in the preceding chapter, i.e. the values for fixed capital, employment and value added obtained from ASI, has been used for the purpose of comparisons and computation. The data for mid-year population have, in addition, been taken from the Indian Census Office estimates for mid-year population to work out per capita values wherever required.[3]

## TRENDS IN THE INTER-STATE DISTRIBUTION OF INDUSTRY

One of the striking features of the industrial development in India is its undulated spread over space. Industry has tended to concentrate in a few regions and within the regions in a few pockets, a point we have already brought home in our survey of literature. However, in order to comprehend the level of industrialisation of the various States in 1961, 1969 and 1981,[4] we take recourse to the share of value added generated by manufacturing sector (VAM) in the respective State domestic products (SDP).

The proportion of VAM and SDP in the various States with their relative ranks is given in Table 4.1. We observe that Maharashtra with 23.50 per cent emerges as the most industrialised State followed by Delhi (22.59%), Gujarat (19.49%), West Bengal (19.15%) and Tamil Nadu (16.24%) in 1961. All these States are more industrialised compared to the remaining ones, by virtue of being above the all India level (14.60%). A somewhat similar trend is observed in the organised manufacturing segment of the total manufacturing in 1961.[5]

By 1978, some changes are observed in the rank ordering of various States. However, it appears that the more and less industrialised States shuffled their ranks within their respective groups. For example, Tamil Nadu moved to second position pushing Delhi and West Bengal to fourth and fifth positions respectively; while Maharashtra and Gujarat maintained their positions. None of the industrially backward States (IBS) developed enough to be considered in the category of industrially developed States (IDS).

It is interesting to observe that ranking of the States in the unorganised segment of the manufacturing sector does not confirm to the rank order of the organised sector. Some of the industrially backward States such as Haryana, Rajasthan and Assam snatch a higher order berth with second, third and fifth ranks according to their shares in value added in the unorganised manufacturing sector (VAMU). By 1978, some more IBS group States emerged as industrially prominent by improving upon their earlier ranks. For example, Kerala, Uttar Pradesh, Punjab and Andhra Pradesh moved to third, fourth, sixths and eighth positions in 1978, from sixth, sixteenth, eighth and fourteenth positions respectively in 1961.

To confirm the association between the organised and unorganised sectors, we work out rank correlation for various years. In 1961 the rank co-efficient of correlation ($r_k$) across States was +0.2848, and +0.1744 in 1978, which turn out to be insignificant (see Table 4.2). It indicates a declining strength of association between these two sectors over time.[6] It leads one to speculate that the unorganised sector is developing independent of the organised sector, and has its own growth impulses across States. It may be party due to the government policies of encouraging the small-scale sector, especially in backward areas.

Table 4.2 also gives a set of relationships between various segments of the manufacturing sector. It is interesting to note that the relationship between the large and small scale organised sectors, though significantly positive, has a declining trend over the years.[7] Whereas the association between the organised small scale (sample) sector and the unorganised sector appears to have strengthened over time. It may plausibly be a case of scalar complimentarity between these two segments of the small scale in the various regional industrial economies in India.[8]

TABLE 4.1: Percentage Share of Value-Added Generated in Manufacturing Sectors as a Proportion of State Domestic Product (SDP)

*(At Constant Prices)*[1]

| Sl. No. | Name of the State | Census Sector[2] | | | Sample Sector[2] | | | Organised (Factory) Sector | | |
|---|---|---|---|---|---|---|---|---|---|---|
| | | 1961 | 1969 | 1978 | 1961 | 1969 | 1978 | 1961 | 1969 | 1978 |
| 0 | 1 | 2 | 3 | 4 | 5 | 6 | 7 | 8 | 9 | 10 |
| 1. | Andhra Pradesh | 2.03 | 3.98 | 4.72 | 0.67 | 0.42 | 0.70 | 2.75 | 4.40 | 5.42 |
| 2. | Assam | 5.94 | 10.00 | 5.27 | 1.06 | 1.15 | 0.40 | 7.01 | 11.15 | 5.67 |
| 3. | Bihar | 6.65 | 7.29 | 7.74 | 0.64 | 0.37 | 0.40 | 7.29 | 7.66 | 8.14 |
| 4. | Gujarat | 10.59 | 12.10 | 12.70 | 2.33 | 2.20 | 1.98 | 12.92 | 14.30 | 14.68 |
| 5. | Haryana | 3.11 | 6.93 | 7.26 | 0.66 | 1.11 | 0.98 | 3.77 | 8.04 | 8.24 |
| 6. | Himachal Pradesh | 2.71 | 3.71 | 2.16 | 0.31 | 0.23 | 0.11 | 3.02 | 3.94 | 2.27 |
| 7. | Jammu & Kashmir | 1.03 | 1.06 | 1.73 | 0.30 | 0.37 | 0.84 | 1.33 | 1.43 | 2.57 |
| 8. | Karnataka | 4.38 | 6.90 | 8.05 | 1.39 | 0.78 | 0.48 | 5.77 | 7.69 | 8.53 |
| 9. | Kerala | 5.10 | 9.20 | 5.91 | 1.58 | 1.06 | 1.03 | 6.68 | 10.26 | 6.94 |
| 10. | Madhya Pradesh | 2.78 | 3.83 | 6.17 | 0.43 | 0.39 | 0.60 | 3.21 | 4.22 | 6.77 |
| 11. | Maharashtra | 15.97 | 20.09 | 20.77 | 2.22 | 1.96 | 2.51 | 18.19 | 22.05 | 23.28 |
| 12. | Orissa | 2.92 | 5.29 | 6.66 | 0.29 | 0.22 | 0.31 | 3.21 | 5.51 | 6.97 |
| 13. | Punjab | 3.17 | 3.94 | 3.87 | 1.40 | 1.78 | 1.32 | 4.57 | 5.72 | 5.19 |
| 14. | Rajasthan | 1.53 | 2.50 | 3.35 | 0.35 | 0.31 | 0.37 | 1.88 | 2.81 | 3.72 |
| 15. | Tamil Nadu | 7.13 | 9.85 | 13.56 | 1.67 | 1.47 | 1.96 | 8.80 | 11.32 | 15.52 |
| 16. | Uttar Pradesh | 2.80 | 4.26 | 4.61 | 0.40 | 0.45 | 0.57 | 3.20 | 4.71 | 5.18 |
| 17. | West Bengal | 13.03 | 13.54 | 11.39 | 1.18 | 1.17 | 0.78 | 14.21 | 14.71 | 12.18 |
| 18. | Delhi | 7.90 | 8.43 | 6.77 | 2.25 | 1.97 | 2.36 | 10.15 | 10.40 | 9.13 |
| | All India | 7.25 | 8.96 | 8.57 | 1.25 | 1.14 | 1.03 | 8.50 | 10.10 | 9.60 |

*(Contd.)*

TABLE 4.1 *(Contd.)*

| Sl. No. | Name of the State | Unorganised Sector | | | Total Manufacturing Sector | | | Census Sector as a proportion of Factory Sector | | |
|---|---|---|---|---|---|---|---|---|---|---|
| | | 1961 | 1969 | 1978 | 1961 | 1969 | 1978 | 1961 | 1969 | 1978 |
| 0 | 1 | 11 | 12 | 13 | 14 | 15 | 16 | 17 | 18 | 19 |
| 1. | Andhra Pradesh | 4.39 | 5.57 | 4.86 | 7.15 | 9.98 | 10.29 | 75.69 | 90.50 | 87.04 |
| 2. | Assam | 7.07 | 7.36 | 4.15 | 14.08 | 18.52 | 9.82 | 84.87 | 89.77 | 92.91 |
| 3. | Bihar | 2.87 | 8.73 | 2.63 | 10.17 | 16.40 | 10.77 | 91.24 | 95.20 | 95.11 |
| 4. | Gujarat | 6.56 | 6.07 | 3.91 | 19.49 | 20.37 | 18.59 | 81.99 | 84.62 | 86.55 |
| 5. | Haryana | 7.46 | 5.53 | 3.42 | 11.23 | 13.57 | 11.67 | 82.49 | 86.23 | 88.16 |
| 6. | Himachal Pradesh | 4.13 | 4.82 | 3.19 | 7.33 | 8.76 | 5.46 | 62.94 | 94.30 | 95.56 |
| 7. | Jammu & Kashmir | 4.67 | 4.35 | 3.84 | 6.00 | 5.79 | 6.42 | 77.45 | 74.27 | 67.20 |
| 8. | Karnataka | 4.02 | 3.42 | 3.48 | 9.80 | 11.12 | 12.02 | 75.92 | 89.81 | 94.33 |
| 9. | Kerala | 6.17 | 4.69 | 6.58 | 12.85 | 14.95 | 13.53 | 76.35 | 89.70 | 85.14 |
| 10. | Madhya Pradesh | 4.49 | 4.81 | 5.30 | 6.60 | 8.71 | 11.59 | 86.59 | 90.70 | 91.11 |
| 11. | Maharashtra | 5.30 | 4.95 | 5.69 | 23.50 | 27.01 | 28.98 | 87.79 | 91.11 | 89.20 |
| 12. | Orissa | 4.68 | 2.78 | 2.50 | 7.90 | 8.29 | 9.48 | 90.88 | 96.00 | 95.51 |

*(Contd.)*

TABLE 4.1 *(Contd.)*

| 0 | 1 | 11 | 12 | 13 | 14 | 15 | 16 | 17 | 18 | 19 |
|---|---|---|---|---|---|---|---|---|---|---|
| 13. | Punjab | 5.54 | 5.49 | 5.31 | 10.08 | 11.22 | 10.51 | 69.43 | 68.90 | 74.48 |
| 14. | Rajasthan | 7.45 | 7.35 | 4.61 | 9.33 | 10.17 | 8.33 | 81.36 | 89.76 | 90.16 |
| 15. | Tamil Nadu | 7.44 | 9.16 | 6.53 | 16.24 | 20.48 | 22.05 | 80.98 | 86.98 | 87.35 |
| 16. | Uttar Pradesh | 4.30 | 4.73 | 5.78 | 7.51 | 9.44 | 10.96 | 87.65 | 90.39 | 89.02 |
| 17. | West Bengal | 4.93 | 5.31 | 4.45 | 19.15 | 20.03 | 16.64 | 91.75 | 92.05 | 93.56 |
| 18. | Delhi | 12.43 | 10.92 | 8.31 | 22.59 | 21.17 | 17.44 | 70.88 | 81.01 | 74.96 |
| | All India | 6.10 | 6.08 | 5.70 | 14.60 | 16.20 | 15.30 | 85.34 | 88.69 | 89.26 |

*Notes:* 1. Data for 1961 and 1969 are at 1960-61 prices and for 1978 at 1970-71 prices except for the State of Assam which had adopted the base year 1948-49 while Andhra Pradesh, Madhya Pradesh, Orissa and Uttar Pradesh have the base year 1970-71 up to 1969-70. For the year 1970-71 onwards, the base year is uniformally the same (1970-71) in rest of all the States.

2. Census and sample sectors' values have been worked out on the basis of their respective proportion in the factory sector (at 1970-71 constant prices) based on the Annual Survey of Industries. For, organised sector in the SDP corresponds to the Factory Sector which is total sum of the two segments, viz. Census Sector and Sample Sector.

*Source:* Percentage are based on the data obtained from the *Estimates of State Domestic Product — 1960-61 to 1982-83*, for all the States, published in June 1984; and for All India from various issues of *National Accounts Statistics*; both published by Central Statistical Organisation, Govt. of India, New Delhi.

TABLE 4.2: Rank Coefficients of Correlation Between the Various Segments of the Manufacturing and Coefficient of Variation of the Segments

| Sl. No. | Rank coefficients of correlation '$r_k$' between[1] | Years | | |
|---|---|---|---|---|
| | | 1961 | 1969 | 1978 |
| 1. | Organised and Unorganised sectors | +0.2848 | +0.4644*** | +0.1744 |
| 2. | Census and Sample sectors | +0.7502* | +0.7101* | +0.4803** |
| 3. | Census and unorganised sectors | +0.2827 | +0.3230 | +0.0712 |
| 4. | Sample and unorganised sectors | +0.4303*** | +0.4202*** | +0.6224* |
| | *Coefficients of Variation* (Per cent) | | | |
| 1. | Organised Manufacturing sector | 70.89 | 61.47 | 62.51 |
| 2. | Unorganised Manufacturing sector | 37.06 | 35.23 | 32.18 |
| 3. | Total Manufacturing sector | 45.11 | 41.39 | 44.54 |

*Note:* * Significant at 1% level of significance
** Significant at 5% level of significance
*** Significant at 10% level of significance

*Source:* Based on the Table 4.1.

Another noteworthy feature is the behaviour of the various sectors in terms of their variation across regions and over time. In the organised and unorganised sectors coefficient of variation reveals a declining trend over time. However, the degree of variation is much higher, almost double, in the former, compared to the latter. Moreover, the decline in the divergence of unorganised sector across States is observed to be more regular compared to the former. Therefore, one can postulate that the main source behind the regional inequalities is the organised sector, and thus it is this sector which needs to be tackled separately.

However, the share of value-added in SDP generated by the manufacturing sector is also likely to depend on the performance of other sectors of the economy, apart from its own. Therefore it might not always reflect the relative strength of the manufacturing sector in the regional economies.[9] Another way to adjudge the level of industrialisation of various regions is to look at the per capita industrial output in the respective State economies.[10]

The per capita value added generated in the organised sector (PCVAO) and total manufacturing sector (PCVAM) by States is given in Table 4.3. Interestingly enough, the table displays almost similar ranks to that when the States are ranked according to VAM. There is hardly any significant deviation from the earlier grouping except that Assam, which formed a part of IBS groups according to the criterion, moves to IDS group in 1961.

Therefore, irrespective of the criterion used, Maharashtra, West Bengal, Gujarat, Tamil Nadu and Delhi emerge as industrially developed States, which register above the national average value. The other category, i.e. of industrially backward States, comprises of Karnataka, Kerala, Punjab, Bihar, Haryana, Andhra Pradesh, Madhya Pradesh, Uttar Pradesh, Orissa, Jammu and Kashmir and Himachal Pradesh, which are below the national average in terms of per capita value added generated in the manufacturing sector. Assam is a case which falls in the IDS category in 1961, however to join IBS later. On the other hand, Punjab and Haryana make an upward movement to join the group of IDS by the year 1978.

In the light of the above discussion, we attempt to understand the growth profile of the various regions between 1961 and 1978, on the basis of the indicators like value-added, employment and fixed-capital pertaining to the registered (organised) manufacturing sector, i.e. the factory sector.

TABLE 4.3: Per Capita Value Added Generated in the Manufacturing Sector by States[1]

*(Value in Rupees at current prices)*[2]

| Sl. No. | Name of the States[3] | Organised Manufacturing Sector | | | Total Manufacturing Sector | | |
|---|---|---|---|---|---|---|---|
| | | 1961 | 1969 | 1978 | 1961 | 1969 | 1978 |
| | Category I - *Industrially Developed States* | | | | | | |
| 1. | Delhi | 73.48 | 112.12 | 226.52 | 163.46 | 229.91 | 432.74 |
| 2. | Maharashtra | 73.08 | 146.85 | 383.22 | 97.38 | 198.52 | 491.30 |
| 3. | West Bengal | 62.95 | 90.94 | 186.44 | 81.90 | 120.26 | 246.25 |
| 4. | Gujarat | 53.09 | 87.73 | 243.09 | 78.84 | 120.19 | 308.93 |
| 5. | Tamil Nadu | 29.26 | 52.55 | 177.76 | 55.18 | 107.20 | 258.22 |
| 6. | Assam | 29.09 | 36.72 | 110.08 | 54.05 | 66.12 | 144.39 |
| | Category II - *Industrially Backward States* | | | | | | |
| 7. | Karnataka | 18.83 | 45.30 | 114.34 | 31.64 | 70.17 | 149.07 |
| 8. | Kerala | 18.18 | 39.45 | 81.12 | 35.15 | 61.36 | 153.74 |
| 9. | Punjab | 16.73 | 41.25 | 131.76 | 37.03 | 79.17 | 272.06 |
| 10. | Bihar | 15.15 | 27.38 | 77.16 | 21.76 | 60.64 | 93.61 |
| 11. | Haryana | 12.33 | 48.60 | 178.56 | 36.75 | 84.42 | 259.49 |
| 12. | Andhra Pradesh | 10.05 | 21.87 | 75.83 | 23.67 | 46.52 | 130.04 |
| 13. | Madhya Pradesh | 9.39 | 18.21 | 61.42 | 19.38 | 38.39 | 104.20 |
| 14. | Uttar Pradesh | 8.88 | 22.35 | 104.54 | 21.38 | 43.17 | 204.69 |
| 15. | Orissa | 6.68 | 23.21 | 66.04 | 18.49 | 40.93 | 90.61 |
| 16. | Rajasthan | 5.31 | 16.00 | 44.93 | 28.59 | 44.11 | 94.84 |
| 17. | Jammu & Kashmir | 3.56 | 5.83 | 30.15 | 16.91 | 32.73 | 99.82 |
| 18. | Himachal Pradesh | 3.45 | 18.74 | 30.20 | 15.81 | 45.78 | 80.37 |
| | All India | 26.33 | 51.08 | 130.67 | 45.71 | 82.36 | 208.43 |

*Notes:* 1. In order to arrive per capita value we took the *Estimates of Mid Year Population* (for various States) published by the Registrar General of India, New Delhi.

2. Value added (per capita) are not available at any single base period for all the State, therefore, estimates suffer with the limitation that interregional price variation effect is not captured.

3. States are arranged in the descending order according to their per capita value added in the organised manufacturing sector in 1961. The categorisation is based taking All India per capita value added as the cut off point, in 1961.

*Source:* As per Table 4.1.

## THE GROWTH RATES

The annual compound growth rates of value-added, employment and fixed capital in the various regions between 1961-1969, 1969-1978 and 1961 and 1978 have been given in Table 4.4. We observe from the table that the States with higher level of industrialisation are not necessarily the 'high growth' ones. To the contrary these are the less developed regions which, by the large, grew at a higher rate. For example, Himachal Pradesh, the least industrially developed State in 1961, registered the highest (17.30%) rate of growth per annum; and the most industrialised States like Delhi or Maharashtra, ranked 11th and 13th respectively in terms of their growth, grew at 4.24 and 5.34 per cent compound rate of growth per annum between 1961 and 1978 in terms of value added.

Similarly, the highest rate of growth in value added during 1961-69 was achieved by Haryana having 13.61 per cent compound rate of growth per annum, closely followed by Himachal Pradesh with 13.83 per cent. Both these States belong to IBS. On the other hand, the last three ranks went to the IDS group where Gujarat, West Bengal and Assam grew at a rate of 3.29, 2.09 and -4.04 per cent compound per annum obtaining 16th and 17th and 18th ranks, whereas in terms of the level of industrialisation they stood 4th, 3rd and 6th respectively. During 1969 and 1978 H.P. grew at the highest rate (14.54%) followed by Rajasthan. The top five States according to their level of industrialisation again ranked 11th, 12th, 14th, 15th and 17th according to the rate of growth (see Table 4.4).

It can be seen from Table 4.4 that though the growth performance of various regions differ according to the variable considered, the fastest growing regions invariably belong to the IBS category. This was observed irrespective of the time period (year) of the variable. On the other hand, most of the last positions were claimed by the IDS group. In fact, all the regions in this group, Tamil Nadu being the only exception grew at a slower than the national average growth.[11]

Therefore, it is quite plausible that the negative association between the level of industrialisation and the rate of growth might have led these States to converge over a period of time, implying thus a reduction in the inter-regional industrial disparities across States between 1961 and 1978. However, as noted earlier, there is always a risk of inconsistency if the conclusion is based only on the behaviour of growth rates. In order to avoid such fallacy we analyse the percentage share of various regions.

TABLE 4.4: Annual Compound Rates of Growth by States[1]

| Sl. No. | Name of the States[2] | Value Added (V.A.) | | | Trend Rate of Growth (V.A.) | Employment | | | Trend[4] Rate of Growth (Employment) | Fixed Capital (Fx) | | | Trend Rate of Growth (Fx) |
|---|---|---|---|---|---|---|---|---|---|---|---|---|---|
| | | 1961-69 | 1969-78 | 1961-78 | | 1961-69 | 1969-78 | 1961-78 | | 1961-69 | 1969-78 | 1961-78 | |
| 1 | 2 | 3 | 4 | 5 | 6 | 7 | 8 | 9 | 10 | 11 | 12 | 13 | 14 |
| Category I - *Industrially Developed States* | | | | | | | | | | | | | |
| 1. | Delhi | 3.97 | 5.39 | 4.72 | 4.24* | 5.27 | 3.85 | 4.51 | 4.11* | 15.78 | 5.64 | 10.30 | 10.32* |
| 2. | Maharashtra | 5.97 | 5.52 | 5.65 | 5.34* | 2.72 | 3.18 | 2.96 | 3.22* | 13.24 | 3.42 | 7.93 | 7.15* |
| 3. | West Bengal | 2.09 | 3.04 | 2.59 | 1.15*** | 1.87 | 0.68 | 1.24 | 0.54 | 11.79 | 4.26 | 2.98 | -0.30 |
| 4. | Gujarat | 3.24 | 6.77 | 5.10 | 6.08 | 2.41 | 4.35 | 3.43 | 3.80* | 13.44 | 7.76 | 10.40 | 9.13* |
| 5. | Tamil Nadu | 6.43 | 6.87 | 6.85 | 6.35* | 6.66 | 3.93 | 5.20 | 5.45* | 21.90 | -0.10 | 9.72 | 8.24* |
| 6. | Assam | -4.04 | 9.15 | 2.73 | 4.76** | 1.66 | 3.99 | 2.89 | 2.82* | 17.76 | -1.14 | 7.38 | 5.56* |
| Category II - *Industrially Backward States* | | | | | | | | | | | | | |
| 7. | Karnataka | 10.08 | 8.08 | 9.01 | 7.45* | 5.39 | 5.00 | 5.18 | 5.92* | 22.40* | 3.69 | 12.11 | 10.76* |
| 8. | Kerala | 10.81 | 2.12 | 6.12 | 6.07* | 3.20 | 2.30 | 2.72 | 3.18* | 18.56 | 6.23 | 11.86 | 13.06* |
| 9. | Punjab[3] | 3.33 | 8.40 | 7.11 | 8.21* | — | 6.79 | 5.12 | 6.36* | -2.78 | 8.89 | 5.84 | 9.12* |
| 10. | Bihar | 3.97 | 5.76 | 4.91 | 4.30* | 3.20 | 4.78 | 4.03 | 3.98* | 9.53 | 11.49 | 10.56 | 9.31* |

*(Contd.)*

TABLE 4.4 (*Contd.*)

| 1 | 2 | 3 | 4 | 5 | 6 | 7 | 8 | 9 | 10 | 11 | 12 | 13 | 14 |
|---|---|---|---|---|---|---|---|---|---|---|---|---|---|
| 11. | Haryana[3] | 13.61 | 9.02 | 10.16 | 10.46* | 5.49 | 4.73 | 4.92 | 4.99* | 3.94 | 5.02 | 4.74 | 5.40* |
| 12. | Andhra Pradesh | 8.48 | 8.92 | 8.71 | 9.56* | 5.89 | 7.53 | 6.75 | 5.42* | 24.17 | 2.66 | 12.28 | 11.90* |
| 13. | Madhya Pradesh | 7.75 | 7.60 | 9.65 | 9.65* | 5.63 | 4.56 | 5.06 | 4.60* | 28.72 | 2.75 | 14.25 | 6.08** |
| 14. | Uttar Pradesh | 7.85 | 4.29 | 5.95 | 6.23* | 2.29 | 7.40 | 4.96 | 6.43* | 23.33 | 5.26 | 13.41 | 12.21* |
| 15. | Orissa | 11.34 | 7.32 | 9.19 | 6.77* | 15.19 | 1.98 | 8.00 | 5.61* | 23.69 | -3.48 | 8.46 | 1.12 |
| 16. | Rajasthan | 10.51 | 11.55 | 11.06 | 11.67* | 7.37 | 6.16 | 6.73 | 7.07* | 29.41 | 6.12 | 16.50 | 15.94* |
| 17. | Jammu & Kashmir | 4.07 | 10.15 | 7.25 | 3.92** | 6.35 | 4.79 | 5.53 | 6.46* | 5.49 | 27.17 | 16.46 | 18.72* |
| 18. | Himachal Pradesh | 13.53 | 14.54 | 14.06 | 17.30* | 24.13 | 5.11 | 13.67 | 16.21* | 45.74 | 19.99 | 31.49 | 35.13* |
| | All India | 5.70 | 6.07 | 5.89 | 5.56* | 3.86 | 4.08 | 3.97 | 3.94* | | | | |

*Notes:* 1. Value used for computing growth rates are at constant 1970-71 prices in the case of V.A. and Fx.
2. States are arranged in descending order according to the note 3 in Table 4.3.
3. Growth rates are for 1966-69, 1969-78 and 1966-78.
4. * Significant at 1 per cent level; of significance.
** Significant at 5 per cent level of significance
*** Significant at 10 per cent level of significance

*Source:* Annual Survey of Industries.

The position or rank of various regions in the industrial skeleton of the country has not changed much over the past twenty years despite the plausible decline in the magnitude of regional inequalities due to the varied growth performance. As is evident from Table 4.5, Maharashtra, West Bengal, Gujarat, Tamil Nadu, Bihar and Uttar Pradesh remain virtually unchallenged throughout the period. In 1961, Maharashtra, West Bengal, Gujarat and Tamil Nadu were the top four States in terms of their contribution to value-added which was 26.97, 20.59, 10.19 and 8.16 per cent respectively. In 1978 also the *status quo* was almost maintained. Similarly, in terms of employment and fixed capital, these States were industrial leaders in 1961. Together, these States contributed 59.25 per cent of the employment and 56.12 per cent of the fixed capital. In 1978 also, their combined share in employment and fixed capital was approximately 50 per cent and 38 per cent respectively.

Therefore, though their absolute share did experience a decline over time, the position remained almost unaltered except that some of the States in the IBS group such as Karnataka and Andhra Pradesh, Uttar Pradesh and Bihar also improved their position substantially. It is interesting to observe that, over time, the States with higher contribution in the various variables lost their share in favour of the States which had a relatively modest share in 1961. However, Delhi, which is a highly industrialised region, is a case by itself with a very small proportion of value-added, employment or fixed capital in the nation. For it is more a city-State than a full-fledged region of any significant size.

Out of all the States which lost in terms of their share over time, West Bengal lost half of its share in terms of value-added (from 20.59 per cent in 1961 to 11.18 per cent in 1978), employment (from 20.23 per cent to 12.87 per cent) and fixed capital (from 19.85 to 6.56 per cent). Other such regions are Maharashtra, Assam, Bihar in terms of value-added, joined by Gujarat and Kerala in terms of employment, and Orissa in terms of fixed capital. The remaining States have tended to gain marginally or substantially over time (see Table 4.5).

However, the relationship between the level of industrialisation and the shares of various States seem to be positive and strong only in the early phase, and seems to be withering over time. For example, rank correlation between these two sets was +0.7812, +0.7668 and +0.6924 in value-added, employment and fixed capital series in 1961, which reduced to +0.5438, +0.5377, +0.4000 respectively in 1978.[12] This is also indicative of a trend of reduction in the inter-regional inequalities in India. In the light of the above discussion, it will be worthwhile to discern the trend and the rate of movement n the regional industrial inequalities over time move precisely.

## REGIONAL INDUSTRIAL INEQUALITIES IN INDIA : 1961-78

As discussed in the methodology, six indices, viz., unweighted coefficient of variation, weighted co-efficient of variation, standard deviation of logs, Thiels Inequality Index, Hirschman-Herfindahl Index and Gini ratios, were computed in order to make an overall assessment about the trends in the inter-regional concentration of industry over States (see Table 4.6). These indices are calculated for value-added, employment and fixed capital across States, for all the years between 1961 and 1978.

The results show a clear trend toward reduction in the level of inter-regional inequalities over the years, which is observed irrespective of the index or variable considered. However, the trend is not completely harmonious or smooth and some undulating years do appear here and there. For example the years 1969 or 1978, where the values of inequality indices have marginally increased, appear somewhat inconsistent. However, they do not seem to distort the overall declining trend.

To further confirm our observation, we computed per cent change between 1961-69, 1969-78 and 1961-78. We found that despite a marginal upward movement in 1969 and 1978, the percentage change has been negative though it varies according to the variable or index. On an average, inequalities decline (as shown by percentage change) by approximately 15 per cent in value added, approximately 21 per cent in employment and around 28 per cent in fixed capital, between 1961 and 1978. The decline between 1961 and 1969 was more marked than in the subsequent sub-period, particularly in the case of fixed capital.[13] To know the exact trend and magnitude of decline we worked out trend rates of growth also, for various indices (see Table 4.6).

As observed from Table 4.6, we notice that inequalities in terms of fixed capital have declined most rapidly compared to the other two variables. Overall regional industrial inequalities, on an average, declined at a compound rate of growth of approximately 1.50 per cent per annum (though the rate varies from index to index due to the procedure of computation) in value added, while in terms of

TABLE 4.5: Relative Shares of States in the Factory Sector

(At Constant Prices 1970-71 = 100)

| Sl. No. | Name of the State/Region[1] | Shares in Value Added (%) | | | Shares in Employment (%) | | | Shares in Fixed Capital (%) | | |
|---|---|---|---|---|---|---|---|---|---|---|
| | | 1961 | 1969 | 1978 | 1961 | 1969 | 1978 | 1961 | 1969 | 1978 |
| 1 | 2 | 3 | 4 | 5 | 6 | 7 | 8 | 9 | 10 | 11 |
| Category I - *Industrially Developed States* | | | | | | | | | | |
| 1. | Delhi | 1.63 | 1.72 | 1.63 | 1.72 | 1.92 | 1.87 | 1.35 | 1.23 | 1.43 |
| 2. | Maharashtra | 26.97 | 26.41 | 25.21 | 20.86 | 19.09 | 17.66 | 20.40 | 15.51 | 14.99 |
| 3. | West Bengal | 20.59 | 14.51 | 11.18 | 20.23 | 17.34 | 12.87 | 19.85 | 13.66 | 6.56 |
| 4. | Gujarat | 10.19 | 8.79 | 9.33 | 10.00 | 8.93 | 9.14 | 8.67 | 6.70 | 9.34 |
| 5. | Tamil Nadu | 8.16 | 9.36 | 10.02 | 8.16 | 10.11 | 9.98 | 7.20 | 9.92 | 7.00 |
| 6. | Assam | 2.76 | 1.28 | 1.66 | 2.09 | 1.76 | 1.76 | 2.05 | 2.14 | 1.37 |

(Contd.)

TABLE 4.5 (*Contd.*)

| 1 | 2 | 3 | 4 | 5 | 6 | 7 | 8 | 9 | 10 | 11 |
|---|---|---|---|---|---|---|---|---|---|---|
| Category II - *Industrially Backward States* | | | | | | | | | | |
| 7. | Karnataka | 3.45 | 5.37 | 6.36 | 4.08 | 4.59 | 4.97 | 3.37 | 4.80 | 4.73 |
| 8. | Kerala | 2.41 | 3.94 | 2.80 | 4.48 | 4.26 | 3.65 | 2.17 | 2.39 | 2.93 |
| 9. | Punjab | — | 2.41 | 2.93 | — | 2.57 | 3.24 | — | 2.87 | 4.39 |
| 10. | Bihar | 6.80 | 5.57 | 5.43 | 5.32 | 5.06 | 5.37 | 12.76 | 7.46 | 14.12 |
| 11. | Haryana | — | 2.07 | 2.66 | — | 1.80 | 1.90 | — | 2.42 | 2.68 |
| 12. | Andhra Pradesh | 2.80 | 3.88 | 4.93 | 5.67 | 6.63 | 8.89 | 3.65 | 5.82 | 5.75 |
| 13. | Madhya Pradesh | 2.88 | 3.31 | 3.77 | 3.46 | 3.96 | 4.13 | 3.09 | 6.59 | 5.98 |
| 14. | Uttar Pradesh | 6.33 | 7.25 | 6.23 | 7.99 | 7.07 | 9.38 | 6.50 | 9.83 | 11.09 |
| 15. | Orissa | 1.22 | 1.74 | 1.93 | 0.83 | 1.89 | 1.58 | 3.19 | 4.94 | 2.55 |
| 16. | Rajasthan | 1.06 | 1.59 | 2.51 | 1.46 | 1.90 | 2.27 | 1.41 | 3.13 | 3.80 |
| 17. | Jammu & Kashmir | 0.10 | 0.10 | 0.14 | 0.25 | 0.30 | 0.32 | 0.10 | 0.14 | 0.28 |
| 18. | Himachal Pradesh | 0.15 | 0.24 | 0.47 | 0.06 | 0.25 | 0.27 | 0.02 | 0.17 | 0.63 |
| | All India[2] | 100.00 | 100.00 | 100.00 | 100.00 | 100.00 | 100.00 | 100.00 | 100.00 | 100.00 |

*Notes:* 1. Serial order and grouping of the States is as per note 3, Table 4.3.

2. The total for all the States may not add-up to 100.00 because of the rounding up of values to the second decimal point, and (b) the fact that all the regions have not been included in the analysis. However the share of all the excluded regions taken together is very insignificant and hardly exceeds 0.80 per cent of the total.

*Source:* As in Table 4.4.

employment the rate was approximately 1.75 per cent per annum and in fixed capital around 2.0 per cent. In all cases, value of $R^2$ were found to be statistically significant.

To further confirm these results we regressed various inequality indices ($I_x$) on time ($t_1$) and its square ($t_2$) postulating the following relationship

$$I = \alpha - \beta_1 t_1 \pm \beta_2 t_2$$

The results are presented in Table 4.7. We observe the postulated relationship to be true. For, all *t* values are negative with significant $R^2$ (at 1% level). This is regardless of the variable and indices. It implies that the regional industrial inequalities have definitely converged over time.

## CONCLUDING OBSERVATIONS

This chapter was devoted to the discussion on the overall behaviour of the industrial sector in the various States, and the consequential trends in regional inequalities, over a period of approximately twenty years. Main findings based on the foregoing analysis are:

(1) the States of Delhi, Maharashtra, West Bengal, Gujarat and Tamil Nadu emerge as the most industrialised States in India;

(2) there does not appear to be any significant relationship between the organised and unorganised sector *per se*. However, the sample and unorganised sectors tent to grow together unlike the census and unorganised sector. Thus, the unorganised sector has it own growth impulses which are independent of at least the large scale sector. Even the relationship between the organised large scale (census sector) and the organised small scale (sample sector) seems to have weakened over time;

(3) there is no significant relationship between the level of industrialisation and the growth rates of various State economies. The States which are relatively on the lower ladder of the industrial development have shown potential to grow at a faster rate, compared to the relatively developed States;

TABLE 4.6: Indices of Regional Industrial Inequality in India

*(Value-Added-Employment-Fixed Capital in Factory Sector)*

| Years | Unweighted Coefficient of Variations (C V u, w) | | | Weighted Coefficient of Variations (C V w) | | | Standard Deviation of Logs | | |
|---|---|---|---|---|---|---|---|---|---|
| | Value Added | Employment | Fixed Capital | Value Added | Employment | Fixed Capital | Value Added | Employment | Fixed Capital |
| 1 | 2 | 3 | 4 | 5 | 6 | 7 | 8 | 9 | 10 |
| 1961 | 121.77 | 107.80 | 108.52 | 140.45 | 120.88 | 123.40 | 1.39 | 1.43 | 1.59 |
| 1962 | 127.98 | 109.07 | 101.18 | 149.06 | 122.44 | 109.09 | 1.58 | 1.33 | 1.61 |
| 1963 | 124.95 | 104.71 | 98.87 | 145.07 | 117.03 | 107.57 | 1.64 | 1.44 | 1.71 |
| 1964 | 121.04 | 101.63 | 87.36 | 140.55 | 113.69 | 93.89 | 1.53 | 1.34 | 1.70 |
| 1965 | 118.02 | 101.71 | 85.94 | 136.81 | 114.07 | 92.57 | 1.44 | 1.28 | 1.50 |
| 1966 | 115.06 | 100.55 | 81.59 | 133.41 | 112.66 | 87.27 | 1.38 | 1.19 | 1.49 |
| 1967 | 117.81 | 99.03 | 80.50 | 136.77 | 110.31 | 85.50 | 1.35 | 1.18 | 1.50 |
| 1968 | 110.26 | 94.74 | 76.34 | 127.82 | 105.36 | 80.86 | 1.26 | 1.17 | 1.46 |
| 1969 | 112.43 | 95.01 | 77.61 | 131.76 | 105.72 | 84.29 | 1.31 | 1.14 | 1.44 |
| 1970 | 111.92 | 93.86 | 76.68 | 130.93 | 104.59 | 85.98 | 1.30 | 1.12 | 1.09 |
| 1971 | 115.12 | 92.63 | 76.83 | 135.04 | 103.02 | 86.89 | 1.21 | 1.12 | 1.01 |
| 1972 | — | — | — | — | — | — | — | — | — |
| 1973 | 112.44 | 91.01 | 73.70 | 130.88 | 101.15 | 85.22 | 1.34 | 1.08 | 0.98 |
| 1974 | 110.49 | 90.71 | 73.73 | 128.12 | 100.87 | 85.40 | 1.31 | 1.11 | 1.22 |
| 1975 | 104.07 | 87.28 | 71.49 | 120.05 | 96.12 | 82.01 | 1.27 | 1.10 | 1.08 |
| 1976 | 102.08 | 85.79 | 73.36 | 117.91 | 95.01 | 84.92 | 1.25 | 1.09 | 1.03 |
| 1977 | 102.86 | 84.20 | 73.90 | 119.18 | 93.12 | 85.36 | 1.19 | 1.10 | 0.98 |
| 1978 | 103.67 | 84.69 | 77.32 | 120.31 | 93.26 | 89.07 | 1.16 | 1.12 | 1.02 |
| Trend Rate of Growth | -1.26 | -1.60 | -2.11 | -1.26 | -1.71 | -1.63 | -1.62 | -1.69 | -3.73 |
| Percentage between | | | | | | | | | |
| 1961-69 | -7.67 | -11.86 | -28.48 | -6.18 | -12.54 | -31.69 | -5.75 | -20.28 | -9.43 |
| 1969-78 | -7.79 | -10.86 | -0.35 | -8.69 | -11.79 | +5.93 | -8.62 | -1.78 | -29.17 |
| 1961-78 | -14.86 | -21.89 | -28.75 | -14.34 | -22.85 | -27.64 | -16.54 | -21.68 | -35.85 |

*(Contd.)*

TABLE 4.6 *(Contd.)*

| Years | Thiel's Inequality Indices | | | Hirschman-Herfindahl (H-H) | | | Gini Ratios Indices | | |
|---|---|---|---|---|---|---|---|---|---|
| | Value Added | Employ-ment | Fixed Capital | Value Added | Employ-ment | Fixed Capital | Value Added | Employ-ment | Fixed Capital |
| 1 | 11 | 12 | 13 | 14 | 15 | 16 | 17 | 18 | 19 |
| 1961 | 33.92 | 25.60 | 24.07 | 13.79 | 12.01 | 12.09 | 0.568 | 0.533 | 0.535 |
| 1962 | 35.75 | 25.98 | 24.48 | 14.66 | 12.16 | 11.24 | 0.583 | 0.535 | 0.528 |
| 1963 | 34.27 | 23.82 | 22.54 | 14.23 | 11.64 | 10.98 | 0.567 | 0.515 | 0.510 |
| 1964 | 31.24 | 22.34 | 16.27 | 13.69 | 11.29 | 9.79 | 0.556 | 0.501 | 0.462 |
| 1965 | 29.18 | 21.84 | 13.80 | 13.29 | 11.30 | 9.65 | 0.551 | 0.503 | 0.462 |
| 1966 | 27.82 | 21.31 | 12.40 | 12.91 | 11.17 | 9.25 | 0.540 | 0.497 | 0.442 |
| 1967 | 30.62 | 21.06 | 10.88 | 13.26 | 11.00 | 9.13 | 0.551 | 0.495 | 0.441 |
| 1968 | 25.16 | 20.16 | 10.07 | 12.31 | 10.54 | 8.79 | 0.523 | 0.480 | 0.418 |
| 1969 | 25.42 | 19.23 | 8.41 | 12.58 | 10.57 | 8.90 | 0.527 | 0.483 | 0.427 |
| 1970 | 25.24 | 18.59 | 6.98 | 12.51 | 10.45 | 8.82 | 0.524 | 0.482 | 0.421 |
| 1971 | 27.12 | 18.48 | 7.02 | 12.91 | 10.32 | 8.83 | 0.526 | 0.478 | 0.419 |
| 1972 | — | — | — | — | — | — | — | — | — |
| 1973 | 24.75 | 17.61 | 6.92 | 12.58 | 10.15 | 8.57 | 0.521 | 0.470 | 0.397 |
| 1974 | 23.62 | 16.10 | 8.00 | 12.33 | 10.12 | 8.57 | 0.518 | 0.473 | 0.397 |
| 1975 | 20.36 | 14.61 | 6.95 | 11.57 | 9.79 | 8.39 | 0.499 | 0.462 | 0.395 |
| 1976 | 20.46 | 13.48 | 7.06 | 11.34 | 9.64 | 8.54 | 0.482 | 0.457 | 0.403 |
| 1977 | 21.59 | 12.72 | 6.91 | 11.43 | 9.49 | 8.59 | 0.482 | 0.452 | 0.406 |
| 1978 | 22.05 | 13.29 | 7.99 | 11.52 | 9.54 | 8.87 | 0.486 | 0.455 | 0.422 |
| Trend Rate of Growth | -3.29 | -4.30 | -8.01 | -1.41 | -1.53 | -1.80 | -1.11 | -0.99 | -1.69 |
| Percentage between | | | | | | | | | |
| 1961-69 | -25.06 | -24.88 | -65.06 | -6.82 | -11.99 | -26.38 | -7.22 | -9.38 | -20.18 |
| 1969-78 | -18.26 | -30.89 | -4.99 | -8.43 | -9.74 | -0.34 | -7.78 | -5.80 | -1.17 |
| 1961-78 | -34.99 | -48.08 | -66.81 | -16.39 | -20.57 | -26.63 | -14.44 | -14.63 | -21.12 |

*Source:* Annual Survey of Industries.

TABLE 4.7: Trends in Regional Industrial Inequality Across States[1]

*(Indices from 1961 to 1978)*

| Indices | .∝ | $\beta_1$ | $\beta_2$ | .$R^2$ |
|---|---|---|---|---|
| *Value Added* | | | | |
| 1. C V u, w | 126.7670 | -1.5034** | +0.0039 | 0.8691* |
| | | (0.6312) | (0.0341) | |
| 2. C V w | 146.3839 | -1.4757*** | -0.0104 | 0.84.20* |
| | | (0.8178) | (0.0441) | |
| 3. σ of logs | 1.5867 | -0.0328** | +0.0005 | 0.70.46* |
| | | (0.0165) | (0.0009) | |
| 4. Thiel's Index | 36.9227 | -1.4713* | +0.0314 | 0.9008 |
| | | (0.3448) | (0.0186) | |
| 5. H.H. Index | 14.4906 | -0.2118** | +0.0017 | 0.8663* |
| | | (0.0808) | (0.0044) | |
| 6. Gini Ratios | 0.5802 | -0.0052** | -0.0004 | 0.9315* |
| | | (0.0018) | (0.0009) | |
| *Employment* | | | | |
| 1. C V u, w | 110.5115 | -1.8748* | +0.0182 | 0.9814* |
| | | (0.2418) | (0.0130) | |
| 2. C V w | 124.2139 | -2.2134* | +0.0206 | 0.9787* |
| | | (0.3084) | (0.0166) | |
| 3. σ of logs | 1.5045 | -0.0582* | +0.0021* | 0.9254* |
| | | (0.0073) | (0.0004) | |
| 4. Thiel's Index | 26.3667 | -0.7624* | -0.0029 | 0.9776* |
| | | (0.1402) | (0.0075) | |
| 5. H.H. Index | 12.3325 | -0.2243* | +0.0033** | 0.9802* |
| | | (0.0267) | (0.0014) | |
| 6. Gini Ratios | 0.5400 | -0.0079* | +0.0002 | 0.9610* |
| | | (0.0011) | (0.0006) | |
| *Fixed Capital* | | | | |
| 1. C V u, w | 112.6300 | -6.2579* | +0.2452* | 0.9662* |
| | | (0.4523) | (0.0244) | |
| 2. C V w | 124.3412 | -7.4915* | +0.3259* | 0.8989* |
| | | (0.8216) | (0.0443) | |
| 3. σ of logs | 1.7869 | -0.0554** | +0.0003 | 0.8306* |
| | | (0.0253) | (0.0013) | |
| 4. Thiel's Index | 29.1242 | -3.4725* | +0.1327* | 0.9676* |
| | | (0.2548) | (0.0137) | |
| 5. H.H. Index | 12.4065 | -0.6328* | +0.0252* | 0.9580* |
| | | (0.0499) | (0.0026) | |
| 6. Gini Ratios | 0.5633 | -0.0245* | +0.0009* | 0.9619* |
| | | (0.0019) | (0.0001) | |

*Note:* 1. Values in the parentheses are standard error of the coefficient

* significant at 1% level of significance

** significant at 5% level of significance

*** significant at 10% level of significance

*Source:* Based on Table 4.6.

(4) in spite of this trend in growth rates, there does not seem to be much effect on the position/ranking of the States over time, barring a few exceptions. There is a strong relationship between the level of industrialisation and the relative share of various States in the registered manufacturing sector of the country, at least in the initial period. The developed States have lost some of their shares in favour of the industrially backward States; and

(5) consequently the inequalities across States in the distribution of industry have declined significantly over time. However, it is also possible that it is the deceleration of some of the industrially developed States and not so much the gain by industrially backward States that narrows the disparities.

This leads us to ask: What are the forces which tend to bridge the gap in inter-regional industrial inequality? We attempt to answer this question in the next chapter.

## NOTES

1. For conflicting evidences owing to the choice of period or inequality measure, see Nair (1982); Dholakia (1982); Dhar and Sastry (1967); Laheri (1969); Saradamoni (1969); Nadkarni (1969) and Jhuraney (1976).
2. For detailed discussion on the inadequacy of any single measure and implications thereof, see Yenterna (1933); Kuznets (1963); Ranadive (1965); Atkinson (1973); Sen (1973).
3. Mid-year estimates for the population are obtained from the office of the Registrar General, Ministry of Home Affairs, Government of India, New Delhi.
4. Share of the manufacturing sector in the total SDP is widely used as an index for the level of industrialisation or an indicator of the relative strength of the manufacturing sector in the region's economy.
5. Co-efficient of rank correlation between organised and total manufacturing sector is found to be +0.9112, which is significant at 0.01 per cent level of significance in 1961.
6. However, $r_k$ for the year 1969 which is +0.4644 turn out to be significant but at 10 per cent level of significance. The year 1969 can be treated as a special case. For it is plausible that the year in question might have carried some impact of the mid-sixties recession effecting these sub-sectors in such a way that both of them seem to have moved in somewhat similar direction, resulting in an improvement in the association. However, it appears to be a random phenomenon. For, in 1978 again the relationship becomes insignificant though positive.
7. The rank correlation between organised large scale and small scale sectors across the States, was found to be +0.7502 in 1961, +0.7101 in 1969 and +0.48.03 in 1978. The first two values were statistically significant at 1 per cent level and the last at 5 per cent level of significance.

8. Rank correlation coefficients between the organised small scale and unorganised sectors were +0.4303, +0.4202 and +0.6224 in 1961, 1969 and 1978 respectively.
9. For example, exceptionally good harvest in a particular year, accompanied by an improved performance of the tertiary sector will obviously tend to reduce the percentage share of the manufacturing sector's contribution to the overall SDP of a region, and vice-versa.
10. For the purpose of analysis we have used per capita value-added to represent per capita output generated in any region.
11. The rank correlations between the level of industrialisation and the trend rates of growth of value-added, employment and fixed capital between 1961-78 were found to be negative and significant at 5 per cent level of significant. The co-efficient values were (-) 0.5418, (-) 0.6491 and (-) 0.4572 respectively for value-added, employment and fixed capital, which are significant at 5 per cent.
12. The value of coefficient of correlation are insignificant at 1 per cent level if ≥ 0.590, at 5 per cent if ≥ 0.486 and at 10 per cent if ≥ 0.400.
13. It may be owing to the heavy investment in the capital intensive public sector in relatively backward States such as Orissa, Madhya Pradesh and Bihar and to some extent Karnataka between 1961 and 1969, Latter, it was seen to have tilted somewhat, in favour of some of the developed States such as Gujarat, Maharashtra, as a consequence of investment in the petrochemical industry.

*ANNEXURE 4.1*

## A Technical Note on the Inequality Measures

As noted earlier, the inadequacy of any single index in measuring inequalities is well documented in the literature (Kuznets, 1963; Ranadive, 1965). Moreover, Sen (1973) and Atkinson (1973) have highlighted the merits and limitations of the various inequality measures in detail. Therefore, without going into the details of these aspects, we present formulations of the various inequality indices like Standard Deviation of Logarithms, Weighted Coefficient of Variation, Unweighted Coefficient of Variation, Gini Coefficients, Thiel's Inequality Index, and Hirschman-Herfindahl Index; used by us for the purpose of gauging the extent of the interState industrial inequalities, from the year 1961 to 1978; where

$n$ = number of states

$X_i, X_j$ = Aggregate variable in question ($x$) for $i^{th}$ or $j^{th}$ state;

$\overline{X}$ = mean value of the variable $X$;

$\hat{X}$ = mean of the log of $x$ values;

$P_j$ = population for the $j^{th}$ state;

$\overline{X}W$ = weighted mean or the average values of x for all the states taken together;

$P_j$ = proportion of nation's population in the state $j$;

$px_j$ = proportion of state $j$ in the aggregate of the variable $x$;

then:

(1) Standard Deviation of Logarithms ($\sigma_{\log}$)

$$\sigma_{\log} = \left[\frac{1}{n-1_j}(\log X_j - \hat{X})^2\right]^{\frac{1}{2}}$$

(2) Unweighted Coefficient of Variation ($CV_{uw}$)

$$CV_{uw} = 100x\left[\frac{1}{n-1}\sum_j(X_j - \overline{X})^2\right]^{\frac{1}{2}} / \overline{X}$$

(3) Weighted Coefficient of Variation ($CV_w$)

$$CV_w = 100x\left[\frac{1}{\sum_j p_j}\sum_j P_j(X_j-\overline{X})^2\right]^{\frac{1}{2}}/\overline{X}W$$

(4) Gini Coefficient ($G$)

$$G = \frac{1}{2n^2\overline{X}}\sum_i\sum_j |(X_i - X_j)|$$

(5) Thiel's Inequality Index ($TII$)

$$TII = \sum_j px_j \log(px_j/p_j)$$

(6) Hirschman – Herfindahl Index ($H.H.$)

$$H.H. = \sum_j px_j^2/100$$

It may be mentioned that the Standard Deviations of Logarithms have been worked out for per capita value added and per capita fixed capital for all the years between 1961 and 1978.

# 5

# INDUSTRIAL STRUCTURE AND REGIONAL GROWTH

THE FINDING that regional inequalities have declined over time, leads to a question : How/why has the change taken place, and what are the underlying forces behind this change? After all, regional inequalities, at least in the early phase of development, arise because some advantageous regions grow faster than the regions having some kind of handicap.

The industrial history of various countries reveals that regional inequalities tend to decline as development proceeds (Williamson, 1965). Logically it would happen if (a) developed regions stop growing and backward regions grow; (b) developed regions grow at a slower pace than the backward regions; and (c) developed regions encounter a declining phase, whereas underdeveloped regions remain even stagnant.

These phases might be witnessed owing to a variety of reasons, such as industry mix of the regions, existing technological linkages and operation of some behavioural factors at regional levels. The government intervention with the market forces is also likely to influence the pattern of growth.

This chapter, therefore, attempts to explore the causes of variations in the growth performance of various regional economies with respect to their industrial structure and impact thereof. However, we do not intend to investigate the causes of the performance of the industrial spatial units. The attempt will be to find some clue to the diverse performance of various States owing to the shifts, in their respective industrial structure, between 1961 and 1978-79.

## METHODOLOGY

In order to understand the industrial structure of the States/regions we have used location-quotients and specialisation co-efficients technique, apart from this simple percentages and rank correlations.'Location Quotient' (L.Q.) is a measure of relative regional concentration of a given industry compared to total national magnitude, which provides the basis for a qualitative judgement about the 'structural base' of the region's industrial economy. The industries with high 'location quotients' (L.Q $\geq$ 1) constitute the industrial base of the region.[1] The specialisation co-efficient (SQ) measured the extent to which a regional economy has a diversified pattern. The lower and upper limits of the specialisation coefficient are zero and one respectively. If a region's industrial economy is as diversified as that of the nation, the specialisation co-efficient will be zero, while if all its industrial activity is concentrated in one industry and which in turn is concentrated only in that region, the specialisation coefficient will be equal to one, reflecting complete lack of diversification. In other words SQ nearer to the zero more diversified will the State be and value approaching one will indicate relative lack of diversification.[2]

The 'shift and share' technique has been employed in order to identify and decompose the forces behind regions' growth. The technique has been widely used as a descriptive device and an analytical tool.[3] Some of the researchers (Greenberg, 1972; Williamson, 1980; Armstrong and Taylor, 1980) have also used it for future projections, which is not considered very desirable (Houston, 1967; Brown, 1969).

The shift and share technique is a method to calculate the extent to which difference between a region's growth and the nation's growth can be explained by the region's industry mix. It decomposes the growth of a regional variable into three components, viz. (i) total shift or national growth effect; (ii) structural shift or industry mix effect; and (iii) differential shift or competitive effect.

Total shift is the overall growth of the economy against which differential performance of the region's is measured. Any region having exactly the same growth rate as the nation will have zero net shift. If it grew faster is will have positive net shift otherwise negative net shift. This net shift is further decomposed into structural and differential shifts.[4]

The structural shift is a measure of region's performance determined by the type of regions industrial structure. The shift is positive when the industrial base of the region constitutes of fast growing industries and is negative or zero when region specialises in declining or slow growing industries.

Finally, the 'differential shift' is that part of the region's growth which remains unexplained and can be given a variety of interpretations. It indicates the extent to which growth of a particular industry in a given region is the result of some region specific factors. It is assumed, more dynamic regions (with better infrastructure facilities, industrial climate, resource endowment and entrepreneurship etc.) are expected to grow faster with a positive shift and *viceversa.* Thus, it hints at some locational or competitive advantage enjoyed by; one region over the other. The methodology of shift and share technique can be expressed in algebraic form as followed

(1) Regional Growth Rate ($g_r$)

$$g_r = \sum_i r_i^t - \sum_i r_i^o / \sum_i r_i^o$$

(2) National Growth Rate ($g_n$)

$$g_n = \sum_i N_i^t - \sum_i N_i^o / \sum_i N_i^o$$

(3) Regional Growth at National Growth Rate Per Industry ($g_m$)

$$g_{rn} = \sum_i [r_i^o(N_i^t / N_i^o)] - \sum_i r_i^o / \sum_i r_i^o$$

where

$r_i$ = regional added in $i^{th}$ industry
$t$ = terminal year
$o$ = initial year
$N_i$ = national value added in a $i^{th}$ industry.

The third growth rate is the most crucial calculation. It is the growth rate that would have occurred in the region if each industry had grown at the same rate as the corresponding national industry during the study period. In other words, national growth rates are applied to the region's industry mix as it existed at the beginning of the study period; in a sense it is hypothetical growth rate.

Now, with the help of these three definitions, the regional growth rate can be divided into three separate elements

$$g_r = (g_m - g_n) + (g_r - g_m) + g_n \tag{5.1}$$

Taking $g_n$ to the left hand side, we get

$$(g_r - g_n) = (g_m - g_n) + (g_r - g_m) \tag{5.2}$$

In equation (5.2), the left hand side term is 'Regional-National Growth' or the difference between the regional and the national growth. On the right hand side, the first element is the structural component. It is the difference between the hypothetical growth of the region (given the industry structure and national growth rates for each industry) and the national growth rate. Finally the last element $(g_r - g_m)$ is simply that part of the region's growth that remains unexplained (for details, see Armstrong and Taylor, 1980 : 301-302).

However, we hasten to note that the shift and share technique has certain limitations which must be kept in mind while interpreting the results. For example, the industrial structure of a region in the base year effects the extent of shift which introduces biases, especially if the period of observation is very long (Houston, 1967).[5] Secondly, the differential shift does not bring out the region-specific factors and this part of the decomposition remains a black-box (Klassen and Paelinck, 1972). The method also neglects the inter-industry linkages and improperly assigns growth, based on these linkages, into the residual rather than structural components (Brown, 1969). And finally, the results are sensitive to the level of sectoral disaggregation used in computation (Udai Sekhar, 1983). However, despite the weaknesses, the technique provides a convenient framework for understanding the inter-regional differences in the growth with reference to the industrial structure.

## DATABASE

We have taken value-added as the representative variable for the purpose of analysis in this chapter. Value-added as a proxy for output is in real terms (at 1970-71 prices). The data have been obtained from the ASI for all the States for the years 1961, 1969 and 1978. The level of industrial disaggregation is 3-digit level of ASI classification. After matching pre-70s and post-70s ASI and NIC classification respectively, we arrived at 53 industry groups for the purpose of analysis at the regional level, also like we did earlier for all India.

## REGIONAL INDUSTRIAL BASE AND ITS DIVERSIFICATION

We attempt a comparative assessment of the 'industrial base', of different regions in India, with the help of the location quotient technique. In multi-regional economy, a region would tend to specialise in those industries for which it has some comparative advantage over the other regions. Hence, the industries with high location quotients (if its value is greater than or equal to one) would constitute the industrial base of the region.

### Industrial Base of the States

Table 5.1 depicts the industrial-base of different States in India in the year 1978-79. These industries have further been classified into nine broad groups according to their end use. What emerges from the table is that the majority of the States have relatively independent blocks or sets of resource based industries comprising their industrial base. The development of capital goods or demand based industries is confined either to some developed States like Maharashtra or West Bengal; or where heavy public sector investment has been made (like in Bihar, Orissa, Madhya Pradesh or Karnataka). To some extent Punjab and Haryana are exceptions. Development of the capital goods sector in Uttar Pradesh is of relatively recent origin. Even in the capital goods sector, activities are confined mainly to repair of motor vehicles or to a lesser extent in some metal products (other than machinery and transport equipment), otherwise, the industrial base of the regions, by the large, reflects resource endowment of the regions.

The industrial base of Gujarat, a relatively developed State, consists of four independent blocks of industries viz., agro-based consumer goods industries; fibre-based (textiles) consumer goods industries; chemical-based intermediate goods industries; and non-metallic mineral based intermediate goods industries. The industrial base of Assam, Jammu and Kashmir and Himachal Pradesh dominated by agro-based industries (like food preservation and canning) or some stray consumer industries like wine and tea, of course along with some intermediate goods industries like wood and wood products or paper and paper products. The capital goods sector, more often than not, is confined to motor vehicle repairs.

TABLE 5.1 Industrial Base/Specialisations of Regions in India — Location Quotient: 1978-79-

| | | Industry Groups | | |
|---|---|---|---|---|
| | | Consumer Goods Industries | | |
| | States | Agro-based | Fiber-based | Others |
| (1) | (2) | (3) | (4) | (5) |
| 1. | Andhra Pradesh (0.4635) | Dairy Products (7.31), Grain Mills Products (3.53), Bakery Products (1.16), Cocoa, Chocolate & Sugar confectionery (4.0), Tobacco Mfg. (6.43) | Other Textiles n.e.c (1.28) | Canning and Preservation of Fish & Seafood (1.25), Wine Industries (9.0), Malt and country Liquor (1.95), Soft Drinks (2.50), Jewellery and Mint (4.54), Distilling and Rectifying & blending of Spint (1.84) |
| 2. | Assam (0.7185) | Canning and fruit Preservation (1.16), Grain Mill Prods. (1.50), Food Prods. n.e.c (10.48) | | |
| 3. | Bihar (0.5218) | Sugar, Gur and Khandsari (1.31), Tobacco & Tobacco Prods. (3.09), | | Mfg. of Footwear (1.44) |
| 4. | Gujarat (0.3097) | Mfg. of Dairy Prods. (1.62), Canning and Fruit Preservation (1.00) | Mfg. of Textiles (2.05) | Canning and Preservation of Fish & Sea Food (1.25), Mfg. of Leather and Leather Prods. n.e.c (1.0), Jewellery & Mint (2.09), |
| 5. | Haryana (0.3416) | Grain Mill Prods. (1.58) | | Soft Drinks (1.87), Malt Liquor, Malt and Country Liquor (2.54), Mfg. of Motor cycles Bicycles (6.83) |
| 6. | Himachal Pradesh (0.6318) | Canning & Preservation of Fruits & Vegetables (4.33), Grain Mills Prod. (1.12) | | Distilling, rectifying and Blending of Spirit (19.63), Watches & Clock (17.54). |

*(Contd.)*

TABLE 5.1 *(Contd.)*

| (1) | (2) | (3) | (4) | (5) |
|---|---|---|---|---|
| 7. | Jammu & Kashmir (0.5252) | Canning and Fruit Preservation (24.83), Grain Mill Prods. (2.93) | Mfg. of Textiles (1.95) | Mfg. Furniture & Fixture (1.43), Mfg. of Miscellaneous Products n.e.c. (15.55); Distilling Rectifying & Blending of Spirit (9.45), |
| 8. | Karnataka (0.3178) | Canning & Fruit Preservtion (4.50) Bakery Prods. (1.08), Sugar, Gur & Khand Sari (1.80), Coco, Chocolate & Sugar conf. (3.50). Tobacco & Tobacco Prods. (1.86) | Mfg. of other Textiles, n.e.c. (1.34), Textiles Garments etc. (1.41) | Canning and Preservation of Fish and Sea Food (1.87), Distilling & Rectifying of Spirit (2.68), Wine Industries (23.50), Malt Liquor & Country Liquor (2.90), Soft Drinks (1.50), Photographic Materials (1.20), Watches & Clock (9.90). |
| 9. | Kerala (0.4644) | Canning and Fruit Preservation (3.66), Mfg. of Food Prods. n.e.c. (3.14), Tobacco and Tobacco Prods. (1.97) Grain Mills Prods. (1.71); | Knitting Mills (36.29), Other Textile n.e.c. (2.54) Mfg. of Textiles (1.12) | Canning and Preservation of Fish & Sea Food (12.25), Distilling and Rectifying & Blending of Spirit (3.78) |
| 10. | Madhya Pradesh (0.3525) | Mfg. of Cocoa Chocolate & Sugar Conf. (1.0), Tobacco & Tobacco Prods. (1.24), Bakery Prods. (1.27), Sugar, Gur and Khandsari (1.22); | | Malt and country liquor (1.54), Miscellaneous Industries n.e.c. (1.60) |
| 11. | Maharashtra (0.2026) | | Mfg. of Textiles (1.02), Knitting Mills (12.11), Other Textiles n.e.c. (1.06), | Soft Drinks (1.50) Furniture & Fixture (2.12); Leather Prods, n.e.c. (2.0); Mfg. of Motor Cycles & Bicycles (1.49), Mfg. of Photographic Material (1.40), Misc. Industries n.e.c. (1.88), |
| 12. | Orissa (0.5430) | | | Canning and Preservation of Fish & Sea Food (2.37) |

*(Contd.)*

TABLE 5.1 *(Contd.)*

| (1) | (2) | (3) | (4) | (5) |
|---|---|---|---|---|
| 13. | Punjab (0.3588) | Dairy Products (8.44); Canning and Fruit Preservation (1.00), Grain Mill Prods, (1.35), Sugar, Gur, Khandsari (1.24), | Mfg. of Textiles (1.11), Knitting Mills (42.70), Other Textile, n.e.c. 3.22 | Distilling & Rectifying Spirit (7.21), Malt and Country Liquor (3.22), Mfg. of Miscellaneous Industries n.e.c. (1.61) |
| 14. | Rajasthan (0.3265) | | Mfg. of Textiles (1.30), Other Texiles n.e.c (1.64) | Malt Liquor & Country Liquor (1.68) |
| 15. | Tamil Nadu (0.2102) | Mfg. of Dairy Prods. (1.14), Grain Mill Products (1.35), Mfg. of Cocoa, Chocolate and Products n.e.c. (3.05), Misc. Food Prod. (1.05). | Mfg. of Textiles (1.16); Knitting Mills (1.82) | Canning and Preservation of Fish & Sea Food (2.0); Leather Prods., n.e.c. (4.0) |
| 16. | Uttar Pradesh (0.2385) | Canning & Fruit Preservation (1.50), Grain Mill Prods. (1.52); Sugar, Gur and Khandsari (3.97), Mis. Food Prods. n.e.c. (1.10), Tobacco and Tobacco Prods. (1.52) | | Distilling, Rectifying & Blending of spirit (4.84), Mfg. of Footwear, except rubber & Plastic (1.55); Leather & Leather Prods. n.e.c. (4.00) |
| 17. | West Bengal (0.2195) | Canning and Fruit Preservation (1.16); Mfg. of Bakery Prods. (2.18); | Mfg. of Textiles (1.12) | Wine Industry (19.50); Mfg. of Foot-wear (except rubber & plastics) (5.00); Mfg. of Watches & Clocks (1.22), Misc. Mfg. Industries n.e.c. (1.50) |
| 18. | Delhi (0.3690) | Mfg. of Dairy Prods. (4.45), Canning & Fruit preservations (1.35); Grain Mill Prods. (1.50), Mfg. of Bakery Prods. (3.62) | Knitting Mills (5.29); Textile Garments (3.34) | Soft Drinks (14.12); Furniture & Fixture Mfg. (1.65); Mfg. of Photographic Materials (1.20); Mfg. of Watches & Clocks (1.22), Misc Mfg. Industries n.e.c. (2.63). |

*(Contd.)*

TABLE 5.1 *(Contd.)*

| (1) | States (2) | Industry Groups: Capital Goods Industries — Basic metal (6) | Machinery (7) | Transport Equipment (8) |
|---|---|---|---|---|
| 1. | Andhra Pradesh (0.4635) | | Manufacturing of Electric Machinery and Appliance (2.47) | Ships and Boat Building (3.84) Transport Equipments n.e.c. (9.16), Repair of Motor Vehicles (2.02) |
| 2. | Assam (0.7185) | | | |
| 3. | Bihar (0.5218) | Iron, Steel and Ferrous Alloys (3.05), Non-Ferrous Basic Industries (1.70) | | Mfg. of Motor Vehicles and Parts (4.26), Mfg. of Transport Equipments n.e.c. (27.66), Mfg. of Transport Equipments n.e.c. (1.16) |
| 4. | Gujarat (0.3097) | | | |
| 5. | Haryana (0.3416) | Mfg. of Metal Prods. (except Mach. & Trans. Equipments) (2.37) | Mfg. of Machinery and Machine Tools (except mach.) (2.61), | Mfg. Railway & Loco Equipment (1.10), Repair of Motor Vehicles (1.19) |
| 6. | Himachal Pradesh (0.6318) | | Mfg. of Mach & Machine Tools (Except Ele. Mach.) (5.42) | Repair of Motor Vehicles (6.88) |

*(Contd.)*

TABLE 5.1 *(Contd.)*

| (1) | (2) | (6) | (7) | (8) |
|---|---|---|---|---|
| 7. | Jammu & Kashmir (0.5252) | | | Repair of Motor Vehicles (3.52) |
| 8. | Karnataka (0.3178) | Non-ferrous Basic Industries (3.64), Mfg. of Metal Prods. (except Mach. & Trans) (1.12), | Mfg. of Electric Machinery & Equipments (2.74), | Mfg. of Motor Vehicles & Parts (1.62), Repair of Motors Vehicles (2.05) |
| 9. | Kerala (0.4644) | Non-Ferrous Basic Metal (4.32) | Mfg. of Electric Mach. & Equipment (1.17) | Repair of Motor Vehicles (1.63), Mfg. of Transport Equip. n.e.c. (17.16) |
| 10. | Madhya Pradesh (0.3225) | Iron, Steel & Ferrous Alloys (2.16) Non-Ferrous Basic Ind. (2.29), | Elect. Mach. & Equipment (2.43) | |
| 11. | Maharashtra (0.2026) | Mfg. of Metal Products (1.39) | Mfg. of Mach. and Mach. Tools (1.11) | Ship & Boat Building (1.35), Mfg. of Transport Equipment, n.e.c. (1.83) |
| 12. | Orissa (0.5430) | Iron, Steel & Ferrous Alloys (4.35), Non-Ferrous Basic Metal Ind. (1.16) | | |
| 13. | Punjab (0.3588) | Iron, Steel & Ferro-Alloys (1.27), Mfg. of Metal Prods. (2.28), | | Mfg. of Motor Vehicle (1.95) Repair of Motor Vehicles (1.10) Air Craft and Parts (6.94) |
| 14. | Rajasthan (0.3265) | Mfg. of Non-Ferrous Basic Industries (6.37) | Mfg. of Machinery & Mach. Tools (except Elect. Mach.) (1.07), Electric Mach. & Appliance (1.19), | |

*(Contd.)*

TABLE 5.1 *(Contd.)*

| (1) | (2) | (6) | (7) | (8) |
|---|---|---|---|---|
| 15. | Tamil Nadu (0.2102) | | Machine & Machinery Tools (except Electric Mach. & Equipment) (1.48) | Railway locomotive equipment Mfg. (1.44), Mfg. of Motor Vehicle & Parts (1.94); Repair of Motor Vehicles (1.42), Mfg. of Transport Equipment n.e.c. (8.00). |
| 16. | Uttar Pradesh (0.2385) | Mfg. of Metal Prods. and Parts (except Mach. & Equip.) (1.39) Non-ferrous Basic Industries (2.21), | Mfg. of Electric Machinery & Apparatus (1.73), | Railway Locomotive Equipment Mfg. (2.42), Repair of Motor Vehicles (1.23) |
| 17. | West-Bengal (0.2195) | Iron Steel & Ferro-Alloys (1.96), Mfg. of Products and parts (except machine & transport equipment) (1.15) | Mfg. of Electric Machinery & Apparatus (1.16) | Ship and Boat Building (2.23); Mfg. of Railways Locomotive Equipments etc. (3.36), Mfg. of Aircraft & Parts (1.78), Mfg. of Transport Equipment n.e.c. (1.83), |
| 18. | Delhi (0.3690) | Mfg. of Metal Prods. & Parts (except Mach. & Transport Equipments) (2.14) | Mfg. of Electric Machinery and Apparatus (1.69) | Mfg. of Motor Vehicles & Parts (1.02); Repair of Motor Vehicles (3.13); Mfg. of Motor cycle & Bicycles (1.85) |

*Contd.*

TABLE 5.1 (*Contd.*)

| States | Industry Groups | | |
|---|---|---|---|
| | Intermediate Goods Industries | | |
| | Basic metal | Machinery | Transport Equipment |
| (1) (2) | (9) | (10) | (11) |
| 1. Andhra Pradesh (0.4635) | Mfg. of Cement and Lime Plaster (2.61), Non-metalic Mineral Products, n.e.c (6.48) | Mfg. of Inedible oil (6.46) | Mfg. of Paper and Paper Board (1.84), Medical Surgical and Scientific Instruments(1.38) |
| 2. Assam (0.7185) | Petroleum Refineries (13.62), Mfg. of Petroleum and Coal Prods. (2.01), Mfg. of Non-Metallic Mineral Prods. (2.14) | | Mfg. of wood and wood prods. (16 27) |
| 3. Bihar (0.5218) | Petroleum Refineries (3.10), Petroleum & Coal Prods. (8.97), Mfg. of Structural Clay Prods. (2.59); Glass and Glass Prods. (1.21), Non-metallic, Mineral products n.e.c. (1.82), | | |
| 4. Gujarat (0.3097) | Mfg. of Petroleum & Coal Prods. (2.09); Structural clay Prods. (1.08), Glass & Glass Prods. (1.60), Earthenware & Chinaware (1.56) | Industrial Heavy Org. & In-Org. Chemicals (1.74); Mfg. of Inedible Oils (2.92), Mfg. of Paints, Varnish Drugs & Chemical n.e.c. (1.12), | |

(*Contd.*)

TABLE 5.1 *(Contd.)*

| (1) | (2) | (9) | (10) | (11) |
|---|---|---|---|---|
| 5. | Haryana (0.3416) | Structural clay Prods. (1.79), Glass and Glass Prods. (1.76), Earth & Chinaware (4.82) Non-Metallic Min-Prods, n.e.c. (2.52) | Rubber and Rubber Prods.(4.35) | Mfg. of paper and paper boards (2.55), Medical, Surgical and Scientific Instruments (1.82) |
| 6. | Himachal Pradesh (0.6381) | Cement & Lime Plaster (1.16), Non-Metallic Prods. n.e.c. (4.47), | Industrial Chemical (1.67) | Mfg. of Wood Prods. (1.29), Printing & Pub. of All Types (2.31) |
| 7. | Jammu & Kashmir (0.5252) | Mfg. of Non-metallic Mineral Prods, n.e.c. (2.39) | Paints, Varnishes n.e.c. (1.25) | Wood & Wood Prods. (7.87), Printing & Publishing (1.50), Tanning & Furnishing of Leather (2.00), Medical, Surgical & Sc. Ind. (15.11), |
| 8. | Karnataka (0.3178) | Mfg. of Structural clay Prods. (1.33), Earth & Chinaware (2.56), Cement & Lime Plaster (1.55), Non-metallic Min, Prods. (2.16) | | Wood & Wood Prods. (2.25) Mfg. of Paper and Paper Board (1.05) |
| 9. | Kerala (0.4644) | Petroleum Refinery (3.73), Structural clay Prods. (5.83), Earthenware & Chinaware (1.13) | Rubber and Rubber Prods. (3.47); Paints Varnishes & Chem. n.e.c. (1.08) | Wood & Wood Prods. (7.43), Paper and Paper Board (1.92), Medical Surgical Sc. Ind. (5.26) |
| 10. | Madhya Pradesh (0.3525) | Mfg. of Cement & Lime Plaster (6.43); | Mfg. of Inedible Oils (2.42). | Wood & Wood Prods. (1.46); Paper & Paper Prods. (1.44); Printing & Publishing (1.42), |
| 11. | Maharashtra (0.2026) | Petroleum Refinery (1.26), Mfg. of Petroleum & Coal Prods. (3.26); Glass & Glass Prods. (1.10) | Industrial Heavy Org. & Chemical & Fert. (1.34), Paints, Varnishes Drugs & Medicines & Chem. n.e.c. (2.15) | Mfg. of Medical, Surgical & Scientific Instruments (1.05) |

*(Contd.)*

TABLE 5.1 *(Contd.)*

| (1) | (2) | (9) | (10) | (11) |
|---|---|---|---|---|
| 12. | Orissa (0.5430) | Mfg. of structural clay Products (9.12) Mfg. of Cement Lime Plaster (1.22) | Indust. Heavy org. Inorg. Chem. and Fertilizer (1.73), Mfg. of Inedible Oil (1.73) | Mfg. of wood & wood Products (1.06); Mfg. of paper & Paper Prods. (3.71) Printing & Publishing (4.81) |
| 13. | Punjab (0.3588) | | Mfg. of Inedible Oil (1.07) | Tanning curing and Finishing of Leather (1.17) |
| 14. | Rajasthan (0.3265) | Mfg. of Earthenware & Chime. ware (1.08), Cement & Lime Plaster (6.47) Nonmetallic Mine, Prods. (2.17) | Rubber & Rubber Products (2.79), Ind. Heavy Org. & Inorg. Chemicals & Fert. (1.70) | |
| 15. | Tamil Nadu (0.2102) | Mfg. of Petroleum & Coal Prods. (1.17), Earthenware and Chinaware (2.35); Mfg. of Cement & Lime Plaster (1.28) | Rubber & Rubber Prods. (1.30), Industrial Heavy Org. & Inorg. Chemical & Fertilizer etc. (1.10) | Printing and Publishing (1.45), Tanning, curing Finishing of Leather (7.10), Mfg. of Medical, Surgical & Scientific Instruments (1.29). |
| 16. | Uttar Pradesh (0.2385) | Mfg. of Glass & Glass Products (2.76) | Rubber & Rubber Products (1.08) | |
| 17. | West Bengal (0.2195) | Mfg. of Glass & Glass Prods. (1.49) | Rubber & Rubber Prodcs. (161) | Mfg. of Medical, Surgical and Scientific Instruments (1.23) |
| 18. | Delhi (0.3690) | Mfg. of Earthenware & Chinaware | Rubber & Rubber Prods (4.07); Paints, Varnishes Drugs, Medicine and Chem. n.e.c. (1.30) | Printing & Publishing (6.87), Mfg. of Medical, Surgical & Scientific Instruments (4.67) |

*Note*: Location Quotients (L.Q.) and specialisation co-efficients calculated for Organised manufacturing (factory) sector, regionwise and industrywise value — added data (at constant prices, base 1970-71-100 for 1978-79, obtained from ASI (CSO). Only the industries with L.Q. equal to or greater than one have been included in the Table. Figures in parentheses in col. 2 indicate the value of specialisation co-efficient of the region and those in other columns, the value of location quotient of respective industry for the specific region/State.

The industrial base of the States like Bihar, Orissa, Madhya Pradesh and Rajasthan is predominated by the capital goods sector and to a lesser extent to some other intermediate goods industries like paper and paper products or wood and wood products due to the local availability of raw-material. The States of Andhra Pradesh and Uttar Pradesh are characterised by a wide range of agro-based or other consumer-oriented industries and mineral based industries. Of late, the capital goods sector has also started emerging. While Punjab and Karnataka have predominance of consumer demand oriented industries along with some capital goods industries. Kerala, though has a relatively diversified base, tends to specialise in intermediate goods industries like wood and wood products, paper and paper products, rubber and rubber products and some mineral based industries. Resource base for these industries is worth the notice. To the contrary Haryana seems to have specialised in the industries which fall under the capital and intermediate-goods sector and for which very meagre resource base is locally available. Somewhat similar is the case of Delhi. Plausibly, some market forces have shaped the industrial structure of these regions.

In order to understand the pattern of structural change in the industrial base of the various States, we compared the Table 5.1, with a somewhat similar table for the year 1965, provided by Alagh *et al.* (1971a). A broad comparison of these two tables reveals that most of the States have attained a more diversified industrial base by 1978 as compared to the earlier period which was mainly confined to the traditional manufacturing, producing mostly consumer goods. *Al biet*, like in 1965, it appears that industrial scene of most of the States is still dominated by the traditional and resource base industries; a tendency towards greater diversification even within this dominant group is noticed distinctly.

## Regional Industrial Diversification

We attempt to examine the relative extent of industrial diversification of the various regions by estimating the region specific coefficient of specialisation. Table 5.2 provides values of the coefficients for the year 1961, 1969 and 1978. Classified in three broad groups, we find that in 1961 Maharashtra, Tamil Nadu, West Bengal and Uttar Pradesh are industrially more diversified States; Gujarat, Karnataka, Madhya Pradesh and Delhi could be grouped in the 'middle level' of diversification, whereas, the remaining regions are found to be less diversified.

TABLE 5.2: Industrial Specialisation Co-efficient for the States – 1961, 1969, 1978

| States/Regions* | Specialisation Co-efficients | | |
|---|---|---|---|
| | 1961 | 1969 | 1978 |
| *Highly Diversified Regions* | | | |
| 1. Maharashtra | 0.1854 | 0.1932 | 0.2026 |
| 2. Tamil Nadu | 0.2182 | 0.2132 | 0.2102 |
| 3. West Bengal | 0.3186 | 0.2331 | 0.2195 |
| 4. Uttar Pradesh | 0.3125 | 0.2805 | 0.2385 |
| 5. Gujarat | 0.4182 | 0.3723 | 0.3097 |
| 6. Karnataka | 0.3686 | 0.3317 | 0.3178 |
| *Moderately Diversified Regions* | | | |
| 7. Rajasthan | 0.4518 | 0.4033 | 0.3265 |
| 8. Haryana | - | 0.3864 | 0.3416 |
| 9. Madhya Pradesh | 0.4128 | 0.3748 | 0.3525 |
| 10. Punjab | - | 0.4040 | 0.3588 |
| 11. Delhi | 0.4179 | 0.3905 | 0.3690 |
| 12. Andhra Pradesh | 0.4742 | 0.4942 | 0.4635 |
| 13. Kerala | 0.4827 | 0.4703 | 0.4644 |
| *Less Diversified Regions* | | | |
| 14. Bihar | 0.6182 | 0.5451 | 0.5218 |
| 15. Jammu & Kashmir | 0.6170 | 0.5321 | 0.5252 |
| 16. Orissa | 0.5936 | 0.6135 | 0.5430 |
| 17. Himachal Pradesh | 0.7929 | 0.6544 | 0.6318 |
| 18. Assam | 0.8067 | 0.8059 | 0.7185 |

* Classification is based on the values for 1978 and the States are given in ascending order accordingly

*Source*: State-wise co-efficients of specialisation calculated from Tables of Location Quotients for the States of India, for the years 1961, 1969 and 1978; and the data on net-output (value-added) in the organised manufacturing (factory) sector were obtained from Annual Survey of Industries, C.S.O.

In the next two decades, almost all the States have diversified their industrial structure except Maharashtra where the tendency seems to be in opposite direction; and Andhra Pradesh and Orissa which became more specialised in some industries in 1969, attained higher degree of diversification in 1978. In the entire period (1961-78) Maharashtra, Tamil Nadu, Bihar, Madhya Pradesh, Delhi, Andhra Pradesh, Kerala, Orissa, Assam, Jammu and Kashmir and Himachal Pradesh showed

## Structural Shifts

The structural shifts during the sixties (the first sub-period 1961-69) are, by and large, negative, except for Delhi and West Bengal in the developed group, and Bihar and Himachal Pradesh in the other (see Table 5.3). It implies that the industry mix of various States has any but positive impact on the growth rates. Whereas, in second sub-period four States viz., Bihar, Haryana, Andhra Pradesh and Orissa had positive impact of industry-mix. But most of important industrial regions (probably with exception of Andhra Pradesh and Bihar) experienced an adverse industrial composition.

However, in spite of the adverse industrial composition most of the States experienced a positive growth over the national rates (especially the regions in the second category). This might have happened due to some other 'rag-bag' factors which, by and large, remain unexplained and are represented by the differential shifts.

TABLE 5.3: A Shift and Share Analysis of Value Added in the States of India: (Registered) Manufacturing (Factory) Sector[1] — 1961-69 and 1969-78

*(Percent)*

| Sl. No. | Name of the States | Percentage change[2] | | Components of the shift-share | | |
|---|---|---|---|---|---|---|
| | | Actual | Hypothetical | Total shift | Structural shift | Differential shift |
| | | $(g_r)$ | $(g_m)$ | $(g_r - g_n)$ | $(g_m - g_n)$ | $(g_r - g_m)$ |
| (1) | (2) | (3) | (4) | (5) | (6) | (7) |
| | **1961-69** | | | | | |
| | Category I: *Industrially Developed States*[3] | | | | | |
| 1. | Delhi | 36.57 | 70.41 | -19.23 | 14.61 | -33.84 |
| 2. | Maharashtra | 56.19 | 52.16 | 1.17 | -3.64 | 4.81 |
| 3. | West Bengal | 18.01 | 60.12 | -37.79 | 4.32 | -42.11 |
| 4. | Gujarat | 29.13 | 39.48 | -26.67 | -16.31 | -10.36 |
| 5. | Tamil Nadu | 69.71 | 44.27 | 13.91 | -11.53 | 25.44 |
| 6. | Assam | -28.11 | 10.71 | -83.91 | -45.63 | -38.28 |
| | Category II: *Industrially Backward States*[4] | | | | | |
| 7. | Karnataka | 115.62 | 52.30 | 59.82 | -3.50 | 63.32 |
| 8. | Kerala | 127.31 | 27.24 | 71.51 | -28.56 | 100.07 |

(*Contd.*)

TABLE 5.3 (*Contd.*)

| (1) (2) | (3) | (4) | (5) | (6) | (7) |
|---|---|---|---|---|---|
| 9. Punjab | - | - | - | - | |
| 10. Bihar | 36.54 | 56.71 | -19.26 | 0.91 | -20.17 |
| 11. Haryana | - | - | - | | - |
| 12. Andhra Pradesh | 91.84 | 36.39 | 36.04 | -19.41 | 55.45 |
| 13. Madhya Pradesh | 81.51 | 33.63 | 25.95 | -12.17 | 48.12 |
| 14. Uttar Pradesh | 83.12 | 43.77 | 27.32 | -12.03 | 39.35 |
| 15. Orissa | 136.18 | 41.47 | 80.38 | -14.33 | 94.71 |
| 16. Rajasthan | 122.54 | 49.14 | 66.74 | -8.66 | 75.40 |
| 17. Jammu & Kashmir | 37.62 | 24.44 | -18.18 | -31.36 | 13.18 |
| 18. Himachal Pradesh | 176.00 | 76.67 | 120.20 | 20.87 | 99.33 |
| All India ($g_n$) | | | | | |
| 1961-69 | 55.80 | | | | |
| 1969-78 | 70.00 | | | | |
| *Category I* | | | | | |
| 1. Delhi | 60.49 | 50.89 | -9.51 | -19.11 | 9.60 |
| 2. Maharashtra | 62.26 | 63.65 | -7.74 | -6.35 | -1.39 |
| 3. West Bengal | 30.99 | 57.15 | -39.01 | -12.85 | -26.16 |
| 4. Gujarat | 80.34 | 67.93 | 10.34 | -2.07 | 12.41 |
| 5. Tamil Nadu | 81.90 | 58.66 | 11.90 | -11.34 | 23.24 |
| 6. Assam | 119.86 | 19.86 | 49.86 | -50.32 | 100.18 |
| *Category II* | | | | | |
| 7. Karnataka | 101.28 | 62.71 | 31.28 | -7.29 | 38.57 |
| 8. Kerala | 120.81 | 43.63 | 50.81 | -26.37 | 77.18 |
| 9. Punjab | 106.78 | 63.07 | 36.78 | -6.93 | 43.71 |
| 10. Bihar | 65.51 | 85.65 | -4.49 | 15.65 | -20.14 |
| 11. Haryana | 117.64 | 222.34 | 47.64 | 152.34 | -104.70 |
| 12. Andhra Pradesh | 115.82 | 77.94 | 45.82 | 7.94 | 37.88 |
| 13. Madhya Pradesh | 93.35 | 68.99 | 23.35 | -1.01 | 24.36 |
| 14. Uttar Pradesh | 46.02 | 37.20 | -23.98 | -32.80 | 8.82 |
| 15. Orissa | 88.88 | 84.05 | 18.88 | 14.05 | 4.83 |
| 16. Rajasthan | 167.43 | 40.39 | 97.43 | -29.61 | 127.04 |
| 17. Jammu & Kashmir | 138.85 | 51.10 | 68.85 | -18.90 | 87.75 |
| 18. Himachal Pradesh | 211.36 | 64.55 | 141.36 | -5.45 | 146.81 |

*Notes:* (1) Disaggregation is at 3 digit level of ASI.
(2) Value Added is in real terms at 1970-71 prices.
(3) Categorisation of developed and backward States is on the basis of per capita value-added generated in the States in the organised manufacturing (factory) sector in 1961, as per Table 4.3.
(4) Percentage change is between the two points of time.

*Source:* Various issues of *Annual Survey of Industries*, Central Statistical Organisation, New Delhi.

**The Differential Shifts**

In 13 out of the 16 regions[10] differential shifts have a higher magnitude, compared to the structural shifts between 1961 and 1969. Moreover in eleven cases they are positive too. Maharashtra and Tamil Nadu in the group of industrially developed States and all the regions except Bihar in the other category exhibit positive differential shift, whereas, in the second sub-period (1969-78) 14 out of the 18 regions experienced this shift in positive direction, with exceptions of Maharashtra and West Bengal in the first category of States and Bihar and Haryana in the other. Differential shifts markedly out-smarted structural shifts in 13 cases, which include most of the industrially important States (in terms of their proportion in the nation's aggregate value-added). Thus, by and large, the proportionality shifts appear to be less important than the differential shifts.[11] This indicates that some other region specific factors have greater bearing on the regions industrial growth than the share of particular sector in the 'initial year' which are slow-growing of fast growing at the national level.

The results based on the technique have to be viewed with caution, and can be taken only as indicative of the trend. No broad generalisations seem plausible. However, it does provide a clue that the cause of interregional variations in the growth performance have to be sought somewhere else, rather than in the industrial composition of the regions.

## CONCLUDING OBSERVATION

We attempted to examine the industrial structure of the regional economies in India. An attempt was also made to decompose the growth performance of the regions in order to assess the role played by the industrial structure of the regions. What broadly emerges is that:

(1) It is heartening to note that the industrial structure has shown a tendency towards change from traditional consumer oriented industries to capital goods sector, at the regional level in India during 1961 and 1978;

(2) while the regions, by and large, have diversified their industrial structure, the resource-base orientation still dominates the industrial scene in most of the regions. However, it appears that most diversified States are the ones which are at a higher level

of industrialisation;

(3) despite an apparent relationship between the levels of industrialisation and diversification, the industrial structure explains very small portion of the regional growth performance. To the contrary, the 'differential shift' dominates as an explanatory component; and

(4) since the shift-share technique side tracks impact of the inter-industry linkages; one has to explore into this technological relationship in order to understand the role of industrial structure in the varied regional growth performance.

## NOTES

1. We may express location quotient (L.Q.) in the following notation.

$$L.Q. = \frac{V_{ij}}{V_j} / \frac{V_i}{V_N}$$

where $V$ = Value added
$i$ = $i^{th}$ industry
$j$ = $j^{th}$ region
$N$ = National Aggregate

2. Specialisation coefficient (SQ) is calculated as

$$SQ = +\sum_{i=1}^{n} \frac{V_{ij}}{V_j} - \frac{V_i}{V_N}$$

symbols as in L.Q. above. We add all the positive (or negative) values.

3. The shift and share technique was developed by Daniel Creamer and later modified by Dunn, Ashby and Marquillaes. For details, see Creamer (1943); Dunn (1960); Perloff *et al.* (1960); Ashby (1964); and Marquillas (1972), among others.
4. The 'national growth effect' is also termed as the share-effect; the 'structural shift' as compositional mix or proportionality shift; and the 'differential shift' as competitive effect or the regional component or residual component.
5. It may be mentioned that the technique is able to eliminate the biased view that the simple growth rates usually portray when the industry base is narrow in the initial year.
6. Average change in the specialisation coefficient for all the regions in 1969 over 1961 was merely about +0.0315 and +0.0324 between 1969 and 1978. Also the rank correlation between the series for 1961 and 1969, and 1969 and 1978 was +0.9764 and +0.9731 respectively, indicating the stability of the relative rank order or the States during these years.
7. Here least specialised State (having lowest value of coefficient of specialisation) is treated as most diversified for the purpose of ranking.

8. We also worked out rank correlation between the level of diversification and the level of industrialisation in terms of per-capita value added generated in the registered manufacturing (feature) sector. In this case also the values of rank coefficient correlation were found to be significantly positive, being +0.4573, +0.5645 and +0.6099 for 1961, 1969 and 1978 respectively.
9. Incidentally this is in conformity to out earlier conclusion that the inter-regional disparities have shown a clear tendency of decline over time between 1961 and 1978 (see Chapter 4).
10. Data for Punjab and Haryana were not available for the first sub-period (1961-69), hence being ignored for the purpose of analysis.
11. To further confirm our conclusion, we worked out rank correlations ($r_k$) between the compound growth rates of the States during 1961-69 and 1969-78 and the two components of the total shifts for the respective sub-periods. The correlation coefficient between the growth rate and structural shift was though positive but quite insignificant with values of +0.1941 in 1961-69 and +0.0278 in 1969-78 period. To the contrary, with differential shifts it turned out to be significantly positive, the coefficients being +0.6394 and +0.5376 for the first and the second period respectively. Implying that the growth rates go more hand in hand with the differential shifts than the structural shifts.

# 6

# INTER-INDUSTRY LINKAGES AND REGIONAL INDUSTRIAL GROWTH

A PRELIMINARY idea about the regional industrial base was given in the previous chapter. However, we are not sure, the extent to which industrial base affects the growth potential of a region. Further, the shift and share analysis has limitation that it side tracks the effect of inter-industry linkages, thereby leaves a major proportion of changes in the interregional variations unexplained. In this backdrop, we shall be exploring the inter-industry linkages effect on the overall regional industrial growth performance.

Linkages in an economy arise owing to the technological relationship among its various sectors through their input purchase (backward linkages) and output disposal (forward linkages). Hence, as Hirschman would have put it, if a sector with high linkages (backward and forward) is chosen as a key sector and more investment is made therein, it is assumed it will induce growth impulses in other sectors of the economy too.[1]

We, therefore, make an attempt to assess the role of these linkages in the growth of various industrial regions. The proposition here is that a region giving high priority to the 'lead' sectors (sectors with high linkages) will tend to grow faster than otherwise.

## METHODOLOGY

The hypothesis to be tested here is that 'the regions which follow the Hirschman strategy of emphasising high linkage industries will, in the long run, be able to achieve higher overall rates of growth than the regions that do not follow it'. To test the hypothesis, as need to devise an index that measures the extent to which a country (region in our case) follows the Hirschman strategy. A simple Hirschman compliance index ($PH_i$) is provided by the region specific correlation between the sectoral total linkages ($LT_j$) and a region's sectoral rate of growth ($g_{ij}$).

It may be mentioned that we have used the total linkage index instead of backward and/or forward linkages.[2] The total linkage index ($Lt_j$) which is based exclusively on the matrix of domestic input co-efficient,[3] and derived from Input-Output table (1979-80) of the Planning Commission used in the Sixth Five Year Plan, is defined as:

$$LT_j = \sum_i d^*_{ij} \quad \text{where } d^*_{ij} = (I - d_{ij})^{-1} \text{ and} \qquad (6.1)$$
$$d_{ij} = a_{ij} - m_{ij}$$

where $m_{ij}$ is per unit requirement of imported inputs.[4] The $LT_j$ are given in Annexure 6.2.

Thus the Hirschman Compliance Index ($PH_i$) is defined as:

$$PH_i = \rho(LT_j, g_{ij}) \qquad (6.2)$$

where $i$ and $j$ denote region and sector respectively.[5]

An alternative formulation incorporating the relative importance of a sector in a region ($w_{ij}$) and accounting for the sectoral income elasticities of demand ($e_{ij}$) is thus defined as:[6]

$$PH_i^* = \rho(LT_j\, e_{ij}, W_{ij}\, g_{ij}) \qquad (6.3)$$

However, it is alleged that the Hirschman hypotheses is based on a rather extreme interpretation of the theory of unbalanced growth in which there is no limit to the desirable degree of imbalance. Therefore, Yotopoulous and Nugent (1973) proposed a balanced growth version of the linkage hypothesis; for, "a sector grows differently from other sectors precisely due to existing differences in linkage indices - all the other factors appropriately weighed. This is the balanced growth version of the linkage hypothesis, which would predict that linkage-balanced countries should grow, over a long period, faster than linkage-unbalanced countries (Yotopoulous and Nugent, 1973: 167).

The linkage-balance index ($VL_i$) for a region is defined as:

$$VL_i = \frac{1}{G_i}\sqrt{\frac{1}{n}\sum_{j=1}^{n} W_{ij}(g_{ij} - LT_j G_i)^2} \qquad (6.4)$$

where $n$ is number of sectors in a region and $G_i$ the overall growth rate of manufacturing sector in $i^{th}$ region. Other notions are as in equation (6.3)

A further adjustment so as to account for difference in income elasticity of demand ($e_{ij}$) between sectors may also be desirable. As such it might be said to combine elements of the structural change theories of Hirschman and Nurkse. Thus the indices corrected for region specific sectoral income elasticities ($e_{ij}$) is written as:[7]

$$VL_i^* = \frac{1}{G_i}\sqrt{\frac{1}{n}\sum_{j=1}^{n} W_{ij}(g_{ij} - LT_j e_{ij} G_i)^2} \tag{6.5}$$

The $VL_i$ index denotes the deviation of a region from the optimum linkage weighted growth proportions of the sectors. It is just a modified version of the coefficient of variation. The hypothesis, thus, will be vindicated by a negative correlation between $VL_i$ index and overall growth rates ($G_i$).

## COVERAGE AND DATABASE

The study analyses the period between 1969-70 and 1978-79. It is assumed that the pattern of economic development, in response to the planning process initiated in the mid-fifties, had not taken concrete shape by the early sixties and the mid-sixties are alleged to have suffered by the economic/industrial stagnation (a controversy, we have avoided at the moment). This prompted us to take 1969-70 as a cut off point, while latest data available for the variables were for the year 1978-79 at the time when exercise was undertaken.

Net output (value-added) data for the years 1969-70 and 1978-79, obtained from the Annual Survey of Industries (ASI), for the census sector only, have been employed to calculate specific compound rates of growth and sectoral weights. The data are available at a very disaggregated level, therefore had to be aggregated to match with the Input-Output (I-O) table (1979-80), used for calculating the linkages. Since information at this level (four, five or sometimes six digit level), in 1969-70, is not available for the sample sector so as to facilitate the aggregation which matches with the I-O table, this sector of manufacturing had to be dropped from the analysis. Moreover, the sectors like electricity generation and distribution, gas and water supply were also excluded, as in earlier exercises, from the analysis.

The Input-Output table 1979-80 was obtained from *A Technical Note on the Sixth Plan of India: 1980-85*, published by the Planning Commission. The data-base and the methodology for calculating sectoral income elasticities is discussed in detail in Annexure 6.1.

## Empirical Findings

The values of 'Hirschman Compliance Indices' ($PH_i$) for the various regions given in column 3 and 4 depict the weighted version of the indices ($PH_i$*) in Table 6.1. Looking at the State-wise indices, one finds very low and negative values of the correlations ($PH_i$) between the sectoral growth and linkages. Among the fast growing States, Andhra Pradesh, Gujarat, Karnataka, Rajasthan and Tamil Nadu have positive association between these two variables whereas Assam, Haryana, Himachal Pradesh, Jammu and Kashmir, Madhya Pradesh, Orissa, Punjab and Delhi have negative association. Among relatively slow growing States Bihar, Maharashtra, Uttar Pradesh and West Bengal have positive association and Himachal Pradesh and Jammu and Kashmir have negative one.

TABLE 6.1: Growth Rates, Hirschman Compliance Indices and Linkage Balance Indices for the Census Sector[1] by States : Value Added[2]

| Sl. No. | States | Annual compound Rate of Growth (1969-70 to 1978-79) | $\rho(H_i)$ | $\rho(H_i)^*$ | $VL_i$ | $VL_i^*$ |
|---|---|---|---|---|---|---|
| (1) | (2) | (3) | (4) | (5) | (6) | (7) |
| 1. | Andhra Pradesh | 9.4026 | +0.0355 | -0.01326 | +0.2959 | +0.5589 |
| 2. | Assam | 7.1859 | -0.3917 | +0.0269 | +0.4190 | +0.7096 |
| 3. | Bihar | 5.7750 | +0.0392 | +0.1155 | +0.3941 | +0.5834 |
| 4. | Gujarat | 6.4843 | +0.1436 | +0.0636 | +0.2241 | +0.5297 |
| 5. | Haryana | 9.5435 | -0.1673 | +0.0392 | +0.2556 | +0.5094 |
| 6. | Himachal Pradesh | 2.9049 | -0.0281 | -0.4585 | +0.8570 | +1.4756 |
| 7. | Jammu and Kashmir | 2.3818 | -0.1636 | -0.3162 | +1.2960 | +1.6701 |
| 8. | Karnataka | 7.0142 | +0.0683 | +0.1030 | +0.4110 | +0.5015 |
| 9. | Kerala | 10.0654 | +0.1022 | +0.0085 | +0.2558 | +0.5317 |
| 10. | Madhya Pradesh | 9.6891 | -0.0126 | -0.2931 | +0.2629 | +0.8232 |
| 11. | Maharashtra | 4.3717 | +0.1452 | +0.0598 | +0.3919 | +0.5622 |
| 12. | Orissa | 6.8350 | -0.1610 | -0.1610 | +0.3100 | -0.7187 |
| 13. | Punjab | 10.5829 | -0.0713 | +0.2409 | +0.2725 | +0.4495 |
| 14. | Rajasthan | 9.1032 | +0.0395 | -0.1862 | +0.4675 | +1.5028 |
| 15. | Tamil Nadu | 8.3036 | +0.1523 | -0.0518 | +0.2064 | +0.5949 |
| 16. | Uttar Pradesh | 4.1021 | +0.2561 | -0.2132 | +0.5076 | +0.7564 |
| 17. | West Bengal | 1.9739 | +0.2557 | +0.1201 | +0.6582 | +0.7890 |
| 18. | Delhi | 6.3683 | -0.1054 | -0.3533 | +0.3423 | +0.7510 |

*Note:* 1. The growth rates are only for Census Manufacturing sector.
2. Value added is in real terms, at 1970-71 prices.
3. Excludes Electricity, Gas and Steam, and Water Works.

*Source:* Base on Annual Survey of Industries, I-O table used in Sixth Five Year Plan and Annexure 6.1 and 6.2.

Similarly, when we consider weighted indices ($PH_i^*$) across regions, the picture by and large remains unchanged, except that Assam, Haryana and Punjab interchange their group with Andhra Pradesh, Rajasthan and Tamil Nadu by encountering a change in their signs. Among the slow growing States only Uttar Pradesh shows a negative association to join Himachal Pradesh and Jammu and Kashmir, otherwise *status quo* is maintained.

One striking feature which emerges from both indices is that most of the industrially important States (in terms of their share in value-added) have positive association between sectoral rates of growth and their linkages. However out of the top six highly industrialised States, except Tamil Nadu and Gujarat, Bihar, Maharashtra, Uttar Pradesh and West Bengal show a relatively low overall rates of growth.

Consequently, when we work out correlation between the region specific $PH_i$ and overall region rates of growth, the relationship turns out to be negative, whether we include all the regions or exclude Himachal Pradesh and Jammu and Kashmir owing to their very meagre industrial base. In the latter case, the relationship is negative but significant only at 10 per cent level of significance (Table 6.2). The association, when indices are properly weighted by the sectoral shares and income elasticities, remains negative but turns out to be insignificant. If, like earlier, Himachal Pradesh and Jammu and Kashmir are included, the association again emerges as significantly negative.

TABLE 6.2: Correlation Coefficient (ρ) Between the Various Linkage Indices and Overall Rate of Growth ($G_i$) of the States (1969-70 to 1978-79)

| Correlation Form | Values of Coefficient of Correlation (ρ) | |
|---|---|---|
| | All State | Himachal Pradesh and Jammu & Kashmir excluded |
| *Hirschman's Compliance Indices* | | |
| (i) ($Gi, PH_i$) | -0.4597*** | -0.4256*** |
| (ii) ($Gi, PH_i$*) | -03.999 | -0.0741 |
| *Linkage Balance Indices* | | |
| (i) ($Gi, VL_i$) | +0.2677 | -0.7288* |
| (ii) ($Gi, VL_i$*) | -0.4464*** | -0.0341 |

*Note:* * Significant at 1 per cent level
*** Significant at 10 per cent level

*Source:* Table 6.1

In the case of linkage balanced approach, the correlation between overall growth rates of the States and State specific linkage balanced indices turns out to be positive when all the States are considered together. Association emerges rather strongly when indices are properly weighted with the sectoral income elasticities. However, when we drop Jammu and Kashmir and Himachal Pradesh, there is a remarkable shift in the result, which displays negative sign and is significant at one per cent level of significance. This apparently lends support to the Yotopoulous and Nugent hypothesis that the regions growing at a higher rate have a more unbalanced structure with a higher weightage to the high linkage sectors than the slow growing ones. However, when we incorporate sectoral income elasticities in the index, the value though negative, turned out to be quite insignificant (see Table 6.2).

Therefore, it is somewhat difficult to associate (i) the sectoral growth with technological linkages (weighted or unweighted) and (ii) overall growth with the indices arrived at on the basis of growth-linkage relationship. However, one possibility for getting such result is that the potential linkages are not being realised within a region and spread, probably, over a wider space.[8] Therefore, it may be more valid to form some macro spatial regions based on the functional spatial linkages by pooling strongly linked (in terms of trade) regions together, in order to assess properly the impact of these linkages and industrial structure on the growth performance of those macro-economic regions rather than States. However, this is difficult for want of inter-regional trade statistics.[9]

## Limitation of the Approach

The limitation of the input output approach may constrain the adequacy of our exercise. Since input-output coefficients are specified in value terms, the relative regional price differences may result in some distortions in the measurement of indices. The use of national technology for the regional mapping as mentioned earlier might further limit the adequacy of our exercise. For the linkage structure and its potential may not be uniform over space. The relationships, which by and large, turn out to be insignificant might also be due to somewhat unrealistic growth rates or due to the partial coverage of the manufacturing sector.

The problems above can be taken care of if: (a) sufficiently disaggregated, region-wise input-output tables, comparable over sectors and the base years; (b) information pertaining to the inter-regional trade for the same year; and data for not only organised large scale (census sector) but organised small scale (sample) sector as well as unorganised sector are available in accordance with the input-output sectors.

## CONCLUDING OBSERVATIONS

An important objective of any growth strategy is not to achieve higher, but maximum attainable rate of growth. In India's case, a strategy based on unbalanced sectoral growth was adopted in the planning process, considering the importance of inter-industry linkages, which were supposed to play a crucial role in fostering the rate of growth. What emerges from the foregoing analysis is that inter-industry linkages and in turn industrial structure have barely played any significant role in the industrial growth, at least at the regional level. Probably, some institutional factors like income distribution, entrepreneurship, infrastructure, industrial climate and the composition of the decision-making body (governments of the States) play an important role in determining the path of development. Therefore, in order to understand the factors underlying the interregional variations, one may have to turn to behavioural factors rather than relying too much on the structural variables and technological relations.

## NOTES

1. The proposition obviously is based on the 'unbalanced strategy of growth' as propounded by Hirschman, Myrdal and Rostow, which refers to a wave of new investment in those (lead) sectors which have high linkages, which act as stimuli to investments (and growth) in other sectors. For detailed discussion see Rostow (1954); Hirschman (1958). Also see, for opposite stand, Rosenstein Rodan (1943); Nurkse (1953); Lewis (1956). And for synthesis of the two views, see Sen (1960); Nath (1962), Bhatt (1965); and Mathur (1966).
2. Forward or backward linkages capture only first round of the forward or backward interactions between industries. In fact an increase (decrease) in the output of an industry has second, third, fourth and subsequent rounds of interactions. The elements of Leontief Inverse capture the sum total effect of the infinite layers of production process. Thus the direct and indirect linkage effect or, as we call it, the total linkages for sector $j$ ($LT_j$), in terms of the elements of the Leontief Inverse, is defined as:

$$LT_j = \sum_i a^{*}_{ij} = (I - a_{ij})^{-1}$$

"It is well known that the inverse of the Leontief matrix can be approximated by $(I-A)^{-1} = I+A+A^2+A^3$.....
The multiplication of A matrix to obtain $A^2$, $A^3$ and so on in the formula involves forward linkages to the extent that going backward *ad infinitum* in a closed system also captures forward Aspects "Yotopoulos and Nugent (1973: 161-162, f.n. 8).

3. We have substituted $a_{ij}$ by $d_{ij}$ which is based exclusively on the domestic input coefficients. For the $LT_j$ based on $a_{ij}$ is misspecified. This index $a_{ij*}$ also captures production linkages with other countries and thus makes the index an erroneous measure of existing linkages within the country. Since some of the intermediate are imported from foreign countries, theoretically the imports should be netted while constructing the total linkages index. That is why we have used exclusively the domestic matrix. This is also suggested by Riedel (1976).
4. Domestic coefficients were arrived at by deducting import transactions (Table 4.9) from the flow matrix (Table 4.3) of the Input-Output tables used in Sixth plan.
5. Here we may clarify that the *national technology* has been used as 'reference technology' for various regions. The ideal way of working out region specific total sectoral linkages would be to use regional input-output tables. But the dearth of comparable (temporally and sectorally) Input-Output tables for all the major industrial regions in India is well known. To our knowledge, one such set of somewhat comparable I-O tables available for the States is for the year 1965. We feel that lot of changes have taken place in the technological relationships with more and more emphasis on the relatively new sectors like petro-chemicals and electronics and likewise. Therefore it might turn out to be somewhat misleading to use the tables based on an outdated technology relations. These tables are prepared, after a painstaking work by Venkataramaiah, *et al.* (1980).

   Though it might not be the *ideal way* to use national technology as reference technology for regions, quite a few researchers have suggested such a use in the absence of such tables at the regional level. Moreover, Chenery and Watanabe (1958) demonstrated that there are international similarities among developed countries, in the pattern of sectoral interdependence, as evidence by their aij, coefficients.

   Also see Lakdawala *et al.* (1972); Alagh 1972); Yotopoulos and Nugent (1973) for arguing in favour of the use of the reference technology.
6. This type of modification is desirable on two counts: (1) A deviation of 100 per cent in the growth rate of an industry that constitutes only one per cent of the total manufacturing value added would be less unbalancing than a 20 per cent deviation of an industry that constitutes, let us say, 30 per cent of the mass. We, therefore, need to weight the industrial sector by the relative importance of that sector in the regional economy. Thus $w_{ij}$ is the share of sector $j$ in region $i$'s total value added with

$$\sum_{i}^{n} w_{ij} = 1.$$

   In the empirical analysis, $w_i$ is given by the ratio of the arithmetic mean of the shares at the beginning and the end of the period, i.e. 1969-70, 1979-80. (2) The sectoral differences in the income elasticity of demand $(e_{ij})$ are also of consequence. For $e_{ij}$'s would play an important role as "... supply is properly distributed among different commodities in accordance with consumer's want... Each industry must advance along an expansion path determined by the income elasticity of consumer demand for its products" Nurkse (1953:250-51).

7. Region specific sectoral income elasticities have been used while computing the index. In some earlier studies on the subject, either sectoral income elasticities have altogether been ignored or the elasticities at the national level have been super-imposed on the regions, assuming that the demand pattern does not vary much across the States as far as manufactured goods are concerned, which is a highly unrealistic assumption. For example for the former type, see Kashyap and Desai (1975) and for later Awasthi (1983).

   Various studies distinctly show that there is significant difference in the demand pattern across regions; see Gupta, 1963; Radhakrishna and Mishra, 1970; Mahajan 1971, among others.
8. While carrying out such an exercise, the regions are treated as closed economies which is not so in reality. The case of iron and steel industry in Bihar, Madhya Pradesh and Orissa is typical one which has more linkages outside the States than within the region.
9. In fact, it is precisely for the non-availability of data on inter-regional trade flows that very few studies relating to spatial interaction and spatial linkage process have been carried out in India, in spite of their importance in exploring economic interaction among regions. Moreover, the studies carried out in this area are based on commodity trade flows by railways and rivers. Transportation by roads, a very crucial variant, is left out on account of the scant availability of information. For example, a study conducted by Berry *et al.* (1966) for the Indian economy with the help of Inland Trade Accounts mainly for the year 1959-60 for 63 commodities brings out four polarised regions oriented to four metropolitan centres viz., Bombay Calcutta, Delhi and Madras, States. Another study by Hashim (1970), based on the Inland (Rail and River borne) Trade accounts for the year 1965-66 for aggregate flows of 61 commodities suggests six macro-regions for the economy on the base of inter-regional trade linkages. The other interesting studies in this streams are by Gidadhubly and Bhat (1960). Thakker (1971) has included trade by roads also but confines to the inter-regional trade of Gujarat *vis-a-vis* other States.

*ANNEXURE 6.1*

## Sectoral Income Elasticities for the Various States in India : Estimates for 1977-1978

With the availability of National Sample Survey (NSS) data on consumer expenditure, a large number of studies have been carried out to quantify the consumer behaviour at national as well as regional level (Iyengar, 1964, 1967; Maitra, 1969; Shah 1972; Murty and Shah 1980). The grouped data published by NSS are usually provided for per capita monthly consumption (in quantity terms) along with per capita monthly total expenditure by commodities and by expenditure classes for rural and urban areas separately. The expenditure elasticities of demand, estimates with this data base, played a vital role in projecting the future demand, as well as understanding the structure of the consumption patterns (Iyengar and Jain, 1960a and 1960b). Initially, the expenditure elasticities of demand were arrived at by considering the cross-sectional demand functions - the Engel Curves. These elasticities were assumed to be invariant during the plant period, for projecting the future demand. Some studies arrived at the demand projections by explicitly incorporating the expenditure distribution (Biswas and Biswas, 1961).

Recognising the need for incorporating the influence of prices, some studies have also simulated complete demand system for India. These studies are structured to incorporate the changes in the expenditure distribution and highlight presence of the rural-urban dualism and income dualism in the demand pattern (Bhattacharya and Chatterji, 1971; Radhakrishna *et al.* 1980; Murty, 1980). In view of the data limitations, however, the demand systems are estimated only for a few commodities constituting the consumer budget.

The broad survey presented above clearly indicates the limited usefulness of the existing estimates of expenditure elasticities for our purpose. This is mainly because of the fact that the sectors considered in the earlier works are only at an aggregate level. Moreover, only expenditure elasticities are available rather than sectoral income elasticities corresponding to the sectoral disaggregation of 1979-80 Input-Output table, used in our analysis. Further, the estimates are not available for all the States as required for the analysis. Therefore, it calls for a fresh exercise to work out sectoral income elasticities for all the States under consideration.

**Database**

We have used two major data sources, viz. 28th round of the NSS providing information on consumer expenditure by States for the year 1973-74 and the Task Force Report (TFR) published by the Planning Commission (1979). The latter report utilised the household information pertaining to the year 1973-74, and provides the Engel Curve estimates for 71 commodity groups of consumption, separately for rural and urban areas and for the people below and above the poverty line.[1] It may be mentioned that complete demand system, i.e. LES has been estimated separately for these groups.

**The Methodology**

We have carried out this exercise in two stages. First, the expenditure elasticities for various sectors at the national level were worked out; and second, on the basis of the national level sectoral expenditure elasticities, the region specific sectoral income elasticities were worked out.

*Sectoral Expenditure Elasticities at the National Level:*

As discussed above, the best fitting Engel Curves are utilised, first to estimate the expenditure elasticities of demand for each population group (people below the poverty line and above the poverty line) for rural and urban areas separately. As provided in the TFR, per capita total expenditure has been utilised to arrive at the sectoral expenditure elasticities of demand at the national level; writing:

$C_j$ = per capita monthly expenditure for the $j^{th}$ group;
$C_{ij}$ = per capita monthly expenditure in $i^{th}$ Sector for the $j^{th}$ group;
$b_{ij}$ and $d_{ij}$ = regression coefficient
$\eta_{ij}$ = expenditure elasticity of demand for the $i^{th}$ sector belonging to the $j^{th}$ group.

The corresponding expenditure elasticity estimates for the various Engel Curves[2] are as follows:

(1) Double log $= \eta_{ij} = b_{ij}$
(2) Semi log $= \eta_{ij} = b_{ij}/c_{ij}$

(3) Log log inverse $= \eta_{ij} = b_{ij} - d_{ij}/c_{ij}$
(4) Log inverse $= \eta_{ij} = -b_{ij}/c_{j}$
(5) Linear $= \eta_{ij} = b_{ij}/c_{ij}$
(6) Hyperbola $= \eta_{ij} = b_{ij}/c_{j}.c_{ij}$
(7) Proportions[3] $= \eta_{ij} = 1$

While carrying out the analysis, some of the functions gave absurd result in predicting the sectoral per capita expenditure.[4] In such cases we inputed directly the values as worked out in the TFR for 13 commodity groups.[5] Where much adjustments were not possible, we took corresponding budget shares of the aggregate expenditure by group - by sector in question.

Weighing diagrams based on the aggregate expenditure of individual groups by sectors are used for estimating the aggregate expenditure elasticity of demand for each sector. Writing thus

$\bar{\eta}_i$ = Weighted average expenditure elasticity for $i^{th}$ sector.

$\bar{\eta}_{ij}$ = Share of expenditure on $i^{th}$ sector by $j^{th}$ group.[6]

then,

$$\bar{\eta}_i = \sum_i W_{ij} \quad \eta_{ij}$$

Estimates for the national level sectoral expenditure elasticities by sector are given in Annexure 6.1a.

## *Region Specific Sectoral Income Elasticities*

Once the sectoral expenditure elasticities were available at the national level, we worked out sectoral expenditure elasticities for the various States in order to finally arrive at the region specific sectoral income elasticities using the data available from 28 round of the NSS, pertaining to the year 1973-74.

The 28th round provides information on consumer expenditure per person for 30 days, for 21 broad groups of items by monthly per capita expenditure classes in rural and urban areas separately, for all the States. We selected 8 out of the 21 broad sectors, corresponding to the 8 groups provided in TFR, and two relevant sectors viz., edible oils and miscellaneous food products in addition to those eight groups. For, 28th round gives separate information on these two groups also; keeping our purpose in mind. We aggregated the information on rural and urban areas by assigning proper weights according to the proportions of the households in respective segments across various expenditure classes in each of the States. Thereafter, following the methodology used in the TFR, we estimated expenditure elasticities by States, for eight major sectors, selecting the formates with highest $R^2$.

Now we had expenditure elasticities for eight major groups at the national level as well as 10 major groups (including 8 corresponding to TFR) by States; and expenditure elasticities for the various manufacturing sectors, constituting the eight broad groups, at the national level.

In order to estimate disaggregated sectoral expenditure elasticities of demand (corresponding to the I-O table 1979-80) by States; first, a weighing diagram, based on the share of $i^{th}$ sector in the aggregate consumer expenditure, was used to work out weighted group expenditure elasticities at the national level. Writing thus

$W_i$ = share of $i^{th}$ sector in the aggregate consumer expenditure

$\bar{\eta}_i$ = expenditure elasticity for $i^{th}$ sector

$\eta_k$ = weighted expenditure elasticity for $k^{th}$ broad group at national level;

then

$$n_k = \Sigma_i W_i \cdot \bar{\eta}_i$$

Thereafter, assuming that the difference between the sectoral expenditure elasticities ($\eta_i$), across States will be found to the extent major group elasticities, i.e. $\eta_k$ and State specific expenditure elasticities of the corresponding broad groups differ with each other. Thus, using the ratio of State group elasticities to the ($\eta_k$) we worked out Statewise disaggregated sectoral expenditure elasticities as

$$\bar{\eta}_{ij} = \eta_{kj} \times \eta_k \times 32\bar{\eta}_i$$

where

$\bar{\eta}_{ij}$ = expenditure elasticity of sector $i$ in State $j$;

$\eta_{kj}$ = expenditure elasticity of broad group $k$ in State $j$; and

$\bar{\eta}$ and $\eta_k$ as above in equation

In view of the fact that the income elasticities rather than expenditure elasticities are to be used in our exercise; some adjustments have to be made in order to convest these $\eta_{ij}$'s into the income elasticities of demand. For this purpose a separate macro consumption function was estimated by postulating the following functional form

$$log\ C_j = \alpha + \beta_j\ log\ Y_j$$

Where

$C$ = per capita consumption expenditure in $j^{th}$ state,
$\beta_j$ = total consumption elasticity w.r.t. per capita income;
$Y_j$ = per capita income in $j^{th}$ state,

The above function was estimated by using time series data on average per capita consumer expenditure (from 1960 to 1979) from various rounds of the NSS consumer expenditure survey; and per capita income (1960-1974) obtained from the Estimates of State Domestic Product (1960-61 to 1982-83), Published by CSO (1984).[7]

The income elasticity of demand ($\eta_{ij}$) for the $i^{th}$ sector in $j^{th}$ region is thus worked out as

$$(\hat{\eta}_{ij}) = \hat{\eta}_{ij} = \bar{\eta}_{ij} \cdot \beta_j$$

We may however note that the income elasticities of demand are subject to so many limitations, precisely due to the data constraints. Firstly, we assumed that the consumption-income relationship at the aggregate level is the same for all the classes of population, and macro-relationship between consumption-disposable income is not important. If these relationships differ, depending on the income share accruing to different sectors, the estimated income elasticity may be under/over Stated. Secondly, the influence of prices are not taken into account and accordingly the estimates suffer from the specification errors. Thirdly, region specific variations in demand due to differences in the taste patterns are ignored. Nevertheless, this was the only way at our disposal to estimate the region specific sectoral income elasticity of demand, given the information base. Moreover, to a great extent it serves our limited purpose. The income elasticities are presented in the Annexure 6.1b.

NOTES

1. In the report (TFR), consumer demand function/Engel Curves have been estimates by fitting the single equation weighted least squares, weights being the proportion of people in each expenditure class for different commodity groups.

The exercise is based on the NSS data on consumer expenditure pertaining to the year 1973-74 (28th round of NSS), adjusted at 19 '6-77 prices. Parameters of the Linear Expenditure System (LES) and Engel Demand Functions were further adjusted for 1977-78 (TFR, 1979:7-8). The estimated per capita expenditure are based on the best fitting Engel Curves, i.e., having highest value of $R^2$ among the various forms of the curve. Further, the internal consistency of the estimates is maintained with 13 broad commodity groups considered in the report.

2. Various forms of Engel Curves (as pep TFR)

(a) Double log *(DL)* = $Log\ C_i = a + b\ log\ C$
(b) Semi log *(SL)* = $C_i = a + b\ log\ C$
(c) Log-log inverse *(LLI)* = $log\ C_i = a + b\ log\ c + d/c$
(d) Log inverse *(LI)* = $log\ C_i = a + b/c$
(e) Linear *(L)* = $C_i = a + bc$
(f) Hyperbola *(Hyp)* = $C^1 = a + b/c$
(g) Proportions = $C_i = bic$

Where; $C_i$ = monthly household per capita expenditure on $i^{th}$ commodity
$C$ = total monthly per capita expenditure of the household on all commodities; and
$bic$ = aggregate consumption proportions per capita per month.

3. In the case of such commodities where data were too inadequate to fit a demand function; aggregate proportions were used so that in each case $n_{ij}$ is equal to 1, estimated by $C_i = bic$ (TFR, 1979:8).
4. For example, in the case of milk and milk products, per capita expenditure by people below poverty line exceeded the corresponding total expenditure on all the commodities.
5. Since our purpose was limited to the manufacturing sector only, we have considered only 8 broad commodity groups, out of 13, from the TFR, These 8 sectors cover all the manufacturing sectors. The groups considered are : Milk and Milk products (3); Other food products (6); Sugar and gur (7); pan, tobacco and intoxicants (8); fuel and light (9); clothing (10); miscellaneous (11) and durable goods (13). However, 28th round of NSS provides information on two more relevant sectors viz. Edible oils and Miscellaneous food articles. Therefore, in addition to the 8 corresponding sectors to TFR, we have considered these two sectors also. Constituent sectors in each of the broad category are given in Annexure 6.1a.
6. It is to be noted that $w_{ij}$ estimates are not provided in TFR and thus the sectorwise groupwise aggregate expenditure are worked out by utilising the best fitting Engel Curve.
7. It may be mentioned that per capita consumption, as a matter of fact, is a function of disposable income rather than total income. However, we do not have information on the disposable income by States. Therefore, we assume it away for the obvious reasons.

*ANNEXURE 6.1a*

## Estimates of Sectoral Expenditure Elasticities ($\eta_i$) – All India (1977-78)

| Sector No. | Name of the Sector | $\eta_i$ |
|---|---|---|
| 1. | Milk and milk products | 1.3351 |
| 2. | Miscellaneous food products | 1.6642 |
| 3. | Sugar | 1.3798 |
| 4. | Gur and Khandsari | 1.1893 |
| 5. | Vanaspati | 1.0387 |
| 6. | Edible oil | 1.0553 |
| 7. | Tea and Coffee | 1.2735 |
| 8. | Other beverages | 1.1572 |
| 9. | Tobacco manufacturing | 0.7129 |
| 10. | Cotton textiles | 2.3716 |
| 11. | Handloom and Khadi | 1.1212 |
| 12. | Woollen and Silk textile | 1.0492 |
| 13. | Art silk fabrics | 1.0069 |
| 14. | Jute textile | 1.0000 |
| 15. | Readymade garments | 1.1386 |
| 16. | Miscellaneous textile products | 0.9292 |
| 17. | Carpet weaving | 1.0000 |
| 18. | Wood products | 2.9084 |
| 19. | Paper and paper products | 1.7001 |
| 20. | Printing and publishing | 2.4289 |
| 21. | Leather and leather products | 1.0000 |
| 22. | Leather footwear | 1.4161 |
| 23. | Rubber products | 1.1724 |
| 24. | Plastics | 1.0000 |
| 25. | Petroleum products | 0.9308 |
| 26. | Miscellaneous coal and petroleum products | 1.0000 |
| 27. | Organic and inorganic heavy chemicals | 1.1997 |
| 28. | Chemical fertilizers and pesticides | 1.0000 |
| 29. | Drugs and pharmaceuticals | 1.1240 |
| 30. | Soaps, glycerine and cosmetics | 2.9742 |
| 31. | Synthetic rubber, manmade fibres, etc. | 1.1997 |
| 32. | Refractories | 2.3058 |
| 33. | Cement | 2.3058 |
| 34. | Other non-metallic mineral products | 2.3058 |
| 35. | Iron and steel | 1.1670 |
| 36. | Casting and forging | 1.6170 |

*(Contd.)*

ANNEXURE 6.1a *(Contd.)*

| Sector No. | Name of the Sector | $\eta_i$ |
|---|---|---|
| 37. | Iron and steel structurals | 1.6170 |
| 38. | Non-ferrous metals | 1.6170 |
| 39. | Metal products | 1.6170 |
| 40. | Tractors and agricultural implements | 1.0000 |
| 41. | Machine tools | 1.0000 |
| 42. | Office, domestic and commercial equipments | 1.0000 |
| 43. | Other non-electrical machinery | 1.0000 |
| 44. | Electrical motors | 1.0000 |
| 45. | Electric cables and wires | 1.0000 |
| 46. | Batteries | 1.0000 |
| 47. | Electric household goods | 1.0305 |
| 48. | Communication and electric equipments | 1.0626 |
| 49. | Other electrical machinery | 1.0000 |
| 50. | Ships and boats | 1.2811 |
| 51. | Rail equipments | 2.6050 |
| 52. | Motor vehicles | 1.8383 |
| 53. | Motor cycles and bicycles etc. | 1.2811 |
| 54. | Other transport equipments | 1.2811 |
| 55. | Watches and clocks | 1.0000 |
| 56. | Miscellaneous manufacturing | 1.1942 |

*Note:* Sectors correspond to the input-output table used in the exercise.
*Source:* As per the text.

## ANNEXURE 6.1b

### State Specific Sectoral Income Elasticities of Demand (1977-78)

| Sector No. | Name of Sector | Andhra Pradesh | Assam | Bihar | Gujarat | Haryana | Himachal Pradesh | Jammu and Kashmir | Karnataka | Kerala | Madhya Pradesh | Maharashtra | Orissa | Punjab | Rajasthan | Tamil Nadu | Uttar Pradesh | West Bengal | Delhi |
|---|---|---|---|---|---|---|---|---|---|---|---|---|---|---|---|---|---|---|---|
| (1) | (2) | (3) | (4) | (5) | (6) | (7) | (8) | (9) | (10) | (11) | (12) | (13) | (14) | (15) | (16) | (17) | (18) | (19) | (20) |
| 1. | Milk and milk products | 1.22 | 1.94 | — | 1.96 | — | — | — | 0.96 | 1.37 | — | 1.31 | — | 0.94 | — | — | 1.05 | 1.57 | 1.34 |
| 2. | Miscellaneous food products | 0.70 | 0.74 | 0.81 | 0.64 | 0.52 | — | 0.57 | 0.58 | 0.60 | 0.77 | 0.69 | 0.55 | 0.56 | 0.62 | 0.57 | 0.61 | 0.80 | 1.09 |
| 3. | Sugar | 1.63 | — | 1.21 | 0.74 | 0.53 | — | — | 0.73 | — | 1.24 | 0.68 | 1.53 | 0.48 | 0.88 | 1.19 | 0.83 | 0.90 | — |
| 4. | Gur and Khandsari | 1.41 | 0.95 | 1.04 | 0.64 | 0.46 | — | — | 0.63 | — | 1.07 | 0.58 | 1.32 | — | 0.76 | — | 0.72 | 0.78 | — |
| 5. | Vanaspati | 0.98 | — | — | 0.67 | — | — | — | 0.67 | — | 1.22 | 0.87 | — | 0.41 | 0.86 | 0.68 | 0.65 | 0.93 | — |
| 6. | Edible oil | 1.00 | — | 1.09 | 0.68 | — | — | — | 0.68 | — | 1.24 | 0.88 | 1.09 | 0.42 | 0.88 | 0.69 | 0.66 | 0.94 | — |
| 7. | Tea and Coffee | 1.50 | 2.00 | — | 1.18 | — | — | — | 1.22 | 0.83 | — | — | — | — | — | 1.21 | 1.77 | 1.91 | — |
| 8. | Other beverages | 0.64 | 1.82 | 1.55 | 1.07 | 0.98 | 1.42 | — | 1.10 | 0.76 | 2.07 | 1.52 | 1.46 | 0.74 | 1.40 | 1.10 | 1.61 | 1.74 | 1.35 |
| 9. | Tobacco manufacturing | 3.25 | — | 0.90 | 0.42 | — | — | — | 0.51 | 0.55 | 1.12 | 0.88 | — | — | 0.82 | 1.07 | 0.85 | — | — |
| 10. | Cotton textiles | 1.44 | 3.82 | 2.60 | 2.66 | 2.35 | — | — | 2.35 | 2.38 | 3.19 | 2.51 | 1.64 | 2.19 | 2.45 | 1.72 | 2.35 | 2.03 | 3.08 |
| 11. | Handloom and Khadi | — | — | — | — | — | — | — | — | — | — | — | — | — | — | — | — | — | — |
| 12. | Woollen and Silk textile | 1.38 | — | 1.15 | 1.17 | 1.04 | 1.36 | 1.12 | 1.04 | — | 1.41 | 1.11 | — | 0.96 | 1.08 | 0.76 | 1.04 | 0.89 | 1.36 |
| 13. | Art silk fabrics | — | — | — | 1.12 | 1.00 | — | — | 1.00 | 1.01 | 1.35 | 1.06 | — | 0.93 | 1.04 | 0.73 | 0.99 | 0.86 | 1.31 |
| 14. | Jute textile | 1.56 | 1.61 | 1.09 | — | — | — | — | — | — | — | — | 0.69 | — | — | — | 0.99 | 0.85 | — |
| 15. | Readymade garments | 2.75 | — | 1.25 | 0.89 | 1.13 | — | — | 1.13 | 1.14 | 1.53 | 1.20 | — | 1.05 | 1.17 | 0.82 | 1.12 | 0.97 | 1.48 |
| 16. | Miscellaneous textile products | — | — | — | 1.04 | 0.92 | — | — | — | 0.93 | — | 0.98 | — | — | 0.96 | 0.67 | 0.92 | 0.79 | 1.20 |
| 17. | Carpet weaving | — | — | — | — | — | — | 1.06 | — | — | — | — | — | — | — | — | 0.99 | — | — |
| 18. | Wood products | 1.54 | 1.57 | 1.92 | 1.94 | — | 2.98 | 2.55 | 1.87 | 2.78 | 3.69 | 2.71 | — | 2.27 | — | 3.33 | 3.22 | 3.03 | 2.51 |
| 19. | Paper and paper products | 2.10 | 1.57 | 1.72 | 1.12 | 0.79 | — | — | 1.06 | 1.15 | 1.54 | 1.33 | 1.35 | 0.93 | 1.31 | 1.09 | 1.17 | 1.37 | — |
| 20. | Printing and publishing | 1.65 | 2.25 | 2.46 | 1.60 | 1.14 | — | — | 1.52 | 1.64 | 2.21 | 1.90 | 1.94 | — | 1.87 | 1.56 | 1.67 | 1.96 | 2.20 |
| 21. | Leather and leather products | 1.94 | — | — | — | — | — | — | — | — | — | 1.63 | — | — | — | 2.00 | 1.93 | 0.80 | — |

(Contd.)

ANNEXURE 6.1b (*Contd.*)

| (1) | (2) | (3) | (4) | (5) | (6) | (7) | (8) | (9) | (10) | (11) | (12) | (13) | (14) | (15) | (16) | (17) | (18) | (19) | (20) |
|---|---|---|---|---|---|---|---|---|---|---|---|---|---|---|---|---|---|---|---|
| 22. | Leather footwear | — | — | — | — | — | — | — | — | — | — | 2.30 | — | — | — | 2.83 | 2.74 | — | — |
| 23. | Rubber products | 1.09 | — | 1.35 | 1.36 | 1.70 | — | — | 1.31 | 1.96 | 2.60 | 1.91 | — | 1.59 | — | 2.34 | 2.26 | 2.13 | 1.77 |
| 24. | Plastics | — | — | — | — | — | — | — | — | — | — | 0.78 | — | — | — | 0.64 | 0.69 | 0.80 | — |
| 25. | Petroleum products | — | 1.11 | 1.21 | 0.79 | — | — | — | — | — | — | 0.94 | — | — | — | — | — | — | — |
| 26. | Miscellaneous coal and petroleum products | — | — | 1.21 | — | — | — | — | — | — | — | 0.94 | — | — | — | 0.77 | — | 0.97 | — |
| 27. | Organic and inorganic heavy chemicals | 0.90 | 1.11 | 1.21 | 0.79 | 0.56 | — | — | 1.75 | 0.81 | 1.09 | 0.94 | 0.95 | — | 0.92 | 0.77 | 0.82 | 0.97 | 1.23 |
| 28. | Chemical fertilizers and pesticides | 1.09 | — | 1.01 | 0.66 | 0.46 | — | — | 0.62 | 0.67 | 0.91 | 0.78 | 0.79 | 0.55 | 0.77 | 0.64 | 0.68 | 0.80 | 0.90 |
| 29. | Drugs and pharmaceuticals | 1.09 | — | 1.21 | 0.79 | 0.56 | 0.89 | 0.91 | 0.75 | 0.81 | 1.09 | 0.94 | — | 0.66 | 0.92 | 0.77 | 0.82 | 0.97 | 1.23 |
| 30. | Soaps, glycerine and cosmetics | — | — | — | 0.64 | — | — | — | 0.61 | 0.66 | — | 0.76 | — | — | 0.75 | 0.62 | 0.67 | 0.78 | 0.88 |
| 31. | Synthetic rubber, manmade fibres, etc. | 3.82 | — | 1.21 | 0.79 | — | — | — | 0.75 | — | 1.09 | 0.94 | 0.95 | 0.66 | — | 0.77 | 0.82 | 0.97 | — |
| 32. | Refractories | — | 2.18 | 2.67 | 2.69 | 3.35 | — | 3.68 | 2.59 | 3.86 | 5.12 | 3.75 | 3.07 | — | — | 4.61 | 4.46 | 4.19 | 3.48 |
| 33. | Cement | 3.82 | — | 2.67 | 2.69 | 3.35 | — | — | 2.59 | — | 5.12 | 3.75 | — | — | 5.71 | 4.61 | — | 4.19 | — |
| 34. | Other non-metallic mineral products | 2.68 | — | 2.67 | 2.69 | 3.35 | 4.12 | — | 2.59 | 3.86 | 5.12 | 3.75 | 3.07 | — | 5.71 | 4.61 | 4.46 | 4.19 | 3.48 |
| 35. | Iron and steel | 2.68 | 1.52 | 1.87 | 1.88 | 2.35 | 2.89 | 2.58 | 1.81 | 2.70 | 3.59 | 2.63 | 2.15 | 2.20 | 4.00 | 3.23 | 3.12 | 2.94 | 2.44 |
| 36. | Casting and forging | 2.68 | — | 1.87 | 1.88 | 2.35 | 2.89 | — | 1.81 | — | 3.59 | 2.63 | 2.15 | 2.20 | 4.00 | 3.23 | 3.12 | 2.94 | 2.44 |
| 37. | Iron and steel structural | 2.68 | — | 1.87 | 1.88 | — | — | — | 1.81 | 2.70 | — | 2.63 | 2.15 | 2.20 | 4.00 | 3.23 | 3.12 | 2.94 | 2.44 |
| 38. | Non-ferrous metals | — | — | 1.87 | 1.88 | 2.35 | — | — | 1.81 | 2.70 | 3.59 | 2.63 | — | — | 4.00 | 3.23 | 3.12 | 2.94 | — |
| 39. | Metal products | 1.65 | 1.52 | 1.87 | 1.88 | 2.35 | — | — | 1.81 | 2.70 | 3.59 | 2.63 | 2.15 | 2.20 | 4.00 | 2.23 | 3.12 | 2.94 | 2.40 |
| 40. | Tractprs amd agricultural implements | 1.65 | — | 1.15 | 1.16 | 1.45 | — | — | 1.12 | — | 2.22 | 1.63 | — | 1.36 | 2.47 | 2.00 | 1.93 | 1.82 | 1.50 |
| 41. | Machine tools | 0.72 | — | 1.15 | 1.16 | 1.45 | — | — | 1.12 | — | — | 1.63 | — | 1.36 | — | 2.00 | — | 1.82 | 1.50 |
| 42. | Office, domestic and commercial equipments | — | — | — | — | 1.45 | — | — | — | — | — | 1.63 | — | — | — | — | — | 1.82 | — |
| 43. | Other non-electrical machinery | 0.72 | 0.94 | 1.15 | 1.16 | 1.45 | 1.79 | — | 1.12 | 1.67 | 2.22 | 1.63 | 1.33 | 1.36 | — | 2.00 | 1.93 | 1.82 | 1.50 |

(*Contd.*)

ANNEXURE 6.1b (*Contd.*)

| (1) | (2) | (3) | (4) | (5) | (6) | (7) | (8) | (9) | (10) | (11) | (12) | (13) | (14) | (15) | (16) | (17) | (18) | (19) | (20) |
|---|---|---|---|---|---|---|---|---|---|---|---|---|---|---|---|---|---|---|---|
| 44. | Electrical motors | 0.72 | — | — | 0.57 | 0.51 | — | — | 0.56 | — | 0.67 | 0.57 | — | 0.47 | 0.43 | 0.53 | 0.47 | 0.60 | 0.61 |
| 45. | Electric cables and wires | 0.72 | 0.65 | 0.58 | 0.57 | 0.51 | — | — | 0.56 | 0.51 | 0.67 | 0.57 | 0.59 | 0.47 | 0.43 | 0.53 | 0.47 | 0.60 | 0.61 |
| 46. | Batteries | 0.72 | — | — | 0.57 | — | — | — | 0.56 | 0.51 | 0.67 | 0.57 | — | 0.47 | — | 0.53 | — | 0.60 | — |
| 47. | Electric household goods | — | — | — | 0.58 | 0.52 | — | — | 0.58 | — | — | 0.59 | — | 0.48 | — | 0.55 | 0.49 | 0.60 | 0.63 |
| 48. | Communication and electric equipments | 0.77 | — | 0.61 | 0.60 | 0.54 | — | — | 0.60 | 0.55 | 0.71 | 0.61 | — | 0.50 | — | 0.57 | 0.50 | 0.64 | 0.65 |
| 49. | Other electrical Machinery | — | — | — | 2.14 | — | — | — | — | — | — | — | — | — | — | — | — | 0.60 | — |
| 50. | Ships and boats | 3.04 | — | — | 2.14 | 2.67 | — | — | 2.06 | 3.07 | — | 2.99 | — | — | — | 3.68 | — | 3.34 | — |
| 51. | Rail equipments | 3.04 | 1.73 | 2.12 | 2.14 | — | — | — | 2.06 | — | — | 2.99 | — | — | 4.55 | 3.68 | 3.55 | 3.34 | 2.77 |
| 52. | Motor vehicles | 3.04 | 1.73 | — | 1.49 | 2.67 | 3.29 | 3.93 | 2.06 | 3.02 | 4.08 | 2.99 | 2.44 | 0.50 | 4.55 | 3.68 | 3.55 | 3.34 | 2.77 |
| 53. | Motor cycles and bicycles etc. | 3.12 | — | — | 0.66 | 1.86 | — | — | 1.44 | — | — | 2.08 | — | 1.74 | — | 2.56 | 2.47 | 2.33 | 1.93 |
| 54. | Other transport equipments | — | — | — | — | — | — | — | — | — | — | 2.08 | — | — | — | — | — | 2.33 | — |
| 55. | Watches and clocks | — | — | 2.12 | 2.11 | — | — | — | — | — | — | 0.78 | — | — | — | — | — | — | — |
| 56. | Miscellaneous manufacturing | 2.90 | 2.96 | 2.23 | — | 1.49 | 2.39 | 2.44 | 2.00 | 2.16 | 2.90 | 2.50 | 2.55 | 1.76 | 2.47 | 2.05 | 2.20 | 2.58 | 2.89 |

*Notes:* (1) State specific sectoral elasticities of demand presented in the table correspond to the input-output sectors are given in Annexure 6.1a.
(2) Only relevant sectoral elasticities, used to construct the various linkage indices, are presented.

*ANNEXURE 6.2*

## Total Linkage Indices ($LT_j$) by Industry

| Sector No. | Name of the Sector | $LT_i$ |
|---|---|---|
| 1. | Milk and Milk Products | 1.6138 |
| 2. | Miscellaneous Food Products | 2.3845 |
| 3. | Sugar | 2.2673 |
| 4. | Gur and Khandsari | 2.3420 |
| 5. | Vanaspati | 2.2773 |
| 6. | Edible oils | 2.0071 |
| 7. | Tea and Coffee | 2.1420 |
| 8. | Other Beverages | 1.9077 |
| 9. | Tobacco Manufacturing | 1.9743 |
| 10. | Cotton Textiles | 2.1197 |
| 11. | Cotton Textile Handloom (Khadi) | 2.2812 |
| 12. | Woollen and Silk Textile | 2.2797 |
| 13. | Art Silk Fabrics | 1.5722 |
| 14. | Jute Textile | 2.5719 |
| 15. | Readymade Garments | 1.7303 |
| 16. | Miscellaneous Textile Products | 1.8943 |
| 17. | Carpet Weaving | 1.2211 |
| 18. | Wood Products | 1.7065 |
| 19. | Paper, Paper Products and News Print | 2.1065 |
| 20. | Printing and Publishing | 1.8156 |
| 21. | Leather and Leather Products | 2.5621 |
| 22. | Leather Footwear | 2.2620 |
| 23. | Rubber Products | 2.1370 |
| 24. | Plastics | 1.7962 |
| 25. | Petroleum Products | 1.0684 |
| 26. | Miscellaneous Coal and Petroleum Products | 1.9100 |
| 27. | Organic and Inorganic Heavy Chemicals | 1.5289 |
| 28. | Chemical Fertilizers, Pesticides, etc. | 2.0607 |
| 29. | Drugs and Pharmaceuticals | 2.1185 |
| 30. | Soaps, Glycerine and Cosmetics | 2.2863 |
| 31. | Synthetic Rubber, Manmade Fibres and Other Chemicals | 1.9037 |
| 32. | Refractories | 1.7875 |
| 33. | Cement | 2.0758 |
| 34. | Other non-metallic mineral Products | 1.9427 |
| 35. | Iron and steel | 2.0439 |

*(Contd.)*

ANNEXURE 6.2 *(Contd.)*

| Sector No. | Name of the Sector | $LT_i$ |
|---|---|---|
| 36. | Casting and Forging | 1.7268 |
| 37. | Iron and Steel Structures | 1.6991 |
| 38. | Non-Ferrous Metals | 1.7838 |
| 39. | Metal Products | 1.6639 |
| 40. | Tractors and Agricultural Implements | 1.5759 |
| 41. | Machine Tools | 2.0401 |
| 42. | Office, Domestic and Commercial Equipments | 1.6569 |
| 43. | Other Non-electrical Machinery | 1.7859 |
| 44. | Electrical Motors | 2.2934 |
| 45. | Electric Cables and Wires | 2.2092 |
| 46. | Batteries | 1.6311 |
| 47. | Electric Household Goods | 1.8401 |
| 48. | Communication and Electric Equipments | 2.0208 |
| 49. | Other Electrical Machinery | 1.7232 |
| 50. | Ships and Boats | 1.7780 |
| 51. | Rail Equipments | 2.1851 |
| 52. | Motor Vehicles | 2.1079 |
| 53. | Motor cycles and bicycles etc. | 1.8863 |
| 54. | Other Transport Equipments | 1.9584 |
| 55. | Watches and Clocks | 1.5462 |
| 56. | Miscellaneous Manufacturing | 1.6305 |

# 7

# INTER-REGIONAL VARIATIONS IN INDIA : Some Explanations

THE DISCUSSIONS in the earlier chapters brought out two interesting findings: (i) inter-regional inequalities in the level of industrial development have revealed a tendency to decline over time in India, and (ii) the analysis of the sectoral composition of industries in the regions leaves a substantial portion of the variations in the industrial growth performance unexplained.

Given the findings, especially the second, one has to seek an explanation of this varied industrial growth in the factors other than region-specific industrial structures. A look at the various location theories might provide some valuable insight into the location dynamics. If the factors which make a region more attractive for industries are identified with the help of these theories, one might make an attempt to explain the regional variations existing in the country's industrial economy.

## CONCEPTUAL FRAMEWORK

In the early theoretical expositions, raw-material availability and transport-cost were assumed to be the most important factors for attracting industries. But with successive technological innovations, these factors were relegated into the background. Researchers laid more emphasis on the historical process of regional industrial development, linking it with the level of economic development. This in turn focused on some other factors like export-base, inter-regional trade, inter-industry linkages, urbanisation, agglomeration economies, human capital and psychic cost of the entrepreneurs, market-size and the government policies.[1]

We start with three widely accepted theoretical propositions: (i) as per capita income increases, there is a distinct shift in the sectoral allocation towards industries (Kuznets, 1957, Clark, 1957), and towards capital goods sector within industries (Haffman, 1958); (ii) regional inequalities increase in the initial phases, but decline subsequently as the economic/industrial development proceeds (Williamson, 1965); and (iii) whatever be the reasons, natural, historical, economic or political, once an economic/industrial activity starts in a particular region, it gets accentuated due to the 'snow-balling effect' via migration, inter-regional trade, transfer of capital (including human) etc. Left to the free play of market forces, these 'backwash effects' operate more strongly than the equilibrating forces leading to the desirability of government intervention (Myrdal, 1958; Hirschman, 1958).

On the basis of these proposition, we can regard regional industrialisation as a sequential process. It can be postulated that with increase in per capita income in a region, industrialisation will also be set in motion. The increase in per capita income may be (if industries were not significant) derived from agriculture, commerce (trade or services). Once income increases, there will be (i) higher demand for manufactured goods (initially consumer goods) owing to their higher income elasticity, and (ii) increase in investible surplus owing to increasing rate of savings which will facilitate industrial development in the region.

However, existing regional demand and investible capital may not be sufficient to foster industrialisation if a critical minimum level of infrastructure is not available. For, raw material can be imported even from distant places if infrastructure (transport, power, banking, etc.) is sufficiently developed.[2]

Another crucial factor is human capital, particularly entrepreneurship along with labour supply.[3] The traditional location theory postulates economic rationality of the entrepreneurs in terms of cost minimisation or profit maximisation. Of late, it has been realised that the "profit maximisation is an unsatisfactory goal for location decision makers", and "location decision, more than most managerial decisions, has to take into account psychic income's influence and other personal factors, which are not easily compatible with narrow definition of economic rationality" (Richardson, 1977: 108-109).

The difference in the entrepreneur's psychic costs and income between regions, apart from some very personal consideration, plausibly depends on his perception of a region's secure and steady environment for business, manifested in the quality (submissive) and cost (cheap) of the labour force, and the response and attitude of the government. Thus, propensity of the labour force to accept some minimum degree of discipline becomes an important factor along with the helping and welcoming government attitude towards entrepreneurs in making a region more attractive for industries.

Government also can play the role of entrepreneur in giving an initial break to the prolonged stagnant region, by locating industries. Public sector investment may also help in creating industrial clusters in a region.[4] Government may also play an important role in providing infrastructure, which is another crucial factor in accelerating the pace of industrialisation.

These and many more likewise factors will attract industries. But their level and scale of operation will further be limited by the size of the market, which again will be determined by the size of the population being served by the industries and the purchasing power thereof. It will be reflected in the per capita income, income distribution, and the type of demand, plausibly varying according to the degree of urbanisation which also, in part, reflects agglomeration and external economies.

One can, therefore, postulate that regional variations in industrial development exist to the extent of regional variations observed in the behaviour of factors such as per capita income, infrastructure, size of the market, urbanisation, agglomeration economies, entrepreneurship, docile labour force, government policies and so on. However, it may be mentioned that these factors operate in a mutually inter-dependent fashion. It is difficult to postulate a unidirectional causal relationship among them. The sources of regional industrial variations are seemingly complex and we are on much less a surer ground in isolating the impact of each of them. Difficulties in quantification of some of the variables like entrepreneurship, government attitude etc., and lack of suitable and adequate database for some other variables like inter-regional trade or agglomeration economies etc., further limit the analysis. An ideal way to examine interdependencies is to adopt a systems approach wherein the cause and effect relationships could be quantified for policy analysis. In view of the data constrain, computer software and resources, etc., the adoption of the system approach in the present context is not feasible.

## EXISTING EMPIRICAL EVIDENCES

In a pioneering study Chenery (1960) tried to understand the varied industrial growth performances of various countries in a deterministic framework using international cross-section data for the 1950s. Using regression technique, he tried to find an answer to the sources of regional variations by considering some factors like regional market size in terms of population, factor proportions, income distribution and government policies, apart form per capita income. Two of his findings are of special interest: (i) the greatest variation in output levels was found to be in the capital and intermediate goods sectors, where *economies of scale are most important*; and (ii) size of the country (in terms of population) is of crucial consequence.

Chenery's study was followed by others using a similar methodology.[5] However most of the studies are by and large cross country comparisons. Very few attempts have been made in the direction of understanding inter-regional industrial growth differentials in regions within a country.

In the inter-regional context of the Indian industrial economy, Sastry's study (1969) deserves special mention. Using a somewhat similar methodology, he tried to offer some explanation for interregional industrial variation in India for the period 1951-61. The study based on a cross-section of the States, using step-wise regression method, observed that change in per capita income and urban population explained nearly 80 per cent of the total variations in 1961. Another interesting finding was that variations in the cost of electricity across States is of no major consequence.

However, taking total net output, as Sastry did, across States to reflect the level of industrial development is somewhat misleading. It does not take care of the size of the regional economy. For example, bigger States like Uttar Pradcsh are likely to have more total output than the States like Punjab and Haryana. Thus size bias creeps into the analysis. Moreover, use of current price net output data cast doubts on the results.

Another study by Gupta (1971) using the Chenery-Taylor framework tried to offer some explanations for the better performance by large States in India. He argued that large size States perform better because of economies of scale, urbanisation and market size. Government participation was found to be of no consequence. The study further observed that better performance of the large States is owing to the unbalanced growth strategies adopted by them.

The conclusions regarding the unbalanced strategy are not only weak on technical grounds (Demery and Demery, 1972); even the data do not support it.[6] The observation about the role of the government also can be taken at best as conjectural.

Other studies have tried to explain the inter-regional industrial variations in India in terms of historical factors, infrastructure, urbanisation, agglomeration economies, entrepreneurship, docile and cheap labour, availability of industrial finance, public sector investment and government attitudes, etc.[7] However, most of the studies are partial in coverage, as they try to explain inter-regional industrial variations in terms of one or two or a small set of variables.

Here, we wish to emphasize that any attempt in the direction of understanding regional variations is most likely to remain incomplete, or partial at best, until and unless all or most of the variables (depending upon the availability of information and suitable indicators) are taken into consideration. Thus, an attempt to incorporate more and more variables appears imperative.

## THE CHOICE OF VARIABLES

### Dependent Variables

We have defined the level of industrialisation in two ways:

(i) Per capita net value added (in real terms) generated in the registered (organised) factory sector. This not only reveals the level of industrialisation across regions but also takes care of the size of the regional economies.

(ii) The proportion of net output generated in the factory (organised manufacturing) sector to the State Domestic Product (SDP) of the respective States. But it suffers from a limitation that its behaviour (share) depends not only on the performance of this sector but also that of the other sectors such as agriculture, services, etc. However it does reveal the weight of manufacturing sector in the economy of the State. Therefore, it may be termed as a structural variable.

**Independent or Explanatory Variables**

For the sake of brevity we initially divide all the independent variables into two groups viz. demand side factors and supply side factors. This classification however is arbitrary because variable like per capita income, may be treated as demand as well as supply side factor depending upon the interpretation. Thus such a classification involves value judgement; and some assumptions inevitably have to be made. Following is the scheme of the variables and their postulated behaviour with respect to the level of industrialisation.

*Demand Side Variables*

This group includes those factors which exercise a pull effect on the industries via increasing demand for manufactured goods. It is postulated that bigger the size of the market, higher will be the demand for the products of all the three major industrial sectors, viz. consumer, capital and intermediate goods.[8] These components of the demand are reflected in:

(i) *Population of the State:* reflecting size of the market;
(ii) *Per capita income*, reflecting the purchasing power of buyers; and
(iii) *Proportion of the population residing in towns with 20,000 or more population:* reflecting urban demand for modern consumer goods.
(iv) *Inter-industry demand:* is reflected by the inverse of the coefficient of specialisation. The assumption here is that more diversified is the industrial structure of the State, higher will be the inter-industry demand[9] for the capital and intermediate goods, leading to a higher level of industrialisation by its pull effect.
(v) *Level of agricultural mechanisation:* is measured by a composite index of (a) number of tractors per 1000 hectares; (b) number of oil engines and pumping sets used for the purpose of irrigation per 1000 hectares; and (c) use of NPK (fertilizer) kg/per ha. It is postulated that higher the level of agricultural mechanisation, higher will be the demand for industrial products, which also will act as a pull factor for boosting

industrialisation in the region.

*Supply Side Factors*

This group consists of factors which make a region more attractive for locating industries. The major factors considered and their postulated relationship with the level of industrialisation is as follows:

(i) *Availability of Raw Material:* The finding, that the industrial structure of most of the States is still dominated by the raw material oriented industries (Chapter 5), suggests that the spatial variability in the availability of raw material will reflect the existing inter-regional industrial variations. This is reflected by the per capita output in forestry, mining and agriculture (Commercial crops).

(ii) *Agglomeration Economies:* The analysis assumes that agglomeration economies are found in urban areas, and that regional agglomeration economies to a great extent depend on the size and spatial distribution of its urban centres (above a threshold size) (Richardson, 1973). We define agglomeration economies as "a composite index of (a) the number of urban centres (above one lakh population) per 1000 km$^2$ of area; (b) relative size of urban settlements, with more weight given to the large centres, and (c) the average inter-city distance between them. Thus the larger the number of cities, the larger the relative size of the leading cities and the smaller is average inter-urban distance, the greater are regional agglomeration economies" (Richardson, 1973: 179). We assume that higher the level of agglomeration index, higher will be the level of industrial development of a region.

(iii) *Infrastructure Index:* It is a composite index of (a) transport network, i.e., the length of roads and railways per 1000 km$^2$ of area and per lakh persons. (b) power availability per capita and rates per kwh; and (c) number of bank offices per 1000 km$^2$ and per lakh population, across States. It is envisaged that higher the level of infrastructural development, higher will be the level of industrialisation.

(iv) *Government Participation:* It is argued that the favourable attitude of the government makes some regions more attractive for investment than others. We divide government participation into two groups viz. direct government participation and indirect participation. The former participation indicates the entrepreneurial role of government, while latter reflects role of government as promotor agency. Though there is no direct measure to quantify the attitude, a composite index of the following indicators is likely to reflect the phenomenon, at least in a conjectural manner:

(1) The direct participation is measured in terms of per capita gross block investment in public sector undertaking and
(2) indirect government participation is reflected by a composite index of (a) per capita loan sanctioned by the non-banking financial institutions such as State Financial Corporations, Industrial Development Bank of India, Industrial Finance Corporation of India, etc. and (b) industrial licences issued to the various States. We postulate a positive relationship between the level of industrial development and the government participations – direct and indirect.

(v) *Entrepreneurship:* Entrepreneurship has widely been recognised as a crucial determinant of the industrial development. Therefore, we postulate that higher the availability of entrepreneurs in a region, higher will be its level of development. Here we make a distinction between two segments of entrepreneurs; (a) local or regional entrepreneurs, who, by and large, are small scale entrepreneurs, are not very mobile and tend to set up their small scale units within or in the vicinity of their place of origin, because of capital constraints, and (b) large-scale entrepreneurs, who operate at the national level and are not tied to any specific region *per se* because of dearth of capital. They tend to move wherever they perceive an opportunity and conducive environment for their unit. Therefore, the first category reflects the availability of entrepreneurship at the local/region level, whereas, the later reflects the preference of the entrepreneurs for a region.

The local availability of entrepreneurs is being measured by a composite index consisting of region specific composite index of (a) number of small scale industrial units per lakh of population; (b) credit-deposit ratio in the commercial banks; and (c) per capita financial assistance disbursed by State Financial Corporations. While first ndicator crudely reflects the entrepreneurship of the population, the other two variables reflect its entrepreneurial ability.

The preference of large-scale entrepreneurs is measured in terms of a composite index of (a) letters of intent for industries issued to a region; (b) per capita assistance disbursed by all India financial institutions; and (c) registrations with the Directorate General of Technical Development (DGTD). In the case of the first indicator, it is assumed that an industrialist will actually apply for a licence only if he finds a location profitable enough for his investment. Similarly, the other two indicators will also reflect his actual choice of a particular region.

(vi) *Availability of Skilled Labour:* Availability of skilled labour at a cheaper rate is seen conducive to the industrial development. We measured it by a composite index of the number of persons undergoing technical training per lakh population which reflects the quantum; and average wages of workers across space in India which reflects the price.

(vii) *Efficiency Wage:* An entrepreneur is likely to be willing to pay even higher wages if he is able to get better returns, than otherwise. Therefore, what matter is efficiency wages than nominal wages. It is argued that the 'efficiency wages' are likely to be lower in those regions which have above average productivity and output growth (Kaldor, 1970). Therefore, we postulate a negative relationship between 'efficiency wages' and the level of industrialisation. Efficiency wage is defined as the index of change in money wages relative to the change in productivity, i.e. V/T where W is an index of money wages (in constant terms) and T is an index of total factor productivity (Richardson, 1973).

(viii) *Labour Indiscipline:* It is argued that submissive and docile labour is more conducive to a healthy industrial climate.[10] But it is difficult to evolve a direct measure of discipline in the labour force. However, there are some measures which, to some extent, reflect the magnitude of indiscipline. So we use them as a proxy for the nature of labour force. It is measured through a composite index of (a) number of mandays lost per 1000 workers due to industrial disputes; and (b) number of trade unions per 1000 workers.[11] Here we postulate a negative relationship between the magnitude of these factors and industrial development at the regional level.

All the above-stated factors are expected to behave in the postulated fashion and affect the levels of industrial development across regions in India, as reflected by the per capita value added generated in the registered factory (organised) sector and the share of net output generated in the organised sector in respective States' SDP.

## DATABASE AND METHODOLOGY

The database for the aforesaid variables and the methods adopted for constructing respective indices, wherever necessary have been described in the Annexure to the chapter.

Now we are interested in finding some clues to answer the following questions: (i) What factors explain interregional variations in the level of industrial development in India between 1961 and 1978?; and (ii) Which of the factors contributed to the decline in the inter-regional inequalities (Chapter 4) in the level of industrial development.

Therefore, first we focus our attention on the empirical verification of the extent to which *inter-state variation in the level of industrial development arise due to the variations in the level of various factors operating in terms of demand and supply side variables.*

The analysis is based on a cross-section of the States at three different points of time, i.e. 1961, 1969, 1978, we have estimated single equation linear models using the method of ordinary least square, and have followed step-wise regression procedure, wherein usual assumptions of classical general linear regression model about the disturbance term apply. Though we recognise the interdependent nature of relationship in such models and consequent simultaneity bias in using unidirectional causal framework, it is assumed that the letter captures the essential elements determining the inter-regional variations.

In the first stage, we have separately estimated the regressions for the demand and supply side variables for each point of time (1961,

1969, 1978) and then for a pool of these cross-sections of States over time. In the second stage we have combined the demand and supply side variables and estimated the relationships to understand the overall behaviour of these variables.[12]

In our next endeavour we made an attempt to isolate some of the major factors which contribute towards decline in the regional industrial inequalities. Here also we adopted the same procedure, i.e., step wise regression method. In the first instance we worked out the inequality indices for both the dependent variables, i.e. per capita value added generated in registered factory sector across States; and proportion of the SDP generated in the organised manufacturing sector of the respective States. Independent variables considered are: population, per capita income, availability of raw-material, infrastructure, financial availability, government participation, availability of technical workforce and labour indiscipline.[13] The inequality indices for dependent variables were regressed on the inequality indices of the independent variables. All the inequality indices, measured in terms of the coefficient of variation were worked out for each of the individual years between 1961 and 1978, across States.

The postulated behaviour of the variables and the equations used for various groups, using step-wise regression procedure, are specified below.

*Specification of the variables:* All the variables considered to explain the inter regional variations and reduction in the interregional inequalities are specified as:

| *Name of the variables* | *Connotations* |
|---|---|
| 1. Dependent variables, i.e. per capita value added generated in the registered factory sector; and proportion of SDP generated in the organised manufacturing sector across the the States, as the case may be | $Y$ |
| 2. Size of the market as reflected by the population of the States | $X_1$ |
| 3. Purchasing power of the buyers as reflected by per capita income of the region | $X_2$ |

4. Urban demand for modern industrial products as reflected by the proportion of urban population in the state, residing in 20000 + population town $X_3$
5. Inter-industry demand as reflected by inverse of the coefficient of specialisation $X_4$.
6. Demand for industrial goods emanating from agriculture sector represented by index of the level of agriculture mechanisation $X_5$
7. Region specific availability of raw materials, represented by per capita output in forestry, mining and cash crops in agriculture $X_6$
8. Agglomeration economies as represented by region specific agglomeration index $X_7$
9. Level of infrastructure development (infrastructure), represented by an index of transport, power and banking facilities. $X_8$
10. Direct government participation as reflected by per capita gross block investment made into public sector undertakings. $X_9$
11. Indirect government participation measured in terms of a index of financial sanction by the various non-banking financial institutions and industrial licences granted by the government. $X_{10}$
12. Availability of skills as represented by an index of the number of persons undergoing technical training per lakh population and wage rate per worker $X_{11}$
13. Efficiency wages, reflecting the wages and productivity in a region $X_{12}$
14. Degree of labour militancy measured in terms of man day lost per 1000 workers and number of trade unions per 1000 workers $X_{13}$
15. Relative size of the urban centres with above one lakh population $A_1$
16. Number of urban centres with lakh + population $A_2$
17. Average inter-urban distance $A_3$
18. Extent of transport facility $T$
19. Availability of power $p$
20. Existing banking facilities $c$

*Variable in the Inequality Index Form (I)*

21. Size of the market (population) $I_1$
22. Purchasing power of the buyers (per capita income) $I_2$
23. Availability of raw material (region specific) $I_3$
24. Infrastructural development level $I_4$
25. Direct government participation $I_5$
26. Indirect government participation $I_6$
27. Inequality indices for the dependent variables *(Y)* $I_y$
28. Error terms $e, e_1, e_2, u$ etc.
29. Time variable $t$
30. Parameters $b_0, b_1, \ldots b_{13}$

**Demand and Supply Side Specifications**

Among the variables specified above, variables $X_1$ to $X_5$ are considered to represent the demand side. Accordingly following linear equation has been postulated:

$$Y = b_0 + b_1X_1 + b_2X_2 + b_3X_3 + b_4X_4 + b_5X_5 + e$$

Similarly the variables $X_6$ to $X_{13}$ are considered to represent supply side variable; and the linear equation postulated is an follows:

$$Y = b_0 + b_6X_6 + b_7X_7 + b_8X_8 + b_9X_9 + b_{10}X_{10} + b_{11}X_{11} + b_{12}X_{12} + b_{13}X_{13} + e$$

Where Y is either per capita value added generated in the registered factory sector, or the proportion of SDP generated in the organised manufacturing sector of the States, as the case may be. In the analysis the estimated equations are presented for each of the three years, i.e. 1961, 1969 and 1978; and also pooling information for all the years.

In another set of equations we have considered all the variables, viz. all the demand side and supply size variables together in the above framework.

**Other Specifications**

We have also considered some other specifications by placing emphasis on agglomeration economies and infrastructural components separately. The factors such as relative size of the urban centres with lakh + population ($A_1$) and number of urban centres with lakh + population ($A_2$) and average inter-urban distance ($A_3$) are assumed to constitute the agglomeration economies; while transport ($t$), power availability ($p$) and banking facilities ($c$) are assumed to represent the infrastructural components. The equations are specified as:

$$Y = b_0+b_1A_1+b_2A_2+b_3A_3+e_1 \text{ and}$$

$$Y = b_0+b_1t+b_2p+b_3c+e_2$$

Following the earlier specifications, the above equations are estimated separately for each year and also for the years pooled together.

**Time Series Variations in Inter-regional Inequalities**

We have considered two alternative specifications wherein the variables, both dependent and independent are transformed into the inequality form. For the equation representing per capita income generated in the registered factory sector and the corresponding independent variables, the Thiel's index of inequality has been constructed; while in the other case we have resorted to the coefficient of variations. Specifications of the equation are:

$$I_y = b_0+b_1I_1+b_2I_2+b_3I_3+b_4I_4+b_5I_5+b_6I_6+t+u$$

It may be mentioned that in this model we have introduced time variable ($t$) to isolate the time trend effect.

## EMPIRICAL RESULTS

As elaborated in the methodology, the results have also been discussed in stages. First, the discussion concentrates on the behaviour of demand side variables, followed by supply side variables. The behaviour of overall variables is discussed subsequently. As a digression, a disaggregated analysis is carried out for sub-variables constituting agglomeration economies and infrastructure, separately. The step-wise regression results corresponding to the above specification are displayed in Tables 7.1 to 7.4.[14] In the second part, we have speculated on some factors which contribute to the decline in the inter-regional industrial inequalities over time. Results of this exercise are presented in Table 7.5.

## Behavioural Factors and the Inter-Regional Variations

### *Demand Side Factors*

The regression show that the values of $\bar{R}^{2}$ ($R^2$ adjusted for degree of freedom) are statistically significant at one per cent level in all the years (see Table 7.1). The results show that in the year 1961, the model explains approximately 69 per cent of the total variation in the level of industrial development across States in India. This explanation is offered by the region specific purchasing power of consumers and inter-industry demand. Both coefficients are significant at one per cent level with right signs as postulated. In 1969, the explanatory power of the model increases to approximately 79 per cent and along with the earlier two, one more variable, viz. the demand for industrial products from agricultural sector also emerges as important in explaining the total variation. However, the sign of this variable is found to be negative (opposite to the postulated one).[15] The impact of other two variables became more pronounced in this year.

Almost similar trend is observed even in 1978, except that the explanatory power of the model declines to aproximately 63 per cent. Although similar variables appear to explain the inter-regional variations in per capita value added generated in the registered factory sector (PCVAFS) the influence of these variables is seen to increase (almost doubled) over the period. Given the pattern of change in the behaviour of the explanatory variables, there is a strong reason to believe that the demand from agriculture sector is contributing adversely to the PCVAFS. In view of the fact that data used in these equations are cross-sectional type, the result exhibits long run nature of the relationships. Therefore it can be argued that the transfer of resources from industry to agriculture, without striking a balance in the industrial developmental activities may adversely affect the level of industrialisation.

TABLE 7.1: Estimated Regression Equations by considering Demand Side Variables

$(Y = b_0 + b_1X_1 + b_2X_2 + b_3X_3 + b_4X_4 + b_5X_5 + e)$

| Dependent Variable (Y): PCVAFS | | | | $\bar{R}^{2}$ | No. of observations | Increase in the $\bar{R}^{2}$ owing to |
|---|---|---|---|---|---|---|
| (a) *Dependent Variable (Y): PCVAFS* | | | | | | |
| 1. $Y_1$ = 44.2963 + | 0.0784*$X_2$ + | 0.1167*$X_4$ | | 0.6896* | 17 | $X_2$=0.5383; $X_4$=0.1821 |
| | (0.0175) | (0.0309) | | | | |
| 2. $Y_2$ = -86.6620 + | 0.1314*$X_2$ + | 0.2315*$X_4$ | -0.7677*$X_5$ | 0.7910* | 18 | $X_4$=0.4314; $X_2$=0.2573; $X_5$=0.1391 |
| | (0.0232) | (0.0402) | (0.2282) | | | |
| 3. $Y_3$ =-138.6260 + | 0.2022*$X_2$ | 0.5152*$X_4$ | -1.3231**$X_5$ | 0.6315* | 18 | $X_4$=0.4160; $X_2$=0.2122; $X_5$=0.0681 |
| | (0.0562) | (0.1247) | (0.7456) | | | |
| 4. $Y_4$ =-152.7429 | 0.2332*$X_2$ | 0.1854*$X_4$ | -0.8754*$X_5$ | 0.5499* | 53 | $X_2$=0.3441; $X_4$=0.2057; $X_5$=0.0345 |
| | (0.0397) | (0.0780) | (0.3855) | | | |
| (b) *Dependent Variable (Y): PSDPOS* | | | | | | |
| 1. $Y_1$= -5.0178 + | 0.0093**$X_2$ + | 0.0292*$X_4$ | | 0.6135* | 17 | $X_4$=0.5052; $X_2$=0.1806 |
| | (0.0041) | (0.0072) | | | | |
| 2. $Y_2$ = -5.819 + | 0.0110**$X_2$ + | 0.0322*$X_4$ | -0.0676**$X_5$ | 0.5021* | 18 | $X_4$=0.4201; $X_2$=0.0690; $X_5$=0.1007 |
| | (0.0048) | (0.0084) | (0.0264) | | | |
| 3. $Y_3$ = -1.0712 + | 0.0102***$X_2$ + | 0.0379*$X_4$ | -0.0886***$X_5$ | 0.5214* | 18 | $X_4$=0.5211; $X_2$=0.0561; $X_5$=0.0023 |
| 4. $Y_4$ = -4.3676 + | 0.0074**$X_2$ + | 0.0325*$X_4$ | -0.0749**$X_5$ | 0.5786* | 53 | $X_4$=0.4825; $X_2$=0.0491; $X_5$=0.0713 |
| | (0.0036) | (0.0043) | (0.0352) | | | |

*Notes:* (1) The suffix 1, 2, 3 and 4 of the variable Y represent the years 1961. 1969, 1978 and pooled data (ph) respectively.
(2) Figures in parentheses are the standard errors of b coefficients.
(3) Only final results are presented. For notations please see the test.
(4) PCVAFS stands for per capita values added generated in the registered factory sector; while PSDPOS connotes proportion of SDP generated in the organised manufacturing sector.
* Significant at 1 per cent level of significance
** Significant at 5 per cent level of significance
*** Significant at 10 per cent level of significance

*Source:* As per the text.

The picture remains, by and large, similar even when the three cross sections are pooled together. However, the regression coefficient of these variables show a different pattern when compared to the year-wise results. This is expected in view of the fact that the pooled regression equations represent a mongrel structure rather than short or long term.

*Supply Side Factors*

We regressed each of the dependent variables on various supply side factors viz. availability of raw material, agglomeration economies, level of infrastructure, direct government participation, indirect government participation, availability of skills, efficiency wages and extent of labour militancy. The values of adjusted multiple correlation coefficient ($R^{-2}$) are significant at one per cent level in all the years; moreover the magnitude of the $R^{-2}$ values for the individual year ranges between 0.75 and 0.92. However, the explanatory power of the models declines over time.[16]

In 1961, indirect government participation along with infrastructure, agglomeration economies and efficiency wages explains about 92 per cent of the total variations observed in the level of industrialisation across States in India. Out of these, only indirect government participation explains approximately 79 per cent of the total variation followed by efficiency wages, infrastructure and agglomeration economies, in the order (see Table 7.2).

A structural shift is observed in 1969 where indirect government participation, agglomeration economies remain important, while infrastructure and efficiency wages are seen to be not important. Degree of labour militancy emerges as an important factor in explaining these variations in 1969. But like agricultural demand in demand side variables; labour militancy has opposite sign to the postulated (negative) one.[17] However, one can expect such behaviour of the variable at least in Indian conditions, where industries are concentrated in a few developed regions of the country. Since these regions have a relatively longer history of industrialisation, it is quite likely that the labour force may become politically more conscious of its rights in these developed regions. Consequently it tends to fight out its claims, leading to more troubled days in such pockets. And that is why, probably, we encounter a positive association between the levels of industrial development and the labour militancy. This phenomenon, however, appears to be short lived, and in 1978 it has right type of (negative) sing.

In the year 1978, infrastructure emerged again, after a lapse, as a dominant factor, explaining approximately 42 per cent of the total variations. It was followed sequentially by agglomeration economies, indirect government participation, availability of raw material and labour militancy. All variables taken together explain approximately 75 per cent of the total variation in 1978.

Another interesting feature is that the availability of raw material is significant only in 1978. In the earlier period it is not so (see Table 7.2). The reason can be traced in the development process itself. when the level of industrialisation in a region is very low, probably it will export its raw material to developed regions. But as growth proceeds, the region itself will tend to industrialise, using its own resources to begin with, in the early phases of industrialisation.

The possibilities of some such thing taking place in India cannot be denied. Because more serious efforts in the direction of balanced regional development in the country started only in the 1970s. Emphasis, to some extent, was also given on the use of locally available resources and skills. That is why, plausibly only in 1978[18] the availability of raw material emerges as one of the more important explanatory variable.

Despite the fact that there is evidence to suggest that structure has been changing over time, we tried to see if some significant deviation from earlier results takes place if the three cross sections are considered together.[19] We found that the pooled regressions results, do not confirm the pattern of any single years; but three most important factor viz. agglomeration economies, infrastructure, and indirect government participation emerge significant. In other years also these factors explained most of the variations along with other factors Another interesting fact is that initially government's indirect participation was most important explanatory variable. But over time some other factors like infrastructure and agglomeration economies became prominent replacing indirect government participation.

When we compare the results of first set with the second set, the picture, by and large, remains the same except that infrastructure dominates the scene most of the time. Agglomeration economies and government's indirect participation, though important till 1969, remain

TABLE 7.2: Estimated Regression Equation by considering Supply Side Variables

$(Y = b_0 + b_6X_6 + b_7X_7 + b_8X_8 + b_9X_9 + b_{10}X_{10} + b_{11}X_{11} + b_{12}X_{12} + b_{13}X_{13} + e)$

| Dependent Variable (Y): PCVAFS | $\bar{R}^2$ | No. of observations | Increase in the $\bar{R}^2$ owing to |
|---|---|---|---|
| (a) *Dependent Variable (Y): PCVAFS* | | | |
| 1. $Y_1$ = 8.7396 + 0.7338**$X_7$ + (0.3965) 0.2711**$X_8$ (0.0990) +0.2735*$X_{10}$- (0.0517) 0.0571*$X_{12}$ | 0.9227* | 17 | $X_{10}$=0.7878; $X_{12}$=0.0982; $x_8$=0.0394; X=0.0165 |
| 2. $Y_2$ = 13.9556 + 1.2369**$X_7$ + (0.6251) 0.4457*$X_{10}$ (0.1087) +0.0062**$X_{13}$ (0.0043) | 0.8043* | 18 | $X_{10}$=0.7451; $X_7$=0.0702; $X_{13}$=0.0235 |
| 3. $Y_3$ = -45.7476 + 1.3413**x6 (0.6001) +2.1072*$X_7$ + (0.4960) 0.9314*$X_8$ (0.1510) +1.9088*$X_{10}$ - (0.4874) 0.1504***$X_{13}$ (0.0927) | 0.7539* | 18 | $X_8$=0.4232; $X_7$=0.1362; $X_{10}$=0.1185 $X_6$=0.0795; $X_{13}$=0.0723 |
| 4. $Y_4$ = -35.66 +1.1025*x7 (0.3036) +0.3621*$X_8$ + (0.1271) 0.8138*$X_{10}$ (0.3241) | 0.4736* | 53 | $X_7$=0.2499; $X_8$=0.1882; $X_{10}$=0.0965 |
| (b) *Dependent Variable (Y): PSDPOS* | | | |
| 1. $Y_1$= 2.5117 + 0.3454*$X_7$ + (0.1066) 0.0489**$X_8$ + (0.0210) 0.0688*$X_{10}$ (0.0151) -0.0181**$X_{12}$ + (0.0089) 0.0500**$X_{13}$ (0.0297) | 0.8287 | 17 | $X_{10}$=0.4724 $X_7$=0.2863; $X_8$=0.0465; $X_{12}$=0.0463; $X_{13}$=0.0305 |
| 2. $Y_2$ = 3.9403 + 0.3227*$X_7$ + (0.1180) 0.2131*$X_8$ + (0.0542) 0.0838**$X_{10}$ (0.0315) | 0.5558* | 18 | $X_8$=0.3800; $X_7$=0.1381; $X_{10}$=0.0900 |
| 3. $Y_3$ = 15.1941 + 0.0979**$X_6$ + (0.0531) 0.3225*$X_8$ (0.0953) | 0.3783** | 18 | $X_8$=0.3272; $X_6$=0.1242; |
| 4. $Y_4$ = -12.6289 + 0.1306*$X_7$ + (0.0394) 0.0525*$X_8$ + (0.0042) +0.0074**$X_{10}$ (0.033) 0.0053**$X_{13}$ (0.0024) | 0.3944* | 53 | $X_8$=0.2185; $X_7$=0.1100; $X_{10}$=0.0597; $X_{13}$=0.0526 |

*Note:* As mentioned in Table 7.1

*Source*: As per the text.

no more significant by 1978. It is because of the fact that infrastructure is more strongly correlated with the proportion of SDP generated in the organised manufacturing sector, than agglomeration economies or indirect government participation, at least in 1969 and 1978. The overall picture of the pooled data is somewhat similar to that of the first set; however labour militancy appears in the second set while it is not in the first set.

*Overall Factors*

At this stage all the demand side and supply side variables were taken together and the dependent variables were regressed on them. All the regressions were found to be significant at one per cent level, as revealed by respective $R^{-2}$. Here also, the trend in the overall explanatory power of the models was found to be declining over time (see Table 7.3).

Table 7.3 reveals that both demand and supply side variables explain approximately 95 per cent of the total variation in the level of industrial development and approximately 79 per cent of the total explanation is provided by indirect government participation alone in 1961. Consumer's purchasing power and inter-industry demand from the demand side and infrastructure, agglomeration economies, efficiency wages and indirect government participation among the supply side factors, emerge as significant factors. All the signs of *b* coefficients are as postulated.

In 1969, consumer's purchasing power loses its place to the demand from the agriculture sector; while inter-industry demand improves its impact by becoming more significant among the demand side variables. Among supply side variables agglomeration economies and indirect government participation retain their significance. In addition labour militancy also emerges as a significant variable. The sings of all the b coefficients are as expected except for the demand from the agriculture sector and the labour militancy. All variables taken together explain approximately 94 per cent of the total variation.

By 1978, inter-industry demand, agglomeration economies and infrastructure are the only factors which explain the regional variations. Taken together these three factors explain about 62 per cent of the total variations. The impact of the remaining factors seems to have declined over time. Another interesting feature of the regression

TABLE 7.3: Estimated Regression Equations by Considering both Demand and Supply Side Variable Together

$$(Y = b_0 + b_1X_1 + b_2X_2 + b_3X_3 + b_4X_4 + b_5X_5 + b_6X_6 + b_7X_7 + b_8X_8 + b_9X_9 + b_{10}X_{10} + b_{11}X_{11} + b_{12}X_{12} + b_{13}X_{13} + e)$$

| Dependent Variable (Y):PCVAFS | | | | $\bar{R}^2$ | No. of observations | Increase in the $\bar{R}^2$ owing to |
|---|---|---|---|---|---|---|
| (a) *Dependent Variable (Y): PCVAFS* | | | | | | |
| 1. $Y_1$ = -8.2837 | 1.007*$X_2$ + | +0.0523*$X_4$ | +0.3101*$X_7$ | 0.9503* | 17 | $X_{10}$=0.7878; $X_{12}$=0.0982; $X_2$=0.0393; |
| | (0.3323) | (0.0213) | (0.0814) | | | $X_4$=0.0165 |
| | +0.1263**$X_8$ | +0.3551*$X_{10}$ | -0.0876**$X_{12}$ | | | |
| | (0.0520 | (0.0410) | | | | |
| 2. $Y_2$ = -35.0963 + | 0.0594*$X_4$ | -0.9712*$X_5$ | +1.5348*$X_7$ | 0.9379* | 18 | $X_{10}$=0.7451; $X_7$=0.1912; $X_4$=0.0186; |
| | (0.0132) | (0.2543) | (0.2004) | | | $X_5$=0.0122 |
| | +0.1462*$X_{10}$ | +0.0638*$X_{13}$ | | | | |
| | (0.0125) | (0.0209) | | | | |
| 3. $Y_3$ =-196.6175 + | 0.3111*$X_4$ | +3.4026**$X_7$ | +1.4026**$X_8$ | 0.6195* | 18 | $X_4$=0.4160; $X_8$=0.1608; $X_7$=0.1080 |
| | (0.0905) | (1.4084) | (0.5617) | | | |
| 4. $Y_4$ =-152 | +0.2349*$X_2$ | +0.3452*$X_4$ + | -1.0676*$X_5$ | 0.5236* | 53 | $X_2$=0.3441; $X_4$=0.1585; $X_7$=0.0316 |
| | (0.0485) | (0.0717) | (0.6594) | | | |
| | +0.7558*$X_7$ | +0.4347**$X_8$ | | | | $X_5$=0.0584 $X_8$=0.0196 |
| | (0.3150) | (0.2313) | | | | |

(*Contd.*)

Overall, the results reveal some interesting features which have certain important policy implications. For example, supply side variables predominate the scene in the early phase. In the later stages, demand side variables become more important. Similarly in both sub-sets indirect government participation is relevant only in the early phases of industrialisation. Later on industrialisation appears to become a self propellant process. Another notable feature is the presence of efficiency wages in the year 1961 only. Probably in the latter stages the compatibility between the wages and productivity would have been maintained across States.[20] In consequence this variable seems to be not an important one in explaining the variations.

## Further Evidence on Agglomeration Economies and Infrastructure

From the above discussion we observe that agglomeration economies and infrastructure are the two important factors from the supply side which substantially explain the regional variations; and have a strong bearing on the industrial growth. Since both these variables are a combination of some of the important factors which are likely to effect the pace of industrial growth; it might be rewarding to look at the behaviour of these individual components. We discuss the influence of these two major variables, viz. agglomeration economies and infrastructure, separately.

### *Agglomeration Economies*

In the foregoing analysis we have defined agglomeration economies as an index of three major components, viz., number of cities above a threshold size per 1000 km$^2$, their relative size with more weight given to the large centres, and the distance between them in a region.[21] The first two components are postulated to influence positively while the last one negatively.

The step-wise regression results are given in Table 7.4. All the models for various years are found to have a good fit, significant at 90 per cent level of confidence. The overall explanatory power of the models seems to be declining over time and the relative size of urban centres is the only variable appearing in the final results.[22] The *b* coefficient for all the years is found to be statistically significant at one per cent level and with right sig.[23]

Table 7.4 reveals that in 1961, a unitory change in the relative size of the urban centres led to 0.2679 unit increase in the level of industrialisation whereas in 1978 it was affected only by 0.1124 unit. It implies that in the early phase, the size of the urban centres plays relatively more important role in the process of industrialisation. Once industrialisation reaches a certain level of development, importance of such centres possibly starts declining. This may be owing to several reasons: (1) some spill-over of industries starts taking place from big and busy urban centres to smaller ones because of the prohibitive cost of the land and other services in the urban agglomeration; (2) diseconomies start operating after a certain stage; (3) probably restrictions imposed by the government, on any further expansion of industries in certain areas may direct growth in some relatively smaller towns.[24]

## INFRASTRUCTURE

The index of infrastructure comprises availability of transport (roads and railways), power and banking facilities. Step-wise regression results are displayed in Table 7.5. All the regressions and *b* coefficients are significant at 99 per cent level of confidence except for 1961 where the level of confidence is 95 per cent. In the present case also only one factor, namely power availability, explains regional variation in a significant manner. The explanatory power of the model has gradually increased over the period. Moreover the influence of power availability has also improved over the period. A unit increase is power availability has induced 0.3946 units increase in the level of industrialisation in the initial period. While it was 1.3032 units increase in 1978. The power being the major constraint for industrial stagnation in India, (Ahluwalia, 1985); and the positive feature of the results obtained would highlight the need for a larger allocation for investment in the power sector.

### Declining Regional Inequalities: An Explanation

The above account helps us in understanding the role of various factors in determining inter-regional variation, but it is not adequate in explaining the reduction in regional inequalities. In consequence a

TABLE 7.4: Estimated Regression Equations — Considering the Components of the Agglomeration Economics and Infrastructure $(Y = b_0 + b_1A_1 + b_2A_2 + b_3A_3 + C_1)$ and $(Y = b_0 + b_1T + b_2P + b_3c + c_2)$

| Agglomeration Economies | $\bar{R}^2$ | n | Infrastructure | $\bar{R}^2$ | n |
|---|---|---|---|---|---|
| (a) *Dependent Variable (Y): FCVAFS* | | | (a) *Dependent Variable (Y): PCVAFS* | | |
| 1. $Y_1$ = 32.4997 + 0.2679*$A_1$<br>(0.0330) | 0.8018* | 7 | 1. $Y_1$ = -3.2685 + 0.03946*P<br>(0.1848) | 0.4013* | 17 |
| 2. $Y_2$ = 50.2702 + 0.183*$A_1$<br>(0.0283) | 0.7072* | 18 | 2. $Y_2$ = -36.1792 + 0.4708*P<br>(0.1598) | 0.3874* | 18 |
| 3. $Y_3$ = 71.6391 + 0.1124*$A_1$<br>(0.0404) | 0.2837*** | 18 | 3. $Y_3$ = 76.3484 + 1.3032*P<br>(0.4551) | 0.3121* | 18 |
| 4. $Y_4$ = 53.3082 + 0.1805*$A_1$<br>(0.0210) | 0.5826* | 53 | 4. $Y_4$ = 45.0227 + 0.4435*P<br>(0.1068) | 0.2377* | 53 |
| (b) *Dependent Variable (Y): FSDPOS* | | | (b) *Dependent Variable (Y): PSDPOS* | | |
| 1. $Y_1$ = 45.1912 + 0.1389*$A_1$<br>(0.0293) | 0.5663* | 17 | 1. $Y_1$ = - 4.7434 + 0.4629*P<br>(0.2092) | 0.2623** | 17 |
| 2. $Y_2$ = 62.8055 + 0.0891*$A_1$<br>(0.0293) | 0.3260*** | 18 | 2. $Y_2$ = - 43.5000 + 0.5829*P<br>(0.2036) | 0.3219* | 18 |
| 3. $Y_3$ = 71.9979 + 0.0624***$A_1$<br>(0.0354) | 0.3102*** | 18 | 3. $Y_3$ = 87.0555 + 0.08373*P<br>(0.2673) | 0.3546* | 18 |
| 4. $Y_4$ = 32.8701 + 0.1029*$A_1$<br>(0.0187) | 0.3010* | 53 | 4. $Y_4$ = 27.3507 + 0.5621*P<br>(0.1989) | 0.3247* | 53 |

*Note*: As mentioned in Table 7.1.
*Source*: As per the text.

separate analysis is carried out, where (as discussed in the methodology) we regressed inequality indices of the dependent variables (IY) on the inequality indices of some of the crucial independent variables (depending on the availability of time series information). It is hoped that the analysis would help in isolating factors (among other) responsible for the reduction in the inter-regional inequalities. The period covered is 1961 to 1978. The postulated model is as:

$$IY = b_0+b_1I_1+b_2I_2+b_3I_3+b_4I_4+b_5I_5+b_6I_6+t+u$$

The postulated behaviour of the various factors, in terms of equality indices measured in terms of coefficient of variation, is that if inter-regional inequalities in the variables like the market size ($I_1$), purchasing power of the buyers ($I_2$), availability of raw materials ($I_3$), level of infrastructure ($I_4$) and indirect government participation ($I_6$) become more uniform across space and over time, the inter-regional inequalities across States would lead to decline as a consequence. Thus the postulated effect of these independent factors is positive w.r.t. the dependent variables.[25] Direct government participation ($I_5$) need some elaboration before we postulate any behaviour of this factor. As envisaged in various government policy Statements and plan documents, public sector investment (here defined as direct government participation) was supposed to be tilting in favour of the backward regions of the country, in order the achieve balanced regional development. Given the objective, one would expect that the pattern of public sector investment is discriminated in favour of the backward areas, at least till they are able to stand on their own. Under these circumstances, the inequalities in the quantum of the public sector investment across States will, at least, not decline. Consequently there will be a negative association between such investment ($I_5$) and the level of regional industrial development ($IY$). We also introduce time variable ($t$) in order to isolate the time trend, if any, and $u$ is the error term. The results are presented in Table 7.5.

Analysis of Table 7.5 reveals that availability of raw material, direct government participation (as reflected by per capita gross block investment in the central/public sector undertakings), and indirect government participation (as reflected by a composite index of per capita availability of the institutional finance and industrial licences issued to various regions) emerge as the major contributory factors that determine the inequalities. The models are significant at 99 per cent level of confidence and are able to explain approximately 67 per cent of the total variations in per capita value added generated in the registered manufacturing sectors across States; and 62 per cent variations in the proportion of SDP generated in the organised manufacturing sector, across the various States.

Out of these three factors, the most significant contribution is that of direct government participation which explains approximately 49 per cent of the total variation.[26] Indirect government participation and availability of raw material follow in that order. The signs in case of both the types of government participation are unexpected. Only raw material availability has the postulated sign. What are the implications of the observed signs, especially the opposite ones?

Let us take the case of direct government participation first. What emerges from the table is that the inequality in public sector investment (per capita) has influenced positively the inequalities in the level of industrial development over time. For regional inequalities, in the level of industrialisation and per capita gross block investment, move in the same direction, or in other words have a declining trends. However, it may be mentioned that the decline in these two inequality indices has altogether different implications.[28] Therefore, one has to consider these results with a bit more caution.

What has actually happened is that in the early sixties, public sector investment favoured backward regions such as Bihar, Orissa and Madhya Pradesh etc. But as the sectoral emphasis changed in favour of petrochemicals and electronics and some other sophisticated industries, especially after sixties, the public sector investment also got diverted to some better off regions such as Gujarat, Maharashtra and Karnataka etc. (see Alagh *et al.*, 1982). This probably resulted into a decline in the overall regional inequalities.[29] Therefore, it appears that instead of helping in reducing the inter-regional inequalities, the public sector investment over time played a neutral or even a negative role. It casts serious doubt on the efficacy of the public policies, geared towards the objective of achieving balanced regional industrial development through public sector investment.

This observation is further strengthened by the negative sign of indirect government participation. It implies that the flow of institutional finances and industrial licences have kept on favouring the

TABLE 7.5: Estimated Regression Equations for Interregional Inequality Trends

(Equation: $IY = b_0 + b_1I_1 + b_2I_2 + b_3I_3 + b_4I_4 + b_5I_5 + b_6I_6 + u$)

| Dependent Variable (Y):PCVAFS | | | | $\overline{R}^2$ | F ratio | D-W | Increase in $\overline{R}^2$ due to |
|---|---|---|---|---|---|---|---|
| *(a) Dependent variable (Y): PCVAFS* | | | | | | | |
| Y = 50.6642 + | $0.1595^{***}I_3$ + (0.0852) | $0.2667^{*}I_5$ - (0.0579) | $0.1187I_6$ (0.3485) | 0.6685* | 11.7577 | 1.9646 | $I_5$ = 0.4900<br>$I_6$ = 0.1681<br>$I_3$ = 0.0725 |
| (n = 17, d.f. = 3, 13) | | | | | | | |
| *(b) Dependent variable (Y): PSDPOS* | | | | | | | |
| Y = 32.4546 + | $0.2084^{*}I_3$ + (0.0834) | $0.2261^{*}I_5$ (0.0577) | $-0.119^{*}I_6$ (0.0347) | 0.6183* | 9.6387 | 2.0268 | $I_5$ = 0.4026<br>$I_6$ = 0.1436<br>$I_3$ = 0.0725 |
| (n = 17, d.f. = 3, 13) | | | | | | | |

*Notes:* 1. Only final results are presented for notations please see text.
2. Figures in the parentheses are standard errors of the *b* coefficients.
3. PCVAFS stands for per capita value added generated in the registered factory sector; while PSDPOS connotes proportion of SDP generated in the organised manufacturing sector.
* significant at one cent level of significance.
** significant at five per cent level of significance.

*Source:* As per text.

better off region, despite the official intentions. It is also clear that mere distribution of raw materials on equalising basis, unless accompanied by favourable direct and indirect participation of the government, may not bring any impressive change in the behaviour of regional inequalities on its own.

Thus the question as to why these regional inequalities in the level of industrialisation have declined over time still remains. May be the technique used for deciphering the factors is not the most appropriate one; or there may be a time lag involved in the relationships, which we are not able to capture; or the list of explanatory variables is not exhaustive. This apart, possibly the inter-regional industrial inequalities might have declined in the natural course of time, because of negative externalities experienced by some points in space (having concentration of industrial activity), consequently some spill over of industries might have favoured backward regions leading to reduction in the inter-regional industrial inequalities. Another related possibility is that the negative government interventions that imposed restrictions on the growth of big industrial agglomerates such as Bombay, Calcutta and Ahmedabad, etc. might have helped in altering the scene. It appears that 'sticks' rather than 'carrots' succeeded in affecting a decline in the regional industrial inequalities.

One can also attempt to explain the phenomenon in terms of the industrial stagnation or decline in the growth rates in some industries since mid/late sixties. It can be argued that the stagnation was also unevenly distributed across States, affecting each of them differently, plausibly in proportion to their level of industrialisation. Consequently the States with a long history of industrialisation might have suffered burnt of the stagnation more severely than the late starters; for the industrial structure of the more industrialised States was having a relatively higher weight of traditional industries which were facing problems of obsolescence. Here late starters probably had an edge over their more industrialised counterparts, in terms of a relatively more recent technology and new plant and machinery.[30]

We are not, however, in a position to provide any specific answers in a precise manner at this stage. All the possibilities mentioned above are, at best, conjectures. Perhaps a more indepth investigation into these propositions might probably help in understanding the complex contours of the problem.

## NOTES

1. For a detailed discussion see Chapter 2. Another school of researchers looks at these regional variations in historical or Marxian framework, stressing the historical forces of colonialism. They view development or underdevelopment as a process of global economic exploitation, better known as 'dependency theory'. See Harold (1975); and Farlane (1982).
2. Economic history of countries like Japan or South Korea will substantiate the point.
3. For example Kerala is endowed with factors like per capita income, saving, infrastructure and large market. But for entrepreneurship and docile labour, it would have made strides in industrial development.
4. Government can further facilitate industrialisation through providing easy access to the capital at a cheaper rate. Government's role is also crucial as an intervening agency for correcting imbalances as envisaged by Gunnar Myrdal.
5. For example see Chenery, Shishido and Watanabe (1962); Chenery and Taylor (1968); and Taylor (1969).
6. See Chapter 6.
7. See Chapter 2 for some of the studies.
8. The demand side variables need some clarification. The assumption is that the regional economies are closed economies; and the demand originating in a region is being met within the region. It may look a bit too heroic assumption. The unrestricted inter-regional trade may limit the effectiveness of the size of the regional markets in determining the regional industrial development, and the demand emanating in a region can be met by imports through inter-regional trade. But the fact that market in India is highly segmented and regional in character due to relative immobility of factors (Ganguly, 1962; Seetharam and Chakraborty, 1979), and small magnitude of inter-regional trade (Hashim, 1970, Hashim, 1971, Thakker, 1971) rules out the above apprehension to some extent. One can thus, quite reasonably argue that given the rigid character of the inter-regional trade; the size of the market and its purchasing power are likely to play an important role in the regional industrial development, at least in the Indian context (Mehta, 1955; Manne, 1967; Sastry, 1970; Gupta, 1971).
9. It may be mentioned here that inter-industry demand, as specified here, only indicates the extent of the region specific industrial diversification, and is not comparable with the inter-industry linkages in an Input-Output sense.
10. Our intention is not to pass a value judgement on the behaviour of labour. It may equally be a consequence of the mismanagement. Exploitative attitude of the employer's is a widely recognised phenomenon and quite a few times workers are forced to go on strike justifiably. Thus workers alone can hardly be held responsible for this mishap. Nevertheless, it does reflect the environment in which industries are operating. Secondly it is also argued that higher the level of organised trade union movement, more conducive will be the industrial climate, whereas a fragmented movement is likely to effect it adversely. For inter-trade union rivalries will make it more difficult to negotiate the issues with the management (sometimes with the connivance of the management also), leading to loss of production.

11. We could have added absenteeism and turnover rates also but they have very insignificant variation across space or over time, unlike the above two measures.
12. Initially all the supply side variables were considered, but later we dropped the variables representing entrepreneurship. For, it was observed that the proxy index for entrepreneurship had high correlation not only with the dependent variables, but also with most of the important variables, may be because the way it was defined. Consequently some of the intuitively important variables did not appear in the results, due to the use of the step-regression procedure; which emerged as quite significant once entrepreneurship index was dropped. Moreover, we feel that it is difficult to ascertain whether entrepreneurship is a cause or the effect of the level of industrialisation, as well as of the other supply side variables. Entrepreneurship, by and large, follows only when other variables reach up to a certain critical minimum level of development. Thus, it reflects the impact of other variables the way the level of industrial development does. This reason also prompted us to exclude this variable from the analysis.
13. But for lack of information for all the years between 1961 and 1978, we would have liked to add some more variables like urbanisation, agglomeration economies, level of agriculture mechanisation etc.
14. Only final results are given in Table 7.1 to 7.4, i.e. the estimates having highers $R^2$ have been selected for the analysis. We have two sets each of the models. Per capita value-added generated in the registered factory sector $Y_1$, reflecting the levels of industrial development of respective States, has been taken as dependent variable in the first set. Whereas second set treats the proportion of the State domestic product generated in the organised manufacturing sector in various States $Y_2$, reflecting the importance of manufacturing in the States economic structure as dependent variable. *As the results will show, there is only marginal difference in the behaviour of independent variables with respect of these indicators of industrialisation. Therefore, focus of the analysis will be on the first set only. However, whenever there is a marked deviation from the pattern in the second set, the later indicator will also be accounted for.*
15. Though a bit difficult to explain, the phenomenon is not altogether surprising. For this is the time when 'Green Revolution' was taking place in India. And, as we know, higher level of mechanisation in agriculture is directly associated with higher use of power in the sector; leading to a situation where power resources have to be diverted to agriculture (sometimes even at the cost of industry). If we accept this as logical, it is quite plausible to encounter the negative impact of agricultural mechanisation on the industrial growth. And possibly this was the period where the agriculture sector might have started vying for the scarce power resources; so important for the smooth and rapid growth of industrialisation; and the negative sign is obvious consequence of this kind of behaviour.
16. It may be mentioned that year to year regressions are not strictly comparable, because structure of the regressions has changed over time in terms of inclusion and exclusion of the explanatory variables.
17. For logic says that healthy and peaceful environment on labour front is a pre-requisite of the industrial development, and a lack of this might prove detrimental, because of the losses suffered in output due to labour unrest.

18. In this context, in the light of the finding that regional industrial inequalities declined over time thus, one can argue, that availability of raw material also might have played a crucial role in achieving regional balances; in whatsoever humble manner.
19. In pooled regression on obvious step would be to introduce time shifters as dummy variables to judge the structural change in relationship examined. However, since the regression analysis of individual years have already indicated the evidence in favour of structural change through time; the purpose of present pooled regression analysis was to identify those common influences which have transcended the time dimension.
20. With more and more access to information, a worker is likely to migrate to a high wage island from the low wage one. If such migration takes place at a slightly higher pace, the increase in the supply of labour in the higher efficiency wage island with decline in supply of the labour force in the later will be the logical outcome. Assuming market mechanism to be operative wages will tend to equalise in both regions.
21. We admit that this is a very crude and imperfect index of regional agglomeration economies. And, How to develop an index of regional agglomeration economies", as Richardson puts it, "is a thorny problem the solution of which requires much more research" (Richardson, 1973: 213).
22. In order to get some explanation as to why the other two variables are ignored, we looked at the correlation coefficient matrix. The results were revealing. What emerges is that relative city size was most strongly and positively associated with the dependent variables, followed by number of urban centres above threshold size. But these two variables are also significantly correlated with each other, whereas average inter-urban distance, though with right type of sign (negative) was weakly (insignificantly) correlated with the dependent variables. This shows that though relationships hold good and direction is also found as postulated, the two variables are dropped out on technical grounds.
23. Here we avoid the controversy whether this variable leads to industrial development or itself is an outcome of the process of industrial development. We have discussed this issue in Chapter 2.
24. Though there is no direct evidence to support at least first two propositions; the restriction imposed on the growth of industries in metropolitan cities like Bombay by the government must have been of some consequence in diverting industries towards some lesser congested regions like Vapi in Gujarat.
25. Since we have *a priori* information that the inter-regional inequalities in the level of industrial development have declined over time, they are postulated to be consequence of the decline in the inequalities in these independent factors.
26. The time trend (t) was not found to be significant in any case.
27. In order to see the trend in the inequality indices of direct government participation ($I_5$) and indirect government participation ($I_6$), we regressed both variable on time (t) and its square ($t^2$) . b coefficients for these two indices were found to be -0.3121 and +0.4276, significant at 5 per cent and 1 per cent level respectively.
28. For example, the decline in the inequalities in the level of industrial development is possibly observed on account of some of the forces operating in favour of the

backward regions, whereas in the other case, probably better off regions gain in the whole deal. Because, *a priority* we know that the public sector investment was initially concentrated in some of the backward States, which, over time, became more evenly spread, due to the investment in relatively developed States.

29. The sectoral shift might also have resulted into a rank reversal within the group of industrially advanced States leading to a decline in the overall regional inequalities. Moreover, decline in the public investment inequalities may be observed even if it is more evenly distributed across more and more backward States over time, than getting concentrated within a few backward States. However, data tends to negate such a possibility as the share of developed States in the gross block investment has increased over time (see Udai Sekhar, 1983).
30. However, the implication of such a hypothesis is that if, as and when, the economy revives and market forces again strike back, the inequalities will tend to increase in all likelihood. We are not able to probe into this aspect in detail, but if the observation for the year 1978-79 is any indication, one finds that inter-regional industrial inequalities have marginally increased compared to the preceding year (see Table 4.6). However, it requires data for more recent years to say any thing more precisely.

*ANNEXURE 7.1*

## A Technical Note on the Data and Methodology Adopted for Constructing the Various Indices[1]

As discussed earlier, we selected certain indicators to be used as proxies for the various behavioural factors affecting interregional industrial structure. Most of these indicators are a combination of some other characters which have to be combined in order to have a single composite index representing a particular variable. Let us take an example to write the methodology. Suppose there are 4 factors to be merged into one index and each factor is spreadover 18 States, i.e. has 18 number of observation.[2] Now let

$CI$ = Composite Index;
$X_j$ = $j^{th}$ variable, where $j = 1, 4$;
$X_i$ = $i^{th}$ observation (State), where $i = 1, 18$;
$X_{ij}$ = $i^{th}$ observation for $j^{th}$ variable;
$X_m$ = maximum value $X_{ij}$ for $j^{th}$ sector, $m = 1,4$;
$X_n$ = minimum value of $X_{ijs}$; for $j^{th}$ sector, $n = 1,4$;
$N$ = total number of State/observations;
$C_j$ = inverse of the coefficient of variation for $j^{th}$ variable;
$X_j$ = mean of the $j^{th}$ series
$W_j$ = Weight for the $j^{th}$ series

then:

$$\hat{X}_{ij} = X_{ij} / X_m - X_n$$

$$C_j = \overline{X}_j / \left[ 1/N - 1 \sum_i (\hat{X}_i - \overline{X}_j)^2 \right] 1/2$$

$$W_j = C_j / \sum_j C_j$$

$$CI = \sum_j \hat{X}_{ij} \cdot W_j$$

All the composite indices were arrived at following the above methodology. At this stage some of the indices need some clarification. For example, *level of agricultural mechanisation*. It is a composite index of (i) number of tractors per 1000 hectares; (ii) number of oil engines and pumpsets per 1000 hectares used for the purpose of irrigation; and (iii) use of NPK (fertilizer) kg/ha. Data for (i) and (ii) are obtained from the Livestock Census for the years 1961, 1971-72 and 1977-78. It is assumed that the values obtained for 1971-72 and 1977-78 hold good for the years and 1969 and 1978, used for the purpose of our analysis. Moreover, hectares are in terms of the gross cultivated area.

Similarly when we considered *urbanisation*, defined as proportion of population living in 20000 + towns. We have not adjusted this proportion for boundary changes. Further, the population for 1971 and 1981 is used as proxy for 1969 and 1978 while working out these proportions.

*Inter-industry demand*: is quantified as inverse of the coefficient of specialisation, which is calculated on the basis of information provided in Table 5.2. Another interesting indicator we have tried to develop is the *index of agglomeration economies*, somewhat as suggested by Richardson (1973).

Agglomeration index (AI) is, thus defined as

$$AJ = \sum_{i}^{z} N_i^{1+\alpha}/Z + \overline{Z} - \sum_{i}\sum_{j} d_{ij} / \frac{Z!}{2!(z-)!}$$

$$(d_{ii}, d_{jj} = 0)$$

($N_i$ = population of $i^{th}$ threshold urban centre in the region; Z = number of threshold urban centres, Z is number of threshold urban centres per 1000 km$^2$, $d$ = distance).

where first term on the right-hand side is the relative size of the urban centres (with lakh + population) with more weight $(1 + \alpha)$ given to the larger centres; second term is the number of these threshold level urban centre per 1000 km$^2$ of area and the last term is the average inter-urban distance between these urban centres. Once we arrive at these three values on the basis of the data obtained from the Census of India, we used the earlier methodology to aggregate these values accordingly (last value being deducted).[3] Inter-urban distance is approximated on the basis of the *Road Map of India*, published by the Geological Survey of India. Weight $(1 + \alpha)$ is the proportion of the population of the city $i$ in the total urban population of the country.[4]

For calculating efficiency wages we need wage rate and total factor productivity. Wage rate for a particular year is defined as the total emolument per worker, calculated on the basis of ASI, while for total factor productivity (TFP), we have used Kendrick's measure defined as:

$$TFP = \frac{V}{aL + bk}$$

where $V$ is index of value added, $k$ and $L$ are the indices for capital and labour respectively, and $a$ and $b$ are the base year weights of the two factor inputs in terms of their proportionate share in value added in the base year.[5]

*Quantification of the degree of labour militancy* is attempted in terms of a composite index of two factors viz. number of mandays lost per 1000 workers owing to industrial disputes; and number of trade unions per thousand workers (here members). It may be mentioned that the information on mandays lost is available only for those disputes which involve more than 10 workers; and reporting of the membership of trade unions is not very regular. However, we have taken average of three years for trade union activities, with assumption that higher number of trade union reflects splited trade union movement.

Data base for other variables is discussed in Appendix I.

NOTES

1. The database has been elaborated in Appendix 1 to the Thesis. However, as and when necessary, important features will be highlighted.
2. In order to aggregate these series, which have different units of measurement, for example length of roads and number of bank offices; we first normalise them by dividing each of the series by the difference of its maximum and minimum values and thus arrive at $X_{ij}$.
3. It is assumed that higher the inter-urban distances, higher will be the cost of transportation, communication and information flow etc., leading to the diseconomies. That is why it is treated as having negative bearing.
4. The weights incorporate the element of urban hierarchy in the national mapping.
5. For details, see Kendrick (1961).

# 8

# THE SUMMING UP

AN IMPORTANT objective of the growth strategy in India is the balanced regional development. It is realised that unless all the constituent regions of the country are imbued to participate in the growth process, the attainable growth will probably remain sub-optimal. Moreover, with the growing sub-nationalist feeling, it is no more possible (neither perhaps desirable) to immolate the cause of any region under the pretext of overall growth. Thus, a need to incorporate explicitly the spatial dimension in the planning approach, accounting for sectoral as well as regional balances, can hardly be over-emphasised. Further, since the industrialisation is thought to be a *sine qua non* for economic development, a more serious thrust has to be given to the spatial dimension of industrial development strategy. This calls for a clear understanding of the regional economies. The present study was, therefore, undertaken to understand the dynamics of regional industrialisation in India. We highlight the major findings subsequently.

The colonial structure of the national economy determined the main contours of the location dynamics of productive forces. On the eve of Independence about two-thirds of the total industrial activity was concentrated in and around the three Presidency towns, namely Bombay, Calcutta and Madras. India's strive for industrial growth was conditioned by the inherited colonial structure. The balanced regional development was not an easy task. The planners and policy-makers during the Second and the Third Five-Year Plans laid emphasis on the objective of achieving balanced regional industrial development. Consequently, substantial public sector investment was made in some of the industrially backward States such as Bihar, Madhya Pradesh and Orissa. However this initial push was, to an extent, short lived due to the shift in the priorities in favour of the high-tech sectors like petro-chemicals and electronics. The implicit assumption of percolation effect of growth, without explicit policy of balanced regional development, at least up to the late sixties, acted probably as a stumbling block for the balanced regional industrialisation.

At the advent of the planning era the industrial base was relatively narrow and confined to the traditional industries oriented to consumer demand and some rudimentary basic industries. Since then, performance of the industrial sector has been quite impressive in terms of quantity as well as quality; so has been the performance of the various regional economies. However, all the regions did not perform alike. Despite the fact that the less developed States grew at a higher than the national growth rate between 1961 and 1978, position of the dominant States did not alter significantly. However a decline was observed in the inter-regional industrial inequality during this period. No significant relationship was observed between the large scale and the unorganised sector. The latter was found to be more evenly spread over space.

We tried to unravel the forces responsible for reduction in the inter-regional inequalities. Initially, we tried to explain the phenomenon in terms of industrial structure. For, the States having a favourable share of fast growing industries (favourable industry mix) were expected to grow at a faster rate and *vice versa*. Thus, if backward States were shifting towards a more dynamic industrial structure than the developed ones, the reduction in tthe inequalities will be the logical outcome. Using shift-share technique, it was observed that the regional industrial composition *per se* explained very small proportion of the growth performance of the respective States. Differential shift component (a sort of residual) emerged more important in offering the explanation. We thought that perhaps inter-industry linkages formed a significant part of the unexplained residual. It was assumed that the favourable linkage-industry mix would be crucial in explaining the inter-regional industrialisation. The empirical results did not vindicate the linkage hypothesis.

We, therefore, shifted our focus on demand side and supply side forces, which probably stimulated the attractiveness of a region for industrialisation.

First, we regressed dependent variables on demand side factors. The results indicated that in 1961 the model explained approximately 69 per cent of the total variations in which approximately 54 per cent of the total variation was explained by the purchasing power. The inclusion of inter-industry demand improved the model's explanatory power. No other variable was found to be statistically significant. In

1969, explanatory power of the model increased to approximately 79 per cent and level of agricultural mechanisation also emerged as an important variable. However, the sign of the agricultural mechanisation was observed to be opposite to the postulated one. *At biet* it is not altogether surprising. For, this was the period when the Green Revolution was swinging across most of the States. Consequently agriculture sector might have started vying for power and thereby adversely affecting industrial growth. Influence of the other two variables was found to be more pronounced in 1969 than in 1961. The same trend was observed even in 1978 except that the explanatory power of the model declined to 63 per cent. The pooled data for the various points of time also did not alter the pattern of results.

In the next stage the supply side variables were taken into account. In the year 1961, indirect government participation emerged as the most important factor explaining about 79 per cent of the total variations, whereas the model explained approximately 92 per cent of the variations. Other important variables were agglomeration economies, infrastructure and efficiency wages. In 1969, a shift in the composition of explanatory variables was observed in favour of labour militancy and against infrastructure and efficiency wages. Overall the influence of agglomeration economies was quite significant along with the indirect government participation. Only sign which was unusual is that of labour militancy.

By the year 1978, the role of agglomeration economies, infrastructure, and indirect government participation became more important and the impact of labour militancy was also according to the theoretical postulates. Raw material availability also assumed importance. Probably by this time some of the backward States started using their natural resources rather than exporting them to the other parts of the world. Here the model explained approximately 75 per cent of the total variation. Overall (pooled) results revealed that the agglomeration economies, infrastructure and indirect government participation were the three important variables which explained the regional variations.

The inclusive analysis (demand and supply) showed that in the early phase, the supply side variables played a more important role in offering explanation for the interregional variations; but subsequently demand side variables emerged more important. Out of all the variables, inter-industry demand and agglomeration economies were important in all the years. Infrastructure lost its importance in 1969, but emerged again in 1978 as an important variable. Indirect government participation and efficiency wages were observed to be important in the early phases only. Among the components of infrastructure and agglomeration economies, power availability from infrastructure and urbanisation index from the agglomeration emerged as significant. Rest of the components namely transport and banking in infrastructural components; and inter-urban distances and regional density of the cities from agglomeration economies did not seem to be crucial. Interestingly enough, between 1961 and 1978 the availability of power became important and the reverse wa true of the urbanisation index.

The behavioural model helped us in understanding the spatial spread of industrialisation. It, however, does not explain the reduction in the regional inequalities. In a separate exercise, we tried to seek some explanations for the reduction in the inequalities. The results revealed that region specific raw material availability and direct government participation had contributed a good deal to the process. Surprisingly, indirect government participation had played only a negative role.

It appears that over time the process of industrialisation had become self-sustaining and the public policies had insignificant impact. Negative association between agriculture and industry leads one to speculate that their relationship may not always be complimentary, if there are competing demands for economic infrastructure. This, also provides some clue to the fact that the unorganised sector tends to grow unrelated to the large scale sector. Probably the small scale enterprises grow with the growth in agriculture. The States such as Punjab and Haryana could be cited as examples in this regard. This implies that planning models will have to work out the infrastructure needs so that the balances between agriculture and industry are not distorted.

A distinct shift from supply to demand side variables was observed in 1969 which was further reinforced over time. This means that the overall industrial policy could no longer be viewed as management of supplyside factors. Demand factors would have to figure crucially in future calculations, both at the national and regional levels. Thus the problem of correcting imbalances may not be amenable to solution through the location of large scale public sector projects, which in any case did not seem to be having linkages with the regional economies. The solution may lie in creating industrial environment where demand side factors are given due importance.

The above discussion has to be viewed in the perspective that recently (since the mid-seventies) the government seems to have given priority to the relatively modern sectors. Incidently, this investment tends to favour some of the developed States. The outcome of the recent policy shift would perhaps be realised by the late eighties. This shift might deter the declining trend in the regional inequalities. Thus some measures safegurding against such a possibility appear to be imperative. Our results indicate that while planning for a proper spatial spread of industries, the emphasis will have to be given on the aspect relating to inter-industry demand, generation of incomes (which are not concentrated in a few pockets), availability of power and agglomeration economies, which are spread over a fairly large number of existing and emerging urban centres.

*APPENDIX I*

## The Database

RELIABILITY OF the emperical result depends on the nature, accuracy and consistency of the data used for the analysis. The data requirements of the present study are determined by the need for analysing (i) industrial growth and trends thereof across States between 1961 and 1978, and (ii) evidence relating to various aspects of inter-State (inter-regional) variations in the level of industrial development in overall macro-economic terms. We outline the sources and nature of the data available for our purpose, in what follows:

### The Data on Manufacturing Sector[1]

The major source of data for the registered factory sector is Annual Survey of Industries (ASI), published anually by the Central Statistical Organisation (CSO), Government of India. The survey covers only registered segment of the manufacturing sector, under sections 2m(i) and 2m(ii) of the Factor Act, 1948. For the purpose of the survey, factories in ASI frame are divided into two sub-sectors namely census and non-census (sample). Generally, factories employing 50 or more workers and using power or employing 100 or more workers without using power constitute census sector and are completely enumerated in the survey; while registered factories employing 10 to 49 workers and using power or 20 to 99 workers without using power are covered on the basis of 50 per cent probability sample annually. The information about large scale factories (census sector) is available on a time series basis for the years between 1961 and 1978-79,[2] except for the year 1972 when survey was not conducted. No separate information about sample sector is available after 1971-72. Moreover, the data for the period 1973-74 to 1978-79 are provisional ones.

Information about the unregistered or unorganised segment of the manufacturing sector is extremely scarce. From no source, data on unorganised sector are available on regular or comparable basis (Somayajulu, 1975). Hence, analysis by and large, leaves out the unregistered or unorganised sector. However, we have used some information provided by the National Accounts Statistics, for this sector.

*Limitations of the Data on Registered Factory*

*Sector*: The limitations in terms of availability and comparability over time as well as across industries have been extensively documented in the literature.[3] Some of the major data limitations are:

(i) The annual survey of industries up to 1965 was conducted for the calendar year while afterwards, it is being conducted for the financial year.
(ii) All the factories covered under the Factory Act do not submit returns punctually. Consequently some proportion of the registered factory sector remains unreported every year. Since no correction is made from year to year for non-reporting units, the comparability over time becomes restricted.
(iii) If any industry group consists of less than three reporting units in a given year, it is included under the classification of industries not elsewhere classified; while the States having less than three reporting units in a particular industry group are pooled together. However, in the footnotes of the industry information, the number of reporting units in respective States is mentioned against their names.
(iv) Another problem was posed in ASI data by change in the industrial classification from ASI to National Industrial Classification (NIC), which is used since 1973-74. As a result industries under NIC do not bear one to one correspondence with ASI in some cases.
(v) The data provided by ASI are at current prices. Therefore comparison over time is not ideal without adjusting the series for price variations.

These limitations make comparison of industries over time and across States somewhat difficult. However, despite the limitations, the ASI data are the best available set for what is termed as registered manufacturing sector in the National Accounts Statistics. Therefore, ASI data have been employed for the purpose of our analysis, after making certain adjustments as follows:

*Adjustment in the Industrial Data*

In order to arrive at registered factory sector, we aggregated the census and the sample sector for the years 1961 to 1971-72 (henceforth referred to as 1971). Since 1973-74, CSO has been publishing information on the registered factory sector as such.

For the purpose of seggregating pooled information, particularly at the States' level, we divided the aggregate information, as given under the column 'others', using proportion of value added of a State among the clubbed States and the number of units pertaining to the State in question as weights; where

- $X_{ij}$ = value of a particular variable $X$ (like fixed capital, employment or value added etc.) in $i^{th}$ industry group in the clubbed $j^{th}$ State;
- $VA_j$ = aggregate value added pertaining to the State $j$;
- $n_j$ = total number of factories mentioned against the State $j$ (in the foot note); and
- $V_j$ = weight of the $j^{th}$ State among all the clubbed States.

Then:

$$V_j = VA_j \cdot n_j / \sum_{j=1}^{n} VA_j \cdot n_j \tag{1}$$

$$X_{ij} = V_j \cdot X_i \tag{2}$$

It may be mentioned that in adopting this methodology there is a change of over or under estimating the region specific values for a variable. However, to provide an overall check on the accuracy of the data, the figures relating to a specific industrial characteristic were aggregated across all the industry groups and compared with the total of that characteristic pertaining to a particular State.

Since the Census Sector and the Sample Sector information can be matched only at the three digit level of disaggregation, the census sector data were aggregated at three digit level of ASI using a key of correspondence in the sample reports. Therefore, NIC sectors also were suitably aggregated to correspond with the earlier period.[4] Though, as mentioned earlier, a one to one correspondence could not be made possible even at three digit level; it was matched to be best possible extent. In all, 53-sector classification of industry groups was arrived at for the purpose of the analysis. Similarly these sectors were further aggregated in order to arrive at use base and input base sectoral classification.[5]

As the data on industries are available at current prices, we feel that the nominal values are somewhat unreliable as indications, given the persistant inflation. It is quite likely that the inflation will effect different industry groups differently. Therefore, any comparison over time will be meaningless, if made on the basis of current prices. The analysis is, thus, carried out taking the series of fixed capital and value added in constant terms, with 1970-71 as the base. The series of value-added were deflated by the appropriate wholesale price indices as provided in Chandhok (1978). There are known limitations in using such price indices,[6] and the ideal way of deflating the series is to use double deflation method. For want of information, we have not been able to do so, and resorted to the single deflation method. Similarly, fixed capital series was deflated by the Index of plant, machinery and transport equipment for the respective yeas. Fixed capital also represents depreciated value of some other fixed assets like land and building etc. along with the other components. Therefore, using the aforesaid deflator may not be very desirable. However, since plant and machinery and transport equipments accounts for the major proportion of the fixed capital, we can use this price deflator as the nearest proxy.[7]

At this juncture one more point may be made clear. The ideal way of deflating various region/State specific fixed capital or value added series is to use region specific, industry-specific, price deflators. But the dearth of such indices is too well known. Therefore, even for the States, we have used all India price deflators. Consequently, the estimates suffer to the extent the regional variations in the price movements across industry groups are not captured. Nevertheless, we are, atleast, able to capture the inter-industry price movements, and are able to correct for the growth of the various States, emanating from the sectoral composition. However, one has to keep these limitations in mind while viewing at the results.

As mentioned earlier, the focus of the study is the organised or registered manufacturing sector. However, the data on unorganised sector has been used to understand the overall variations in the manufacturing sector and its sub-sectors namely organised and unorganised; and relationship between these segments across States in the Chapter 4. The data are obtained from the *Estimates of State Domestic Product (ESDP): 1960-61 to 1982-83*, published by the CSO (1984); and the various issues of the *National Acccounts Statistics* (NAS).

**Other Data**

In analysing the determinants of inter-regional industrial variations and testing the various hypotheses, we required variety of data on a number of variables; which offer some explanations for the inter-regional industrial variations and declining regional industrial inequalities.

Apart from our major data sources namely ASI, NAS, and ESDP; we obtained information from the various government reports and documents. Thus, for working out inter-industry linkages (see Chapter 6) we used Input-Output table obtained from *A Technical Note on the Sixth Plan of India (1980-85)*, Planning Commission (1981). Similarly in order to compute State specific sectoral income elasticities, we obtained data from the *28th Round of the National Sample Survey* (NSS); and the *Task Force Report* published by the Planning Commission (1979).

In order to gauge the impact of some of the behavioural, we selected some proxies to represent these variables. Thus, data related to the various sets of population was obtained from the various volumes of the *Census of India*: road statistics from the various issues of the *Basic Road Statistics of India*, Ministry of Shipping and Transport, Government of India; information on length of railways in the various States was obtained from the various issues of *Indian Railway Year Book*, Ministry of Railways, Railway Board, on banking and credit deposit ratios from *Chart Book on Financial and Economic Indicators, Reserve Bank of India* (RBI) (1978); on forest, mining, agriculture, power, mandays lost, trade unions, geographical area of the various States from the various issues of the *Statistical Abstract : India* (CSO); inter-urban distances from the *Road Map of India*, Geological Survey of India, (1981); on the performance of non-banking financial institutions from the *Report of Development Banking in India*, Industrial Development Bank of India (1980-81), *Operational Statistics* of IDBI, Various reports, on *Currency and Finance*, RBI; on registration of companies with the Directorate General of Technical Development, from the various annual reports on the *Working and Administration of the Company Act, 1956*, Department of Company Affairs, Government of India; on gross block investment in the public sector undertakings from *Annual Report on the Working of Industrial and Commercial Undertakings of the Central Government*, Bureau of Public Enterprise, Government of India; on industrial licences issued to various States from *Hazari Committee Report on Industrial Licensing*,

Planning Commission (1969) and *Assochem Parliamentary Digest* (No. 9, April 1984); data on tractors, oil engines and pumping sets used for irrigation were obtained from the various rounds of *Quiquennial Livestock Census*, Directorate of Economics and Statistics, Ministry of Agriculture; while fertilizer use data were obtained from the various issues of *Fertilizer Statistics*, Fertilizer Association of India. For working out values in per capita terms for non-census years, we used mid-year population projection obtained from the *Report of the Expert Committee on Population Projection*, Office of the Registrar General, Government of India (1978). All the data in monetary terms were suitably deflated by the relevant delators, as given in Chandhok (1978), at 1970-71 prices. If data for the corresponding years were not available, we have taken the nearest possible information in terms of time to represent that year.

## NOTES

1. It may be mentioned that we have analysed only registered factory sector or registered manufacturing sector in the inter-regional context of India.
2. However, now information is available for years now, i.e. for 1979-80 to 1981-82. At the time of our actual analysis, latest data were available up to 1978-79 only.
3. For example, see Krishna (1972); Srinivasan and Vaidyanathan (1972); CSO (1978 and 1979); Ahluwalia (1985) among others.
4. The aggregation scheme is presented in Appendix II.
5. See Sections B and C of the Appendix II.
6. For example in adopting this method we implicitly assume that the prices of inputs change at the same rate a that of the output. As an illustration, the use of the single deflation method affects the trends in the petroleum products group in particular since the output prices diverge markedly from the input prices (Ahluwalia, 1985: 178).
7. It may be mentioned that no adjustments have been made to correct for the vintage involved in the plant and machinery.

# *APPENDIX II*

| Sl. No. | Name of the Industry Group (ASI) | ASI Code | NIC Aggregation (Name of the industry groups and NIC Codes) |
|---|---|---|---|
| 1 | 2 | 3 | 4 |
| (A) | **Aggregation of National Industrial Classification (NIC) corresponding to Anual Survey of Industries (ASI) Classification Code** | | |
| 1. | Manufacturing of dairy products | 202 | Manufacturing of dairy products (201) |
| 2. | Canning and preservation of fruits and vegetables | 203 | Canning and preservation of fruits and vegetables (202). |
| 3. | Canning and preservation of fish and sea food | 204 | Canning, preservation and processing of fish, crustacean and similar foods (203) |
| 4. | Grain mill products | 205 | Grain mill products (204). |
| 5. | Manufacturing of bakery products | 206 | Munufacturing of bakery products (205). |
| 6. | Sugar, gur and khandsari | 207 | Manufacturing and refining of sugar (206) + Production of indigenous sugar, *boora, gur* and khandsari etc. (207). |
| 7. | Manufacturing of cocoa, chocolate and sugar confactionery | 208 | Manufacturing of cocoa, chocolate and sugar confectionary (including sweet marts) (209). |
| 8. | Food products, not elsewhere classified (n.e.c.) and meet products | 201-209 | Slaughtering preparation and preservation of meet (200) + production of common salt (208) + manufacture of hydrogenated oils, *wanaspati ghee* etc. (210) + other edible oils and fats etc. (211) + Tea processing (212) + coffee curing roasting and grinding (213) + cashewnut processing (214) + Animal roods (216) + manufacture of starch (217) + Munufacture of food products (n.e.c.) (219) + cold storage (741). |
| 9. | Distilling rectifying and blending of spirits | 211 | Distilling, rectifying and blending of spirits (220). |
| 10. | Wine industries | 212 | Wine industries (221). |
| 11. | Malt liquors, malt, country liquor and toddy | 213 | Malt liquors and malt (222) + Productiton of country liquor and toddy (223). |
| 12. | Soft drinks and carbonated water industries | 214 | Soft drinks and carbonated water industries (224). |
| 13. | Manufacturing of tobacco and tobacco products | 220 | Manufacture of *bidi* (226) + Manufacture of cigar, cigarettes, choroots and cigarette tobacco (227) + manufacturing of chewing tobacco, sarda and snuff (228) + tobacco and tobacco products (n.e.c.) (229). |
| 14. | Manufacturing of textiles | 231 | Cotton spinning, weaving, shrinking sanforising and finishing of cotton textiles (231) + Printing, dyeing and bleaching of cotton textiles (232) + Cotton spinning other than in mills (*charkha*) (233) + Production of Khadi (234) + Cotton textiles in handloom other than khadi (235) + cotton textiles in powerlooms (236) + cotton textiles (n.e.c.) (239) + Wool spinning weaving and finishing in mills (241) + Wool spinning and weaving other mills (242) + Dyeing and bleaching of wool textiles (234) + Manufacture of wool (n.e.c.) (244) + Spinning, weaving and finishing of silk textiles (245) + Printing, dyeing and bleaching of silk textiles (248) + Silk and synthetic fibre textiles (n.e.c.) (249) + Jute and mesta-spinning and weaving (251) + Dyeing, printing and bleaching of jute textiles (252) + Preparing, spinning, weaving and finishing of hemp and other coarse fibre (253) + Manufacture of jute bags and other jute textiles (n.e.c.) (259) + Embroidery and making of crepes, laces and fringes (262) + weaving carpets, rugs and other similar textile products (263) + Dyeing and Bleaching of silk textiles (246) + spinning, knitting and finishing of other textiles (247). |
| 15. | Knitting mills | 232 | Knitting mills (260). |
| 16. | Manufacturing of all types of threads cordage, ropes, twines, net etc. | 233 | Manufacture of all types of threads, ropes, twines, nets etc. (261). |

*Contd.*

APPENDIX II *(Contd.)*

| 1 | 2 | 3 | 4 |
|---|---|---|---|
| 17. | Other textiles (n.e.c.) | 239 | Cotton gining, cleamning and baling (230) + wool cleaning, baling and processing (240) + Jute and mesta pressing and baling (250) + manufacture of made up textile goods (except garments) such as curtains, mosquito nets, etc. (266) + manufacture of waterproof textiles (267) + of coir and coir products (268) + manufacture of textiles (n.e.c.) (269). |
| 18. | Manufacture of footwear (except rubber and plastic) | 241 | Manufacture of footwear except rubber and plastic footwear (291). |
| 19. | Tailoring, umbrella, raincoats and textile garmets | 243 | Manufacture of all types of textile garments including wearing apparels (264) + Manufacture of umbrella, raincoats, hats, etc. (265). |
| 20. | Munufacture of wood and wood products | (251+252 + 253) | Manufacture of veneer, playwood and their products (270) + Sawing and plaining of wood (other than plywood) (271) + Manufacture of wooden and cane boxes, crates, drums, containers, baskets, reeds, and ratten etc. (272) + Manufacture of structural wooden goods (273) + Manufacture of wooden industrial goods (274) + Cork and cork products (275) + Manufacture of wood and wood products, n.e.c. (279). |
| 21. | Manufacturing of furniture and fixtures | 260 | Manufacture of wooden furniture and fixtures (276) + Bamboo and cane furniture and fixtures (277) + Manufacture of furniture and fixtures primarily of metal (342). |
| 22. | Manufacturing of paper and paper products | 271 | Manufacture of pulp, paper and paper board including news print (280) + Manufacture of pulp products n.e.c. (282) + Manufacture of paper and paper board articles n.e.c. (283) + Manufacture of boxes of paper and poper boards (281). |
| 23. | Printing and publishing of all types | 280 | Printing and publishing of newspapers (284) + Printing and publishing of periodicals, books, atlases, maps, journals, etc. (285) + Printing of bank notes, currency notes, postage stamps etc. (286) + Engraving, etching, blockmaking etc. (287) + Book binding (288) + Printing publishing and allied activities, n.e.c. (289). |
| 24. | Tanning, curing and finishing of leather | 291 | Tanning curing, finishing, embossing and japanning of leather (290) |
| 25. | Manufacturing of leather products n.e.c. | 293 | Manufacture of wearing apparel of leather and substitute of leather (292) + Manufacture of leather consumer goods (other than apparel and footwear) (293) + Scrapping, curving, tanning, bleaching and dyeing of fur and other pelts for the trade (294) + Manufacture of wearing apparel of fur and pelts (295) + Manufacture of fur and skin rugs and other articles (296) + Manufacture of leather and fur products n.e.c. (299). |
| 26. | Rubber and rubber products | 300 | Tyre and tube industries (300) + Manufacture of footwear made of rubber and plastics (301) + Manufacture of rubber products n.e.c. (302). |
| 27. | Manufacture of industrial organic and in organic chemicals, fertilizers and pesticides, turpentine, synthetic resins and fibres, explosive and fireworks, etc. | 311 | Manufacture of basic industrial organaic and inorganic chemicals (310) + Manufacture of fertilizers and pesticides (311) + Manufacture of terpentine, synthetic fibre and resins, etc. (316) + Manufacture of explosives, ammunition and fireworks (318). |
| 28. | Manufacture of inedible oils | 312 | Manufacture of inedible oil (315). |
| 29. | Manufacture of paints, varnishes, drugs and medicines and chemicals, n.e.c. | 319 (313+319) | Manufacture of paints, varnishes and lacquers (312) + Manufacture of drugs and medicines (313) + Manufacture of perfumes cosmetics and other toilet preparations (314) + Manufactures of matches (317) + Manufacture of chemical products n.e.c. (319). |
| 30. | Petroleum refineries | 321 | Petroleum refineries (304). |
| 31. | Manufacture of petroleum and coal Products | 329 | Petroleum products, n.e.c. (305) + Production of coaltar in coke ovens (306) + Manufacture of other coal and coaltar products n.e.c. (307). |
| 32. | Manufacture of structural clay products | 331 | Manufacture of structural clay products (320). |
| 33. | Manufacture of glass and glass products | 332 | Manufacture of glass and glass products (327). |

*Contd.*

APPENDIX II (*Contd.*)

| 1 | 2 | 3 | 4 |
|---|---|---|---|
| 34. | Manufacture of earthenwere and chinaware | 333 | Manufacture of earthenware and earthen pottery (322) + Manufacture of chinaware and porcelainware (323) + Manufacture of earthen and plastic, Manufacture of earthen and plastic statues and other products. |
| 35. | Manufacture of cement, lime and plaster | 334 | Manufacture of cement, lime and plaster (324). |
| 36. | Manufacture of miscellaneous non-matallic mineral products, n.e.c. | 339 | Manufacture of mica products (325), Manufacture of structural stone goods, stone ware, stone dresisng and crushing (326) + Manufacture of asbestos, cement and other cement products (328) + Manufacture of miscellaneous non-matallic mineral products, n.e.c. (329). |
| 37. | Manufacture of iron and steel and ferroalloys | 341 | Iron and steel industries (330) + Foundaries for casting and forging iron and steel (331) + Manufacture of ferro-alloys (332) + Manufacture of structural material products (341). |
| 38. | Non-ferrous basic industries | 342 | Copper manufacturing (333) + Brass manufacture (334) + Aluminium manufacturing (335) + Zinc manufacturing (336) + Other non-ferrous metal industries (339) . |
| 39. | Manufacture of metal products and parts (except mechinery and transport equipments) | 350 | Manufacture of fabricated Metal products (340) + Manufacture of hand tools and general hardware (343) + enamelling, japanning, esequering, galvanising, planting, and polishing of Metal products (344) + Manufacture of Metal utensils cutlery and kitchenware (345) + Manufacturing of metal products except Machinery and transport equipments n.e.c. (349) |
| 40. | Manufacture of mechine and machine tools (except electrical machinery) | 360 | Manufacture of agricultural macheniry and equipment parts (350) + Manufacture of drills, coal cutting machine, earthmovers, lifting and houseing machinery, cranes, conveyors and road rollers and other heavy machinery and equipment used construction and mining industries (351) + Manufacture of prime movers, boilers and steam generating plants (352) + Industrial machinery for food and textile industries (353) + Industrial machinery other than food and textile industry (354) + Manufacture of airconditioners, refrigerators, fire fighting equipments and parts (355) + Non-electrical general items, machinery, parts and components n.e.c. (356) + Manufacturing of machine tools and there parts (357) + Manufacture of office computing and accounting machinery and other parts (358) + Manufacture and repair of non-electrical machinery equipments components and accessories n.e.c. (359). |
| 41. | Manufacture of electric machinery and apparatus | 370 | Manufacture of electrical industries machinery and apparatus and parts (360) + Manufacture of insulated wires and cables (361) + Manufacture of dry and wet batteries (362) + Manufacture of electrical apparatus, appliances and their parts (363) + Telecommunication and transmission equipments and parts (364) + Radiographic X-Ray apparatus and tubes and parts (365) + Manufacture of electronic comupters, control equipments and other equipments (366) + Manufacture of electronic components and accessories n.e.c. (367) + Manufacture of electrical Manufacture of electrical machinery, aappliances and parts n.e.c. (369). |
| 42. | Ship and boat building | 381 | Ship and boat building and repairing (370). |
| 43. | Railway loco equipments etc. | 382 | Manufacture of locomotives and parts (371) + Manufacture of railway wagons and coaches and parts (372) + Manufacture of other rail-road equipments (373). |
| 44. | Manufacture of motor vehicles and parts | 383 | Manufacture of motor vehicles and parts (374). |
| 45. | Repair of motor vehicles | 384 | Rapair of motor vehicles and motor cycles (373). |
| 46. | Manufacture of motor cycles and bicycles | 385 | Manufacture of motor cycles, scooter and parts (375) + Manufacture of bicycles, cycle rickshaw and parts (376). |
| 47. | Manufacture of air-crafts and parts | 386 | Manufacture of aircrafts and parts (377). |
| 48. | Manufacture of transport equipments, n.e.c. | 389 | Bullock carts, push carts and hand carts etc. (378) + Manufacture of transport equipment, n.e.c. (379). |
| 49. | Manufacture of medical, surgical and scientific equipments | 391 | Manufacture of medical, surgical and scientific equipments (380) |

*Contd.*

APPENDIX II (*Contd.*)

| 1 | 2 | 3 | 4 |
|---|---|---|---|
| 50. | Manufacture of photographic materials | 392 | Manufacture of photographic and optical goods (381). |
| 51. | Manufacture of watches and clocks | 393 | Manufacture of watches and clocks (382) |
| 52. | Manufacture of jwellery and mint | 394 | Manufacture of jewellery and palated articles (383) + Minting of coins (384). |
| 53. | Manufacture of miscellaneous products, n.e.c. | 399 (395+399) | Manufacture of ice (215) + Manufacture of plastic products n.e.c. (303) + Manufacture of reports and atheletic goods (385) + Manufacture of musical instruments ( 384) + Manufacture of stationery articles (387) + Manufacture of miscellaneous products, n.e.c. (389). |

**(C) Aggregation of ASI Sectors (at 3 digit level) According to Use-based Classification**

| **Name of use-based Sectors:** | **Industry Groups to constitute the sectors (ASI 3 digit based classification):** |
|---|---|
| 1. Basic goods | 311 + 334 + 341 + 342 |
| 2. Intermediate goods | 232 + 233 + 251 + 291 + 300 + 312 +321 + 329 + 331 + 339 + 350 |
| 3. Capital goods | 360 + 370 + 381 + 382 + 383 + 386 + 389 |
| 4. Consumer goods | |
| (a) Consumer durables | 260 + 384 + 385 + 391 + 393 + 394 |
| (b) Consumer non-durables | 202 + 203 + 204 + 205 + 206 + 207 + 208 + 209 + 211 + 212 + 213 + 214 + 220 + 231 + 239 + 241 + 243 + 271 + 280 + 293 + 319 + 332 + 398 + 399 |

**(B) Aggregation of ASI Sectors (at 3 digit level) According to Input-based Classification**

| **Name of the input-based sector :** | **Industry Groups Constituting the Input-based sectors:** |
|---|---|
| 1. Agro-based | 202 + 203 + 204 + 205 + 206 + 207 + 208 + 209 + 211 + 213 + 214 + 220 + 231 + 232 + 233 + 239 + 241 + 243 + 251 + 260 + 271 280 + 291 + 293 + 300 + 312 |
| 2. Chemical-based | 311 + 319 + 321 + 329 + 392 |
| 3. Metal based | 341 + 342 + 350 + 360 + 370 + 381 + 382 + 383 + 384 + 385 + 386 + 389 + 391 + 393 + 394 + 399 |
| 4. Non-matallic mineral-based | 331 + 332 + 333 + 334 + 339 |

*Notes:* (1) Sectors are aggrerated to the nearest possible inter-related group.

(2) An industry group if defined as a constituent of a particular sector if more than 75 per cent of its products directly contribute to that sector.

*Source:* Based on the information published by the ASI (CSO).

# BIBLIOGRAPHY

## (A) Articles and Books


Acharya, H. (1956), "Urban-Rural Relations", *IEA*, 39 (Conference No; Part I).

Acharya, Hemlata (1965), "Urban-Rural Relations", 39th Conference Number, Part I, December, *IEA*, 39 (Conference No; Part I).

Adhvaryu, H.J. (1983). "Area Development and Theory of Multiplier", *ARVIK*, 9 (1 & 2).

Aguiar, A. and S. Ravindranath, (1983), "Plant Location: The Crucial Choice", *Business India*, (November-December).

Ahluwalia, I.J. (1985), *Industrial Growth in India, Stagnation Since the Mid-Sixties*, Delhi, Oxford University Press.

Aiyar, R.P. (1973), *Power Resources for Industrial Development*, in Vakil (ed.).

Alagh, Y.K. (1962). "Formulation of State Plan : Rajasthan A Case Study", *EW*, 14 (27).

Alagh, Y.K. (1969), "Formulation of Plans at the State level in India", Seminar on Union-State Relations in India, Simla, Indian Institute of Advance Studies.

Alagh, Y.K. (1972), *Regional Aspects of Industrialisation*, Bombay : University of Bombay.

Alagh, Y.K., K.K. Subrahmanian and S.P. Kashyap (1971a), "Regional Industrial Diversification in India : Some Factual Analysis", *EPW*, 6 (5).

Alagh, Y.K., K.K. Subrahmanian and S.P. Kashyap (1971b). "Inter-Regional Industrial Structure in a Developing Economy : A Conceptual Framework with a case study", in *JRS*, 11 (3).

Alagh, Y.K. and P.G. Pathak, (1973), "Industrial Development in Gujarat : Regional Structure and Policies" *ARVIK*, 9 (1 & 2).

Alagh, Y.K., S.P. Kashyap, J.V. Shah and D.N. Awasthi (1982), "Indian Industrialisation : Regional Structure and Planning Choices", *Business Standard*, Annual Number.

Alexander, P.C. (1963), *Industrial Estates in India*, Bombay, Allied Publishing House.

Alonso, W. (1964), *Location Theory* in Friedmann and Alonso (ed.).

Alonso, W. (1968), "Urban and Regional Imbalances in Economic Development", *EDCC*, 17 (1).

Amin, S. (1976), *Unequal Development*, New York : Monthly Press Review.

Antia, F.P. (1973), "Transport Facilities for Industrial Development", in Vakil (ed.).

Armstrong, H. and J. Taylor (1980), *Regional Economic Policy and Its Analysis*, Oxford : Philip Allen.

Ashby, L.D. (1964), "The Geographical Redistribution of Employment: An Examination of the Elements of Change", *Survey of Current Business*, Vol. 44.

Asthana, P. (1980), "A Review of Ongoing Programmes for Development of Backward Areas : With special Reference to Industrial Development", in *IDBI*.

Atkinson, A.B. (ed.) (1973), *Wealth Income and Inequality*, Penguin Book.

Atkinson, A.B. (1973), *On the Measurement of Inequality*, in Atkinson (ed.).

Awasthi, D.N. and Jayashree Shah (1981), "Spatial Diversification of Manufacturing Industries in Gujarat", a paper presented in the *13th Gujarat Economic Conference*, October 31-November 1, Adipur.

Awasthi, D.N. (1983), "Sectoral Income Elasticities for the Indian Economy : Estimates for 1977-78", Paper presented in *21st Annual Conference of the Indian Economic Society*, January 10-January 12, Annamalai University, Chidambaram.

Awasthi, D.N. (1983), "Patterns of Inter-Regional Industrialisation in India : A Retesting of Linkage Hypothesis", in *GIDS*.

Bagchi, A. (1970), *Long Term Constraints in India's Industrial Growth, 1951-1968*, in Robinson and Kidron (eds.), London.

Bagchi, A. (1972), *Private Investment in India, 1900-1939*, Madras; Orient Logman.

Bagchi, A. (1976), "De-Industrialisation in India in the Nineteenth Century : Some Theoretical Implications", in *JDS*, 12 (2).

Bandopadhyaya, K. (1969), *Industrialisation Through Industrial Estates*, Calcutta : Bookland Pvt. Ltd.

Banerjee, Nirmala (1969), "What Course of Urbanisation in India", *EPW*, Special Number, 4 (28-30).

Baran, P.A. (1957), *Political Economy of Growth*, New York : Monthly Press Review.

Barathawal, R.R. (1980), "The Pattern of Inter-State and Inter-Industry Dispersion of Companies in Indian Corporate Sector", in *IJRS*, 12 (1).

Bardhan, P. (1984), "Some Observations on Economic Growth in India", *EPW*, 19 (51-52).

Berry, B.J.L. *et al.* (ed) (1966), *Essays on the Commodity Flows and Spatial Structure of Indian Economy*, Paper No. 111, Chicago: University of Chicago.

Bharati, R.K. (1978), *Industrial Estates in Developing Economies*, New Delhi: National Publishing House.

Bhat, L.S. (1981), "A Case for Spatial Planning and Decentralisation of Planning Process", Nair (ed.) (1981).

Bhat, V.V. (1965), "Some Notes on Balanced and Unbalanced Growth", *EJ*, 75 (297).

Bhattacharya, A.K. (1973), "Economic Regions in the Context of Development: Some Basic Considerations", *ARVIJ*, 15 (1).

Bhattacharya, N. and G.S. Chatterji (1971), "On Rural Urban Differentials in Consumer Prices and Per Capita Household Consumption in India by levels of Living". *Sankhya*, 33B (3 & 4).

Biswas, A.K. and H.P. Biswas (1961), "Engel elasticity of Consumption expenditure on some selected items and increase in their demand during the Third Five Year Plan", *Studies Retaining to Planning for National Development*, No. 238, (micrographed), Indian Statistical Institute.

Bose, Ashish (1961), "Population Growth and Industrialisation and Urbanisation Process in India", *Man in India*, 41 (October-November).

Bose, Ashish (1970), *Urbanisation in India*, Delhi, Institute of Economic Growth.

Bose, A.N. (1971), "Continuing Semi Colonial Character-Basic Problem of Indian Metropolies", *IJRS*, 3 (1)

Bose, D.K. (1969), "Urbanisation, Industrialisation and Planning of Regional Development", *EPW*, (Special Number) 3 (28-30).

Frank, A.G. (1969), *Capitalism and Underdevelopment in Latin America*, New York: Monthly Review Press.

Friedman, John (1966), *Regional Development Planning: A Case Study of Venezuela*, Cambridge: Mass.

Friedman, J. and W. Alonso (eds.), (1964), *Regional Development Planning: A Reader*, Cambridge, Mass.

Furtado, C. (1961), See Rosenstein Rodan.

Furtado, C. (1971), *Development and Underdevelopment*, Berkley: University of California Press.

Ganguly, B.N. (1962), *Significance of Inter-regional Trade Balance with special reference to India*, in Rao, *et al.* (eds.), (1962).

Ghosh, B.N. and Roma Ghosh (1980), "Public Enterprise and Economic Development: Some Observations", *Lok Udyog*, 8 (1).

Gidadhubly, R.G. and L.S. Bhat (1961), *Economic Regions and Regional Flow*, in Gupta and Sdasyuk, (1968).

Giri Institute of Development Studies (GIDS) (1983), *Seminar on Development and Inter-regional Disparities in India*, Lucknow: Giri Institute of Development Studies.

Godbole, M.D. (1978), *Industrial Dispersal Policies*, Bombay: Himalaya Publishing House.

Goswami, A. (1981), "Assam's Industrial Development: Urgency of New Directions", *EPW*, 16 (21).

Goyal, V. (1975), "Area Development Strategy: Diffusion of Growth Process", *ET*, December (17).

Griffin, Keith. B. (1966), "Reflections in Latin American Development", *OEP* (New Series), 8 (1).

Gupta, K.L. (1971), "Development Patterns: An Inter-regional Study", *QJE*, 85 (November).

Gupta, P.S. and G. Sdasyuk (1968), *Economic Regionalisation of India: Problems and Approaches*, Census of India: 1961, Monograph Series, 1 (1).

Gupta, S. (1973), "The Role of Public Sector in Reducing Regional Income Disparities in Indian Plans", *JDS*, 9 (2).

Gupta, Shaibal (1981), "Non-Development of Bihar: A Case of Retarded Sub-Nationalism", *EPW*, 16 (37).

Gupta, T.R. (1963), "Statewise Differences in Distribution of Consumer Expenditure in Rural and Urban India", *ARVIJ*, 5 (2).

Habib, Irfan (1975), "Colonisation of the Indian Economy: 1957-1900", *Social Scientist*, 3 (8).

Hashim, S.R. (1969), "Location Flows and Problem of Regional Development: Some Views Along with Review of Indian Situation", *IEA*, 52 (Conference Number).

Hashim, S.R. (1970), "Interregional Linkages and Economic Regionalisation", *IJRS*, 2 (1).

Hashim, S.R. (1971), "Interregional Linkages and Changes in the Pattern of Commodity Flows in India, 1950-51 to 1959-60, *IEJ*, 19 (2).

Hashim, S.R. (1978/79), "Regional Variations in Industrial Development since Independence", *Journal of the M.S. University*, Baroda: 27/28.

Hayami, Y. (1969), "Industrialisation and Agricultural Productivity: An International Comparative Study", *The Developing Economies*, 8, (1).

Heston, A. (1967), "Regional Income Differences in India and the Historical Pattern", *IEJ*, 15, (2).

Hirschman, A.O. (1958), *The Strategy of Economic Development*, New Haven: Yale University Press.

Hoffman, W.G. (1958), *The Growth of Industrial Economies*, Manchester: Manchester University Press.

Horowitz, I.L., J. de Castro and J. Gerassi (eds.) (1969), *Latin American Radicalism: A Documentary Report on the Left and Nationalist Movement*, New York: Monthly Press Review.

Houston, D.B. (1967), "Shift and Share Analysis – A Critique", *Southern Economic Journal*, 33, (4).

Hurd, J. (1973), "The Influence of British Policy on Industrial Development in the Princely States in India", *The Indian Economic and Social History Review*, 12, (4).

I.D.B.I. (1980), *Report of the Seminar on Industrial Development of Backward Areas*, Bombay: Industrial Development Bank of India.

Isard, W. (1956), *Location and Space Economy*, Cambridge: MIT Press.

Isard, W. and J.H. Cumberland (1961), *Regional Economic Planning-Techniques of Analysis for Less Developed Areas*, Paris: European Productivity Agency.

Isard, W. and T. Reiner (1961), "Regional and National Economic Planning and Analytical Techniques for Implementation", in Isard and Reiner (eds.).

Iyengar N.S. and R.S. Jain (1960), "On a Problem of Estimating Increase in Consumer Demand", *Sankhya*, 22 (379-390).

Management Development Institute (1977), *Backward Area Development : Strategies and Policies*, New Delhi: MDI.

Macrae, J. (1971), "The Relationship Between Agriculture and Industry with Special Reference to Development of Punjab Economy from 1950 to 1965", *JDS*, 1, (4).

Mahajan, B.M. (1971), "Inter-Regional Homogeneity of Consumer Behaviour in India", *ARVIJ*, 13 (1).

Manne, A.S. (ed.) (1967), *Investment for Capacity Expansion*, Cambridge: MIT Press.

Marquillas, J.M.E. (1972), "Shift and Share Analysis – Revisited", *RUE*, (2).

Mathur, A. (1966), "Balanced Vs. Unbalanced Growth – A Reconcilatory View", *OEP*, (New Series), 18 (2).

Mathur, O.P. (1971), *Manual on Industrial Estate Planning*, Hyderabad: SIETI.

Mathur, P.N. and P. Venkatramaiah (1969), *Economic Analysis in Input-Output Framework*, Vol. II, Bombay: Input-Output Research Association.

Mathur, P.N. and S.R. Hashim (1969), "*A Model for Optimum Location and Flows*", in Mathur and Venkatramaiah (eds.).

Mathur, P.N. and S.R. Hashim (1972), *Multiregional Analysis in a Dynamic Input Output Framework*, in Brody and Carter (eds.).

McFarlane, B. (1982), *Radical Economics*, London: Groom Helen.

Mehta, M.M. (1955), *Structure of Indian Industry*, Bombay: Popular Book Depot.

Mera, K. (1973), "On the Urban Agglomeration and Economic Efficiency", *EDCC*, 21 (2).

Meyer, J.R. (1968), *Regional Economics: A Survey*, In Needleman (ed.).

Michalopaulous, C. (1971), "Inter-Industry Relations, External Economies and Regional Economic Development", in *UNIDO*, (1971).

Misra, R.P. (1972), *Growth Pole Policies for Regional Development*, in Lahiri (ed.) (1972).

Misra, T. (1980), "Assam – A Colonial Hinterland", *EPW*, 15 (August).

Mitra, A. (1965), *Levels of Regional Development in India*, Census of India: 1961.

Mitra, A. (1977), *Terms of Trade and Class Relations*, London: Frank Cass.

Mitra, Ashok (1983), *Problems of India's Economic Unity*, Ahmedabad: The Seventh Ajit Bhagat Memorial Lecture, April (9 and 10).

Medhora, P. (1968), *Industrial Gross Since 1950*, Bombay: Bombay University Press.

Mohan, Rakesh (1983), "The Regional Pattern of Urbanisation and Economic Development of India", *GIDS*, (1983).

Moore, W.E. (1969), *The Impact of Industry*, New Delhi: Prentice-Hall.

Murty, G.V.S.N. (1980), "Complete Demand Systems for India: A Series of Experiments with the LES". Paper presented at the 1st World Congress of Econometric Society", Aixen Province, France".

Murty, G.V.S.N. and Niresh Shah, (1980), "Poverty Inequality and Levels of Living in Gujarat", Paper Presented in Seminar on Development of Gujarat: Problems and Prospects", *Paper No. 39*, Sardar Patel Institute of Economic and Social Research, Ahmedabad.

Myrdal, G. (1958), *Economic Theory and Underdeveloped Regions*, (Reprint), Bombay: Vora and Co. Publishers.

Nadkarni, N.V. (1969), "Regional Imbalances in India", *IEA*, 52 (Annual Conference Number).

Nagia, D. (1971), *Industrial Estates Programme: The Indian Experience*, Hyderabad: SIETI.

Nagia, D. (1980), "Incentives, Subsidies and Concessional Finance: Impact on Industrialisation of Chittoor and Khammam Districts", in IDBI.

Nair, D.P. (1980), "Efficiency of State Enterprises Investment in Kerala", *Lok Udyog*, 14 (5).

Nair, K.R.G. (ed.), (1981), *Regional Disparities in India*, New Delhi: National Council of Applied Economic Research.

Nair, K.R.G. (1982), *Regional Experience in a Developing Economy*, New Delhi: Willy Eastern.

Nath, S.K. (1962), "The Theory of Balanced Growth", *OEP*, 14 (2).

Nath, V. (1967), "Regional Planning in the National Plan", *ARVIJ*, 9, (1).

Nath, V. (1971), "Regional Development Policies", EPW, 6, Special Number, (July).

Needleman, N. (ed.) (1968), *Regional Analysis* London: Penguin.

94, 148, 163, 176, 185, 187
level of, 151, 153, 129
process of, 37
Inequality measures, 100
Input-output table, 134
technique, 24
Inter-industry demand, 152-53, 166, 169
impirical findings, 128
linkages, 125, 147
Interpretation, variety of, 104-105
Inter-regional industrial disparities, 87
industrialisation, 185
variation determination, 33-34
Inter-regional inequalities, problems of, 17-18, 23-24
trade, 34, 147
time series variations in, 160
trends, 175-76
variation, 147, 161, 186
impirical results, 150, 160
Inter-state industrial regional inequalities, 32
Issues, 22
Iyengar, N.S., 134

Jain, R.S., 134
Jammu & Kashmir, 18, 60
Jhuraney, J.C., 23

Kanpur, 23
Karnataka, 18, 90, 106
Kashyap, S.P. 36
Krishnaiah, T., 28
Kundu, A., 17, 27
Kuznets, S., 51, 100, 148

Labour indiscipline, 155-57
militancy, 183-84
problems, 37
Lahiri, R.K., 23
Lakdawala, D.T., 24, 35
Lampard, E.E., 35
Location quotient, 103, 107
Low growth industries, 48-49

Madhya Pradesh, 30, 106, 174
Madras, 23, 26
Madurai, 23
Mahalanobis model, 43, 44
Maharashtra, 18, 94
Manifestations, 15
Manufacturing sector, 67, 78, 80, 81, 86, 130, 189
classification, 75
Market, 34, 149
distortion, 30
forces, 78-79
size, 34-35
Mathur, P.N., 30
Mera, K., 35
Methodology, 156, 160,181, 191
Migration, 14
Mineral based industries, 116
Mitra, A., 28
Misra, T., 15, 26
Modern industries, 67
Moore, W.E., 13
Myrdal, G., 14, 37

Nadkarni, N.V., 23
Nair, K.R.G., 36
National growth rate, 104
National Sample Survey (NSS), 134
Non-Banking financial institutions, 31

Organised sector, 85
Orissa, 18, 30, 60, 106, 120, 174

Pandit, M.L., 36, 37
Papola, T.S., 36, 37
Pathak, C.R., 17, 29, 37
Pauperisation, 14
Per capita consumer expenditure, 138
value added, 86
Petroleum and petroleum products, 48-49
Planning Commission, 126, 127, 135, 193, 194
Port-town, developments of, 16
Poverty, 13
Pricing policy, 30-31
Profit maximisation, 148
Psychic cost, 147
Public policies, 27, 174, 187
Public sector investment, 173, 174
project, 29, 187
Punjab, 18, 26, 34, 37, 116, 136, 150, 187
Purchasing power, 34

Radhkrishna, R., 134
Raina, M.K., 30
Rajasthan, 18, 60, 80
Rakesh Mohan, 35
Rao, C.R., 30
Raw material, availability of, 153-54
Raza, M., 16, 17, 25, 27
Regional industrial economy, 103, 122
Regional growth, industrial structure, 102
    performance of, 119
    rate, 104
Regional imbalances, 36-37
Regional industrial base, 106
    disparities, 68
        causes of, 18-19
    diversification, 116
    economic, 78, 118-19
    growth, 14, 15, 125
    inequalities trends in, 22, 78, 91, 97, 176
        indices of, 95
    structure, 24
    variation determinants of, 25-26
        extent of, 149
Regional industrialisation, dynamics of, 184-85
Regional-national growth, 105
Registered factory, 190-191
    sector, 161
Registered manfac uring sector, 50, 192
    classification 71
Regression meth l, 157
Reserve Bank of India (RBI), 193
Resource endowment, 104
Richardson, H.W., 35, 148
Robinson, E.A.G., 13
Rudra, A., 33

Saradamoni, K., 23
Sectoral expenditure elasticities, 135-37, 140
    income elasticities, 134-36
        demand, 142-43
Shift-share technique, 123
Sixth Five Year Plan, 126
Skilled labour, availability of, 155-56
Small industries development corporation, 32
Small scale sector, 80
State Domestic Products (SDP), 79
Structural shifts, 120-21
Subrabaniam., C., 15
Sundaram, K.V., 30
Supply side factors, 163-64
    specifications, 159
    variables, 166

Tamil Nadu, 18, 94
Task Force Report (TFR), 135
Taylor, L.J., 103
Technical note, 181
    workforce, 157
Technological clusters, 24
Thavaraj, M.J.K., 26
Third Five Year Plan, 28, 44, 184
Thomas, T., 36
Total Factor Productivity (TFP), 183
Transport cost, 147

Udai Sekhar, A., 23, 29, 105
Unbalanced sectoral growth, 131
Unorgainsed sector, 80, 94, 192
Urbanisation, 35, 147,-49, 182
    index, 181
Uttar Pradesh, 18, 56, 90, 150

Value added, 51, 54, 57, 61, 78, 90, 105, 127, 129
    growth rates of, 87
    percentage share of, 81
Variables, 173
    choice of, 151
    dependent of, 151
    demand side, 152
    explanatory, 152
    name of, 157
    specification, 157
Variations, causes of, 102-103
Venkataramiah, P., 36

West Bengal, 87, 94, 106
Williamson, J.G., 14, 102, 148
World War I, 16

Yotopoulous, P.A., 126

Bibliography

[illegible] (1990) "Location [illegible] and [illegible] Regional Development" [illegible]

[illegible]

[illegible] "[illegible] in [illegible]", *Journal of the* [illegible]

[illegible]

[illegible] *The Theory of Economic* [illegible]
Yale University Press.

[illegible]

[illegible]
and Cheltenham.

[illegible] Development, Edward [illegible]